THE ULTIMATE COLLEGE SURVIVAL GUIDE

FOURTH EDITION

JANET FARRAR WORTHINGTON AND RONALD FARRAR

THOMSON
PETERSON'S

Australia • Canada • Mexico • Singapore • Spain • United Kingdom • United States

THOMSON

PETERSON'S

About Thomson Peterson's

Thomson Peterson's (www.petersons.com) is a leading provider of education information and advice, with books and online resources focusing on education search, test preparation, and financial aid. Its Web site offers searchable databases and interactive tools for contacting educational institutions, online practice tests and instruction, and planning tools for securing financial aid. Thomson Peterson's serves 110 million education consumers annually.

Dedication

To Gayla Dennis Farrar, who provided the "mo."

For more information, contact Peterson's, 2000 Lenox Drive, Lawrenceville, NJ 08648; 800-338-3282; or find us on the World Wide Web at www.petersons.com/about.

Library of Congress Cataloging-in-Publication Data
    Worthington, Janet Farrar.
        The ultimate college survival guide : proven tips and techniques for
      success / Janet Farrar Worthington, Ronald Farrar.
           p. cm.
        Includes index.
        ISBN 0-7689-0010-7
        1. College student orientation—United States. I. Farrar, Ronald T. II. Title.
    LB2343.32.W672   1998
    378.1'98—dc21   98-15003
                                                                       CIP

Printed in Canada
10 9 8   06 05

Acknowledgments

This book would not have been possible without the advice, encouragement, and experiences of many people—too many to name here. We tried, but the result looked like a telephone book and had about as much personal meaning. So instead of listing everybody (and inevitably missing somebody), we would simply like to thank the students, friends, family members, and colleagues who have helped us the very most, including:

Mark Worthington, for everything. Blair Elizabeth and Andrew Truman Worthington, for inspiration. Gayla Dennis Farrar, for indefatigable research and support. Bradley T. Farrar, for excellent counsel, legal, and otherwise; Carole Ayre Farrar, Sally Worthington, Marion E. Glick, for her help on AIDS and other topics; Channa Taub, for her insight, and Doretha Johnson, for her gift of protected time to write this book. We would also like to thank Melissa Sweeney, Ruth Freishtat, Carol Anne Strippel, Marjorie Centofanti, Patrick C. Walsh, Sheila Plumlee Sanders, Scott Charles Worthington, Leara Rhodes, Martha Merrell, Tim Schaefer, Laura Sanders, Tom Heacock, Edith Nichols, and Megan Sweeney.

CONTENTS

INTRODUCTION

You're about to drive to somebody's house. It's dark, you know there will be few road signs, it's starting to rain, and you're not sure how to get there. What do you do? You get good directions before you start out.

You're traveling in a foreign country. You can barely remember to keep the car on the left side of the road, and you have no idea where you're headed. What's the first thing you do? Buy a road map.

You're running fast to catch a train. You make it; you're breathing hard, and you collapse gratefully into an empty seat. In a few minutes, when the conductor comes by, you buy a ticket to ride this train you just caught.

Why are these images of travel in a book called *The Ultimate College Survival Guide*? Because you're getting ready to start on what may be the biggest journey of your life so far: College. This book is your head start, your directions, your road map, your ticket to the train. It's counsel, wisdom, and fun and practical suggestions, resulting from many people's experiences and gleaned by us in a variety of settings—formal and informal focus groups of college students and recent graduates, one-on-one interviews, classroom discussions, and telephone interviews.

There are many stories here—all true—by current and former college students who have been where you are now.* It's their sound advice you're getting, and also ours. We, the authors, are a not-too-long-ago college graduate and her father, a college professor with 30 years' experience teaching and advising students.

This book, in three previous editions (formerly titled *College 101*), has been around for nearly 15 years. Over the years, it has helped thousands of students make the big, sometimes scary transition to college life. A lot of the material in this latest edition is new; we kept all the

---

*Almost all the students and graduates interviewed for this book said they felt freer to offer advice and talk about their experiences if we agreed not to give their real or entire names.

good advice and valuable information and—we hope—have made it even better by including other people's voices and experiences.

Make the Most of the Info

Take what you read here—as you should take all advice—with a grain of salt. Talk to other college students and read everything you can find that can help you get ready for college. The good news, as Thea, a sophomore at the University of South Carolina, says, is that "you don't have to know everything the first day." However, anything you can do *now* to prepare yourself for this new adventure will almost certainly come in handy later.

And perhaps the best news—at least, the most important point we can make here—is that there is always help when you need it. You may have to look for it, but it's there somewhere. When you get right down to it, the whole purpose of universities is to turn out productive, useful people. Helping students is part of the deal.

College is one of the very few situations in life in which hundreds of people exist simply to help you find your way. Counselors, faculty and resident advisers, financial aid people, health-care workers, librarians, campus security, members of the clergy—they're all there for you. (If you're hesitant about taking advantage of their services, remember that your tuition helps pay for their presence.)

Don't ever think that you're all alone, with no one to turn to, because you're not.

The more you know about college ahead of time, the easier your adjustment will be. Of course, everybody's experience is different. But some things—including many aspects of being a freshman—are universal. Whether you're at a private school, a state university, or a community college or junior college, you'll probably experience some of the same emotional jolts and go through many of the same adjustments as freshmen everywhere.

Which brings us back to travel. As Abraham Lincoln once pointed out, "Nobody ever got lost on a straight road." The route through college is one of the best trips you'll ever take—but it's not a straight road. In fact, it can be a winding, sometimes confusing, and occasionally bumpy road to travel. This book is designed to alert

The good news is that you don't have to know everything the first day.

you to the hairpin turns and the places where avalanches occur and to help you over some of those rough spots along the way.

College is a series of choices. If you'll be living away from home, you'll probably have more freedom than you've ever had before, and with this new freedom come countless more choices. Some of them are mundane—what clothes to bring or wear or wash, for instance. Others are more important—to drink or do drugs, or not. To have a sex life, or not. To study hard, or not. To explore many career paths and expand your intellectual, spiritual, and philosophical horizons, or not.

You're in charge now.

Now go out there and make the most of it! We hope this book helps.

The route through college is one of the best trips you'll ever take—but it's not a straight road. In fact, it can be a winding, sometimes confusing, and occasionally bumpy road to travel.

Are You Ready for College?

Take this quiz and find out. The answers can be found by reading the rest of this book.

1. You're doing your laundry in the dorm. You leave for a while, only to return and find your moist clothes in a heap on an orange plastic chair and a lone tube sock—with somebody's muddy boot mark—on the floor. You suspect this is the work of someone you know only as Selfish Laundry Guy, who certainly
   a. Took your clothes out of the dryer to save himself the cost of a dryer load
   b. Helped himself to your new Tommy Hilfiger shirt
   c. Will get beaten up one day
   d. Can be thwarted by the simple act of doing your homework in the laundry room.

2. Body piercing and tattooing
   a. Can help you achieve the desirable look of a human fishing lure
   b. Can lead to chronic infections with no cure
   c. Can cause you to be rejected as a blood donor
   d. Are best done by an artistic friend

3. Despite strict dorm policy and the watchful eye of your RA, you accidentally made a few dozen holes in your wall when you hung up some pictures. Now it is check-out time, and you want to avoid a fine. Match the toothpaste with the color of the wall it can be used to plug.
Crest	White
Aim	Blue
Pepsodent	Green
Aquafresh	Rose

4. You're trying to dress well without racking up the debt of a backwater nation. Your best bet is to
   a. Establish a close working relationship with a fashion consultant at a store near campus, who knows your sizes, tastes, and penchant for luxury
   b. Shop at home with your parents
   c. Save the shipping and handling fees of several small purchases with one or two mail-order frenzies

5. It is okay to
   a. Give out your ATM pin number to a bank officer if she clearly identifies herself
   b. Let a store employee copy your MasterCard number on a check, particularly if you have an out-of-state bank
   c. Make the minimum payments on several credit cards for the rest of your life

6. College means
   a. If you don't show up for every class, don't sweat it. This isn't high school, and it probably won't affect your grade
   b. You may have only two tests per semester
   c. You may have to speak up in class to get a good grade

7. Match the appropriate statements in each column.
   Incomplete   A = D
   Pass/Fail   Selling your soul to the devil
   Dean's List   May show up on a transcript twice, may not
   The Repeat Option   Looks good on a résumé

8. Professorial politics: bad idea or good idea?
   a. Having sex with your professor
   b. Asking your professor if you missed anything important during that class you skipped.
   c. Questioning your professor closely about his tenure status
   d. Calling your professor at home for insight into tomorrow's essay exam
   e. Blowing off your appointment during your professor's office hours. Whether you show up or not, she has to be there anyway, right?

True or false:

1. College work-study will kill you academic career

2. The best way to get established is to latch onto your old friends from high school—a ready-made clique.

3. Your high school academic and social performance will determine your destiny in college.

4. You can get paid for taking part in student government.

5. If someone you know passes out from drinking too much, it is best to let him or her sleep it off alone.

6. Hazing can't be dangerous because your fraternity is part of the university, and thus is sanctioned.

7. You are a fifth-year junior. You drink fifty-five six-packs a year, but it's only beer, so it's okay.

The Ultimate College Survival Guide

CHAPTER 1

Settling In

The big move to dorm life is just days away, and you're getting all your stuff ready to go.

Now take a break. Before you pack so much as a toothbrush, go to your room and just sit there for a minute. Imagine four walls made out of concrete block—a box, about 10' x 10'. Put an imaginary twin bed in there. Add a desk, half of a dresser, and a tiny, inadequate closet.

This is probably not too far removed from what you'll be living in when you get to college. And do you notice something? Already, it's almost full.

Not a large amount of space. Now, imagine this room with the barest necessities—a couple of towels, a change of sheets, a pillow or two—and a few personal essentials—toiletries, shoes, some clothes. Cram in a semester's worth of textbooks, a typewriter or personal computer if you're lucky enough to have one, stuff for your desk, a laundry basket, hair dryer, hot pot, lamp, some boxes, and cans of food.

Where's the CD player going to go? Where are you going to put the TV? What about that little refrigerator you were thinking of getting?

This is bad. Your college dorm room is starting to look more like somebody's yard sale than a home.

Get the picture? Less is more. It's a lot easier to add a few things at a time from home, as you need them, than to begin college living in a storage closet. (Actually, some dormitory rooms are even smaller than the law requires the minimum prison cell space to be!)

In packing for college, as in almost all things, moderation is your key to happiness. So restrain yourself now. You'll thank us later—particularly if any of your belongings get stolen or trashed during a party by some of your roommate's (or your own) rowdy friends.

JEANS, SWEATS, TEE SHIRTS . . . WHAT CLOTHES TO PACK?

School starts in the fall, right? There's a cool breeze in the air that hints of wood smoke from bonfires; of corduroys, flannel shirts, and wool sweaters; of tailgate parties on warm, plaid blankets; of autumn leaves turning riotous colors.

Wrong! Most of this eventually does happen, but not for about two or three months in most parts of the country. Yes, these are great images. That's why they're so familiar. Think of the fall catalogs you get in the summer from J. Crew, Land's End, and L.L. Bean and magazines such as *Seventeen* with its crisp "Back to School" layouts. They'd be pretty boring if they showed you what the weather is really like in most places when school starts—hot and sticky.

Some schools wait until after Labor Day to start; others begin classes in late August. In any case, it's usually the tail end of the dog days of summer. Some classrooms don't even have air conditioning.

Now is not the time to model your new fall wardrobe.

"I went to school in Nashville, Tennessee, at Vanderbilt," says Jason, a recent graduate. "In the summer, it's no exaggeration to say it was a festering hell. Very humid, and oppressively hot. The worst part about this for me was that it made me very sleepy—especially in the classes just after lunch. I had to sit in the front row just to force myself to stay awake."

His twin sister, Jennifer, remembers the day of her first class. "I got up early and spent 45 minutes fixing my make-up and my hair—which died the minute I stepped outside. The skirt I had ironed the night before wilted, too. I was just so hot and miserable. The next day I wore a nice pair of shorts and a cool shirt, and felt a lot better."

Well, there's another myth shot down—that college is just like it appears in all those fall fashion layouts. Sometimes it is; but often it's not. So dress for the weather, whatever that is where you are. It makes good sense that if you're comfortable physically, you're more likely to become comfortable in other ways—and start to feel like you belong.

If you're planning to return home within the next few weeks, don't be like Rachel (see right) and take your whole wardrobe. That's silly; there's no point. Take enough summer clothes to survive those first few sweltering weeks, and some transitional clothes—a few sweaters and a jacket.

TOO MUCH OF A GOOD THING IS TOO MUCH

"It was really embarrassing," laughs Rachel, a student at the University of Maryland. "I brought everything I owned: casual clothes, enough outfits to get me through a whole week's worth of parties, even two formal dresses that I had worn to junior and senior proms. It was August—I had winter clothes, I had summer clothes, I had transitional clothes. You name the occasion, I was prepared for it." Rachel can admit it now: she was afraid that somehow she wouldn't have the right clothes for college. So she reasoned that some of her wardrobe might not be appropriate for college, but all of it wouldn't be. "As it turns out, I ended up wearing about the same clothes to class as a college freshman that I did in high school—except maybe they're more casual."

What seems so funny now is that Rachel wasn't coming to Maryland from across the country or even from another state. Her parents' home in a Baltimore suburb was only 45 minutes from the College Park, Maryland, campus. The problem was that when Rachel packed for school, she panicked. She took everything.

"I didn't even leave any clothes behind to wear when I'd come home for a weekend—I had to bring some of them back from my dorm room! I had to pack just to go home." By fall break, Rachel ended up taking about half of her wardrobe home again.

WHY YOU SHOULD BUY CLOTHES AT HOME

A tip many future freshmen have found useful: Buy clothes at home, before you go off to school—even though you may be tempted to wait until you get to campus so you can be sure of getting the "in" styles.

There are a couple of good, practical reasons why this is a good tip: One reason is that the shops near most college campuses tend to be overpriced. They know they've got you, especially if you don't have a car. (You're kind of a captive audience, or consumer.) They also know they can count on fairly steady business from visiting parents and wealthy alumni.

But come on: $50 for a shirt you could get for $16 on sale at home? Ouch! It hurts to pay through the nose for stuff like that. Investigate for yourself. You'll probably find out, as have many of the students we polled, that the farther away you get from campus, the more reasonably priced things are.

The second good reason is a theory that works for many students. If you buy clothes at home, your parents are more likely to foot the bill. If you buy your clothes at school, you may have to pay for them with your own spending money, which also must stretch to cover such necessities as books, laundry, and food. For many students, the budget meter doesn't start running until after they arrive at school. So, in other words, if your mom or dad buys now, you won't have to pay later.

Tips for packing smart

First, don't take obvious summer clothes. After all, fall is just around the corner. This means, don't take the white shoes, pants, or suit you wore just after Easter. Labor Day is traditionally considered the cut-off day for such springtime garments. Basically, these clothes will just take up valuable space in your closet. Nobody's going to come and admire them as they hang there, so just leave them at home, and wow your friends with your stylishness next spring.

Instead, take clothes that can do double duty. You know what we're talking about here: Jeans and khakis (shorts, pants, skirts) are always in style. Denim or chambray shirts, skirts, and pants can pretty much be worn year-round. The same goes for tee shirts and polo shirts; they can be worn by themselves or layered under sweaters or other shirts. So can button-down cotton shirts and flannel shirts. Also, items such as thermal underwear are great for layering. Avoid flowery and obviously "summer" prints. By fall, they are old news.

By the same token, avoid "winter" clothes—there's no point in packing corduroys until you can wear them. In sweltering weather, just looking at them is enough to make you hot! Remember that winter lasts until almost the end of March. The warm weather we're so tired of in the fall takes its own sweet time getting here in the spring. So leave your heavy winter clothes at home. You'll have plenty of opportunities to wear these things later.

Again, just use your head. Instead of simply emptying a drawer's contents into your suitcase, think about each individual item of clothing you pack. Imagine yourself wearing it with at least two outfits. Make it earn its place in your crowded dorm room. Chances are, you won't wear half the stuff you bring anyway.

And finally, if you get into trouble, there's always mail order—either from a catalog or, better yet, from the "Parent Express." Almost any garment can be safely boxed and shipped to your campus post office within a few days. This certainly includes the warm coat or sweater hanging in your closet at home. (Your fragile senior prom dress, on the other hand, may be more of a risk—and a pain—to ask someone to mail.)

Should I Pierce Anything? What About a Tattoo?

Sure. Pierce anything you want. Put enough jangly things in your head to make you look like a human fishing lure. Knock yourself out. The odds are good that this phase will pass fairly quickly. Most people who get something pierced—tongue, belly button, eyebrow, nipple, nose, or various private parts—may put up with one bout of infection, or even two, but finally decide that the redness, inflammation, tenderness, and discomfort outweighs any conceivable aesthetic benefit by far.

Now, about tattoos: Hmm. A quick perusal through the current Baltimore, Maryland, *Yellow Pages* shows several tattoo parlors. On the next page is a huge ad for tattoo removal. The ad reads, in part: "Now it's finally possible to safely and effectively remove all types and colors of homemade and professional tattoos without scarring or surgery." The doctor, a board-certified dermatologist, offers two forms of laser treatment that—a bonus—remove tattoo ink pigment but not normal skin tissue. Hey!

If you really feel the need for a tattoo or permanent eyeliner, do whatever you think is best; however, here are our two cents on the subject:

- Start with a fake. The same artists who draw the real ones can do temporary tattoos, which can last several weeks. This will give you a chance to see if a tattoo is really for you. Actually, *mehndi*, an ancient Indian art of body painting with henna, is a very hip alternative: Trendy *mehndi* masterpieces have been seen on Hollywood types including Mira Sorvino, Demi Moore, and Liv Tyler. The designs are elaborate; the process takes hours. The henna "sets" in the skin within a few days, and fades after a few weeks. The bonuses: It's temporary, the dye is natural, and (a biggie) it doesn't hurt. And unlike tattoos, no needles are required.
- Avoid artistic friends with needles. Your odds of getting hepatitis C (see Chapter Twelve) are infinitely lower if you have a professional—licensed and regulated by the health department and other organizations—trained in sterile procedures.

The doctor, a board-certified dermatologist, offers two forms of laser treatment that—a bonus—remove tattoo ink pigment but not normal skin tissue. Hey!

FINDING BATHROOM PRIVACY AWAY FROM HOME

This isn't a big deal for everybody, and it's not something many people will even talk about. But when a group of recent graduates from colleges in several states—Florida, Kentucky, Tennessee, Maryland, Indiana, and Arizona—met to discuss issues for this book, the subject of bathroom privacy came up. Obviously, we can't give you numbers here (not that you'd really want them), but some new freshmen do have a real problem performing all their daily bathroom activities—we think you know what we mean here—in a communal bathroom.

So, if you have this problem, what can you do? First, figure out the peak hours, when your floor's bathroom is busiest. And don't use the bathroom then. Go in the off hours—in the middle of the afternoon, or late at night.

Another good tip: Scout the campus for out-of-the-way, seldom-used restrooms. Nearly every campus building—particularly classroom or office buildings—has a few of these. They may not be as nice as your bathroom at home or even in the dorm, but privacy is privacy. Make it work for you.

- Ask about their hygienic procedures. Look for words like "autoclave sterilization" (involving intense heat), also called "hospital sterilization," and "universal precautions," steps to avoid transmitting AIDS, hepatitis, and other blood-borne diseases. Better still, look for places that offer disposable needles AND—this is important—disposable ink.
- DO NOT DONATE BLOOD. Your intentions are noble; you want to help. But because tattoos (even permanent eyeliner) involve the use of needles, and because some of these needles may not have been properly sterilized (see above), you will probably be disqualified from giving blood for up to a year—particularly if the tattoo or piercing was done at home or by a friend. After a year, your blood can be tested to make certain you are free from infection. The Los Angeles Red Cross estimates that it turns away nearly one percent of people who want to donate blood because of recent tattoos or piercings.

THE BATHROOM IS DOWN THE HALL

For many students, one of the biggest adjustments is getting used to a communal bathroom. For one thing, it's inconvenient. Everything has the potential to be a bigger deal than normal. Say, for instance, you're in the middle of a shower and realize you forgot to bring the shampoo. Oops.

You have several options: Bag washing your hair today—just get it wet and hope it looks clean. Attempt to wash your hair with the bar of soap. Borrow somebody else's shampoo. Hope for the kindness of a passing stranger—one you can entrust with your dripping-wet room key, which you hand over from behind the shower curtain. Or, worst case, drag your wet, soapy self back to the room and start over, hoping in the meantime that no one will take your spot in the shower.

Our strategy for successfully dealing with the group bathroom is simple: Be prepared. The best defense is a good offense. Figure out what you'll need in the shower, put it all together in one container, and use it.

Bathroom essentials

Essential bathroom items are whatever you use most often as you perform your daily personal maintenance. The basic list probably includes:

- Toothbrush
- Toothpaste
- Soap
- Shampoo
- Conditioner
- Razor
- Shaving cream
- Deodorant
- Comb

Other items, such as a hair dryer, brush, and other hair necessities, may be best left in your room, where they'll stay dry. *Note: Don't ever take your hair dryer into the shower stall with you!* Even if it's on a pretty dry, out-of-the-way shelf, you don't want to risk getting it wet.

Other essentials: Shower thongs. Unfortunately, athlete's foot is a common malady in residence halls. Don't just wear them to get to the shower, wear them in the shower. This advice comes from Ben, a student at Wittenberg University in Ohio, who thought we needed to spell this out. He came to college with thongs, but took them off once he got in the shower. He got athlete's foot. "I took showers in high school every day after gym class, and this never happened to me," he says with disgust. "Maybe that's because the showers were open there, and easier to clean or something!" *Note: Athlete's foot needs a warm, moist environment to grow—like the same pair of tennis shoes worn every day.* So you should rotate your shoe lineup and try not to wear the same pair two days in a row; give your sneakers a chance to air out. (If your school is already in a warm, moist environment—a hothouse like New Orleans, for example—it may even be worth it to have two sets of thongs, and to alternate them so they can dry out between showers.)

Also, you'll need something to wear as you travel between your room and the shower. A bathrobe is good; so is a wrap-around beach towel, with elastic and Velcro along the edges so it stays up by itself, leaving your hands free to carry other stuff.

THE BATHROOM BUCKET

For many, there is a key to successful showering, a linchpin on which rest many trouble-free trips down the hall to the bathroom: The bucket.

The well-stocked bathroom bucket or plastic tray (guys may prefer a shaving kit) is your friend. The specifics—what you put in it and the kind of bucket you choose—are up to you. It's a personal decision. "I had two buckets my freshman year," says Ruth, a recent University of Maryland graduate. "One was a gift for my high school graduation. It was huge, like a bathtub. It had my name personalized on it. But it was so huge that I ended up getting rid of it. Then I found a little heart-shaped bucket, which I loved."

But Mark, a recent graduate of Arizona State University in Tempe, Arizona, scoffs at the bucket idea. "I never heard of that! I just use a shaving kit. It's got everything you need, plus, you're ready to go at the drop of a hat if you leave campus for a weekend."

Whatever. The idea is the same—a container, where all your essential toiletries can reside conveniently together in one place.

TIPS FOR HASSLE-FREE LAUNDERING

Save your quarters. Put them in a special, secret place in your room (a sock in a drawer, for instance) where your roommate or dorm buddies won't find it and "borrow" a quarter or two. It's no fun trying to hit people up for change for a dollar late at night—particularly if you've got wet clothes that can't go in the dryer until you get 50 more cents.

Avoid the marathon laundry session by washing smaller loads more often. In the end, it's less time-consuming.

Invest in a folding clothes rack. Some students save lots of money and time by never paying to dry their clothes. Instead, they wash them and then bring them back, wet, to hang up in their rooms. Their towels may not be as fluffy, but they don't seem to mind. (Some drawbacks: These racks do take up space, and the damp clothes can make a small room humid.)

Wash clothes on weeknights. Good times are during the day between classes, in the late afternoon, or right after dinner (before other people get their act together and decide to do the same thing). Sunday nights are generally terrible.

Wash like colors together if you're planning on doing more than one load. It is the sadder but wiser student who washes red socks with white tee shirts in hot water. If you're washing whites or lights, use hot or warm water (warning: we've found that institutional hot

Linens

If you can, take two sets of sheets, pillowcases, towels, and washcloths. You may have great intentions, but it's likely you won't do laundry until it's absolutely necessary. It's good to have a spare. (It's particularly handy to have a spare in case a friend, parent, or sibling comes to visit and spends the night.) *Note: Designer linens are nice but unnecessary. Go to Kmart or a similar store or, better yet, a linen outlet and buy them cheap.* That way, in the event of an unfortunate laundry incident (like washing brand-new blue jeans with your pristine white sheets) or spill, you won't see dollar signs instead of the humor of the situation.

THE PORTABLE MEDICINE CABINET

Sooner or later, it's going to happen: You'll get a headache while you're trying to study for tomorrow's test. Or you'll cut yourself shaving or wake up with a horrible cold.

Such maladies are inevitable, and they rarely respect normal business hours. What are you going to do? Again, the answer is to be prepared. Loading up on a few supplies today will definitely come in handy tomorrow. Get them cheap; go to a discount or warehouse store.

What you'll probably need

- **Something for a headache.** You can get brand names, or you can buy generic medications, which are generally just as good and a lot cheaper. Let's face it, aspirin is aspirin, no matter who makes it. The same holds true for Tylenol (the key compound is called acetaminophen) and Advil or Motrin (the key ingredient in both is ibuprofen). Important note: Some of these pain relievers DO NOT MIX WELL WITH ALCOHOL. The U.S. Food and Drug Administration recently proposed putting labels on some nonprescription painkillers, warning anyone who drinks three or more alcoholic beverages a day to check with a doctor before taking one of these pills. Why? Well, for starters, you could damage your liver or stomach. Acetaminophen can cause permanent liver damage if combined with alcohol. Alcohol and other drugs, such as aspirin, ibuprofen, and naproxen (found in Aleve), can irritate the stomach, even causing it to bleed.

- **Antihistamines or decongestants for cold symptoms.** Some of these can make you sleepy, so read the label. *Tip: Some of these also can make you wired.* This can be a real problem if you need to sleep; so it may be better to buy remedies that need to be taken every 4 to 6 hours, instead of the 12-hour kind. This way, no matter how they affect you, they'll wear off a lot sooner.
- **Cough drops or cough syrup.** There's nothing worse than a hacking cough when you (and others) are trying to take notes during a lecture. Do you want a cough suppressant—something to soothe your throat—or an expectorant—something to loosen up congestion in your chest? Make sure you choose the right one for your symptoms. A pharmacist will be happy to advise you on which one to buy, if you are not sure.
- **Bandages.** Get a multipurpose box, with a variety of sizes. Again, almost any brand will do.
- **Antacids.** Some people prefer the kind you drink; some prefer the pills you chew. A bonus: Tums and similar pills contain calcium—which, as the ads say, your body needs anyway.
- **Medication for diarrhea or an upset stomach.** You definitely don't want to have to go shopping for this when you need it desperately—say, the night before a big exam.
- **Cotton balls, tissues, cotton swabs, tweezers and a sewing needle (for splinter removal).**

What else? Ask your mother. For one reason, she knows. For another, it'll make her feel like she's still taking good care of you, even though you're farther away.

KEEPING UP APPEARANCES

Keeping up appearances means looking halfway decent, if that's a goal for you, or, at least, keeping your clothes (and sheets, towels, and washcloths) clean and free of unwanted holes, tears, or rips, with no buttons missing,

water can be extremely hot). If you're washing colors, use cold water. If you're washing everything in one load and you know nothing is going to "bleed," it's probably safe to use warm. If you're washing everything in one load and you're not sure, use cold water.

Investigate local laundries that will wash your clothes for you. Some places offer "laundry by the pound" and charge differently depending on what you want done—if you want them dried or folded or both. At Muhlenberg College in Pennsylvania, some students in an entrepreneurial class have started their own highly successful laundry service. Best of all—they deliver!

What else might you need for your medicine cabinet? Ask your mother. For one reason, she knows. For another, it'll make her feel like she's still taking good care of you, even though you're farther away.

THE LAUNDRY RULE

Here is a good measuring stick for how many clothes to bring: How often will you be washing your clothes? As Mark, an Arizona State graduate, points out: "Guys may wait a lot longer than girls—until every single thing they have is dirty—to do laundry. Therefore, they may need to bring more clothes. There's nothing worse than wearing something you've already worn that should have been washed first." Bring enough clothes—particularly underwear!—to accommodate your own individual laundry habits. If you're planning to do laundry at least once a week, fine; running out of clothes probably won't be a cause for concern. If, however, you're planning to wash clothes in, say, monthly marathon sessions, you might want to do your friends a favor and stock up on tee shirts, undies, and socks.

and making sure that your shoes are in fairly good shape. It also means handling details like minor sewing repairs. Therefore, you might want to consider these:

- **A small sewing kit,** with a needle; some thread in various shades (if nothing else, you can get by with a spool each of white and black thread); safety pins, and iron-on, double-sided sewing tape (this stuff is great—instant hems!) for quick repairs.
- **Shoe paraphernalia**—extra laces, some polish, or a quick-fix sponge kit that adds instant shine to real or fake leather of any color.
- **An iron**, if you iron a lot. Some dorms furnish a communal iron and ironing board (there's usually one for each floor or so). You can't always count on the reliability of these irons, though, and you may not want to wait if there's a line and you're running late. You can get a portable, half-size ironing board that stows under your bed. However, many people make do by ironing clothes on the bed or on a clean rug or towel on the floor.

But mostly, keeping up appearances means doing laundry.

Laundry paraphernalia you'll probably need

- **A laundry basket.** It's bulky, but you'll probably keep it forever if you get a good one. Also, you can use it to store dirty clothes or loose gear—particularly when you're moving in and out. One small bonus here is that you're more likely to be confronted with your dirty clothes, and therefore (this is only a theory) you may be reminded to wash them more often.
- **Or a laundry bag.** This may be the way to go if space is a problem. It probably holds just as much, and it can be stored much more easily. The only problem here, for those of you who don't wash clothes very often or who live in swampy climates, is the potential for mildew if damp washcloths or towels sit for a week or two in this enclosed bag in your closet.
- **Powder or liquid detergent.** The best buy is a box of concentrated detergent that only takes one scoopful for each load. This can last a long

time—probably a couple of months. The worst use of your money is to buy limited amounts of detergent that might be available in the laundry room. For one thing, sometimes these vending machines don't even work, so there go some valuable quarters or tokens.

- **Spot or stain remover.** There's a variety to choose from, including some you can even spray or rub on days before you actually get around to doing the laundry.

Optional:

- **Fabric softener sheets for the dryer.** These make your clothes smell nice, and they can help control static cling.
- **Liquid soap for hand-washables or delicate clothes** if you don't want to dry-clean them. But another option is . . .
- **A mesh bag for delicate items.** This is great for delicate items such as lingerie that you probably should, but don't want to, wash by hand.
- **Clothes pins and a portable clothesline** if you plan to dry your clothes in your room.
- **A folding drying rack.**

Guerilla Laundry Warfare: Why you should keep an eye on your clothes

A bit of laundry-room advice: Don't leave your clothes in the washing machine or dryer.

Many people disagree with this, and there are certainly some exceptions (if it's late at night, for example, and you're the only one around and don't feel comfortable staying). Yes, it is a colossal waste of time to just sit there and wait for the spin cycle. So bring a book, study, write a letter—all of these things are time-consuming, and they might as well take up your time while you're washing your clothes.

The justification for babysitting your clothes is an unsavory fact we call "Guerilla Laundry Warfare." It's not rampant, but it's not that rare, either.

The basic problem here is that some people are not as courteous as you are. Some people are basically selfish. Say one of these cretins—we'll call him Selfish Laundry Guy—wants to wash his clothes. Now.

Your clothes have been washed; they're sitting there, damp, in the washer, waiting for you to take them out

It is the sadder but wiser student who washes red socks with white tee shirts in hot water.

Selfish Laundry Guy hates to wait. He opens the washer with your clothes, takes them out and—if your're lucky—dumps them on a nearby table. Selfish Laundry Guy is not nice. He doesn't feel bound by basic rules of common courtesy. One day, somebody's going to beat him up.

ESSENTIALS FOR STUDYING

• A good dictionary. A lot of dictionaries out there have the name "Webster's" attached to them. This doesn't necessarily mean they're all equally good; some of them are better than others. Read some sample entries.

• A thesaurus. A real essential for those times when your vocabulary fails you or even when it doesn't but you need writing inspiration. Sometimes, just looking at a stream of related words can suggest new ideas. Note: Even if your computer has a thesaurus—most likely compiled by some geek who thinks "prehistoric" means the mainframe era—it's probably not as good as the old-fashioned kind that you can buy in the bookstore.

• A style manual, showing the correct form for footnotes and bibliography.

• One or two exceptionally well written papers from your high school days. You can use the format and outline for guidance in case your skills have dulled a bit since you last sat in a classroom (the summer before college has this effect on some people).

and put them in the dryer. They keep sitting there—because you're grabbing a bite to eat, or you're on the phone, taking a nap, whatever.

Selfish Laundry Guy hates to wait. He opens the washer with your clothes, takes them out, and—if you're lucky—dumps them on a nearby table. (One Florida State student, Jules, had his clothes dumped on a muddy floor. Not only did he have to pay to wash them again, but he was angry and felt, he said, "violated.")

Selfish Laundry Guy also strikes loads of clothes that are in the dryer. Sometimes he takes out still-damp laundry to make free use of the dryer time somebody else just paid for. (Selfish Laundry Guy is cheap.) Sometimes he takes clean, fluffy clothes and puts them on the table or elsewhere. Sometimes, if Selfish Laundry Guy likes what he sees, he has been known to help himself to a particular garment.

Selfish Laundry Guy is not nice. He doesn't feel bound by basic rules of common courtesy. The problem is, there's usually at least one Selfish Laundry Guy (or Gal) on every college campus. But Selfish Laundry Guy is also gutless; he doesn't dare try his tricks if the owner of the clothes is sitting right there, watching him.

Note: If you just can't abide sitting in the laundry, another option may be to time the washer and dryer cycles, know exactly how long you can stay away, and return the instant your clothes are done.

THE WELL-STOCKED DESK

Office warehouse stores are wonderful places. If there's one near you, visit it before you go to school. Whatever you buy there will almost certainly be cheaper than anything you'll be buying at the school bookstore. If you can't find such a store, return once again to our favorite discount stores—Kmart, Wal-Mart, or Target. This is a fact: There are certain things you're going to need. It's better to have them before you go, and it's definitely better to have them before you realize at an inconvenient time that you need them ASAP—say, a binder for the midterm paper that you've ended up finishing in the middle of the night, despite all your good intentions of working on it a little bit at a time in a responsible fashion throughout the semester. So plan ahead.

Okay. Got your shopping list? Here are some items that should be on it:

- **Scissors.**
- **Tape.** Clear is best for projects; however, a roll of strapping tape comes in handy for mailing packages, and duct tape is useful for fixing things (such as your old, overstuffed suitcase that comes apart an hour before you're scheduled to fly home for Christmas vacation).
- **Paper clips.** Big and small; if you have to pick one size, just get the jumbo clips—it's better to have overkill on a small paper than an inadequate clip that can't hold a 20-page document together.
- **A stapler and staples.**
- **Ballpoint pens and pencils.** Get a good number— at least fifteen—of each; they tend to disappear as either you lose them or people permanently "borrow" them.
- **Paper, paper, paper.** One notebook for each class. Blank paper for use on computer printers or typewriters. Use this or buy some stationery for writing your family, high school friends, and future employers. Envelopes. Again, if you have to pick, go big. You can't go wrong with legal envelopes rather than the letter-sized ones.
- **A box of pre-formatted computer disks—**for homework, downloaded Internet files, back-ups, etc.
- **Stamps.** Get a roll of 100 and hide them in a sock. They should last for most of a semester. (Note: And, now that you have them, write some letters to the folks back home.)
- **A small, cheap address book.** This will do the job until some relative gives you a nicer one for graduation.
- **A highlighter** for marking key passages in your books. We prefer a light yellow (it's less annoying), although some opt for fluorescent green or pink. Whatever works for you.
- **White-out** for covering your writing mistakes. At least one bottle. This stuff has an irritating tendency to dry out, and there's nothing worse than trying to dilute it so you can disguise that one last typo.
- **Small note pads or "yellow stickies"** for phone messages. You can't have too many of these; like pens, they tend to vanish.

There are certain things you're going to need. It's better to have them before you go, and it's definitely better to have them before you realize at an inconvenient time that you need them ASAP.

MAKING A HOME AWAY FROM HOME

Little things mean a lot, particularly in a cramped dorm room. It's the small, personal touches that say the most about you. A lot of people have a TV (a lot of people, in fact, have the same TV). But only *you* have Mr. Bunny. You'll never forget your mom buying him in the hospital gift shop the day you had your tonsils out.

Only you have that crazy photo of the canoe trip where everything, and everybody, wound up overboard. And here's you and your best friend—both barefoot—at graduation. What a couple of nuts.

This doesn't mean you should take your entire scrapbook, or every single familiar thing in your room. Actually, it's a good idea to leave a lot at home. For one thing, there's the space problem. For another, it's a good morale booster to have a rotating collection on exhibit. Also, there's always the risk that when you take anything anywhere, you'll lose it or it'll get stolen or broken. So if you're worried, leave your most priceless keepsakes at home.

- **A calculator**. You'll need it for subjects such as math, economics, and engineering. You'll also need it for balancing your checkbook every month.
- **A bookbag or backpack**. You won't need it for your desk, but you'll almost certainly need it for class.

Better living through hardware

Electrical outlets are your friends. Like all real friendships, they're all too rare. Some dorm rooms, for example, only have two or three outlets. So you know what this means: extension cords and special electrical adapters that let you plug in four or six cords instead of the usual two per outlet.

A lamp is one of the best investments you can make for your room. It doesn't matter what this lamp looks like; you can get a cheap plastic one for less than $10 at a discount store. And what a difference a lamp makes! For one thing, it means you're not solely dependent on the harsh overhead glare from the hideous ceiling light. For another, this gives you some flexibility; you can study into the wee hours at your desk without disturbing your roommate. Lamps make a room look more like home. One lamp is essential. A second one—by your bed or on your dresser—is also great.

What else? An alarm clock—unless you're one of those people who, like a rooster, naturally rises at dawn—is pretty much of a necessity. So is a radio. A clock radio, particularly one with a snooze alarm, is a fine way to have both. Some people prefer the old-fashioned kind of clock that sounds an alarm loud enough to wake the dead. If you remember to wind them, these windup clocks are more reliable—and, unlike electric clocks, they don't stop working if there's a power failure or an accidental unplugging.

At some schools, such as the University of Maryland at College Park, the computerized telephone system is so sophisticated that students can even get their own "wake-up" calls. Using their touchtone phones, they tell the computer when they want to be awakened. (For more on this, see the box on page 16.)

A hot pot or hot plate is nice if the dorm allows it. College students, because they tend to keep odd hours, tend to crave food at odd hours. You probably won't be any exception, particularly when you're studying late, and you may not want to leave your room to find a snack. *(Note: It's a good idea to bring several cans of soup, chili, beans, or stew and a pan of some sort for making emergency meals if you run out of money or miss the cafeteria's closing time.)*

Many students find they can't live without a popcorn popper. One University of Washington chemistry major, Tim, who wasn't allowed to have a hot pot, actually cooked in his popcorn popper. We don't recommend this. If your dorm floor has a microwave, you may prefer to invest in a case of microwave popcorn packets.

If you can afford it, a small refrigerator is a great luxury. Many schools make these available (some schools, such as the Johns Hopkins University in Baltimore, Maryland, offer a microwave-refrigerator "combo") for a rental fee every semester, and certainly one option is for you and your roommate to split this charge. However, for the cost of a couple semesters' worth of refrigerator rental, you could buy a new one. One way to justify this expense—say about $100—is to decide to buy fewer meals out and eat in more often or buy cases of soft drinks so you don't have to pay 75 cents for a single can (you serious soda drinkers know how this adds up!). Remember: You can always sell the refrigerator later to your roommate or to some younger student.

Optional:

- **A small TV.**
- **A cassette/CD player.**

At your own risk:

- **Anything expensive and likely to get stolen.**

Don't look here for the stamp of approval to bring that sweet stereo system you worked all those weekends at the mall to afford. Don't tell us, you're still paying for it? Even worse. Please, do us a favor: bring such luxuries, including video games and equipment, at your own risk. Read Jim's cautionary tale on this page, and then decide if it's worth it.

Many students who decide to bring their stereos, TVs, VCRs, microwaves, and other appliances end up taking them back home for long weekends and fall, Christmas, or spring breaks, when campus security might not be as tight. This is probably a good idea.

IF IT'S TOO SPECIAL, LEAVE IT AT HOME

One of the treasures that Jim, a University of California, Davis student, brought to his freshman dorm room was a glass brandy snifter, engraved with his and his girlfriend's signatures. He had bought it as a memento of their senior prom date.

"I wasn't obsessed with it or anything," he says. "But it was on my desk, and I knew it was there. It reminded me of my girlfriend," a freshman at the University of Southern California.

One Sunday night, Jim returned from a weekend at home to discover the snifter was missing (along with, he learned later, one of his rugby shirts). He confronted his roommate, Marcus, who admitted that he'd had a few friends over Saturday night. Their get-together had turned into a rowdy party, involving a case of beer, during which the room was trashed. When Marcus (who, like the room, had been a little the worse for wear after the party) woke up Sunday morning and began cleaning up the mess, he discovered some broken glass and realized what had happened. Somebody had smashed Jim's snifter.

"At least he offered to pay me for it," Jim comments.

Jim's advice: "Don't bring anything to school you can't afford to lose." Because chances are, you might lose it.

NOT YOUR MOM'S OLD DORM ROOM: A COLLEGE GOES HIGH-TECH

Several years ago, the University of Maryland in College Park spent $32 million to buy its own state-of-the-art digital telecommunications system. "It was the largest single-site installation AT&T ever put in," says Thomas Heacock, manager of the university's Telecommunication Technical Services.

What the university got for its money, Heacock believes, was well worth the price. For starters, there are 13,000 voice mailboxes—one for every resident student and faculty member—and 20,000 phone lines. "We have more phones in College Park than there are in some small countries," Heacock jokes.

One remarkable feature here is that all students living on campus have their own telephone and their own voice mailbox.

"The students love it," says Heacock, "If they're on the phone, the second call automatically goes to their voice mailbox, so they never miss a call. They've really learned to use it in a variety of ways." For example, he continues, some professors leave messages in their voice mailboxes "and have students call it for their current class assignments."

Also, by using voice mail, a student who needs to get in touch with a professor can simply leave messages in the professor's voice mailbox.

If you're determined to have your CDs and great sound, a boom box or personal CD players may be the best solution. These are a lot more portable and definitely less of a pain to cart around (call us paranoid, but we must note that this convenience also may appeal to a thief).

Personal computers: The big exception

The big exception to the "don't bring anything expensive" rule is the personal computer. (Many schools feature "hard-wired" dorm rooms; even if yours isn't, and you have a modem, you're good to go.) Depending on your major, this may be more of an essential than a luxury, and it's invaluable in terms of convenience—no waiting in line at the computer lab—and reliability—no sudden, big system crashes. (By the way, if you're using the school's computer system, minimize potential loss by saving your document frequently. Know that something bad—like the screen freezing or the system going "down" and remaining out of commission for 6 hours until somebody fixes it—will probably happen when you least expect it.)

How can you protect yourself and your computer from theft? First, get in the habit ASAP of making one or more backup disks so you don't have to rack your brains in a feverish panic to remember your seven-point thesis the day before it's due. Second, check with campus police. Among other things, they may be able to give or sell you a security cable (which looks something like the cable used to lock up bicycles) that connects the insides of your computer to a plate firmly attached to the wall; also, they can probably loan you an etching device so you can give your computer a permanent identification number—the sight of which may deter a potential thief.

DECK THE WALLS

Some people—monks, for instance—find bare walls a source of solace and comfort.

Most people find them a little depressing.

You should decorate your dorm room walls. We're not talking fine art here; anything—a cheap poster, a snapshot, a clock—is better than nothing.

Here are a few suggestions:

- **At least two posters.**
- **Several photographs of your family and friends, framed or not.** They may make you homesick; they may comfort you. They also make fine conversation starters when your neighbors are visiting.
- **A bulletin or memo board** for messages, deadline reminders, or notes.

A word of warning: Your college, like many others, may have annoying, threateningly worded policies about driving nails in or putting tape on walls. (However, all this means—at least, er, so we've been told—is that when you leave, you fill the holes you put in the wall; see page 18.) What these dorms would have you do is use masking tape or inadequate, wadded-up mounds of a gummy adhesive to stick your posters on the walls. We have had little success with this kind of adhesive. However, for posters without frames, we have found that clear, "magic" tape works just fine and, if used correctly, comes right off with the poster when you take it down. If you decide to drive a nail, put a piece of clear tape over the spot before you put the nail in. This often helps protect plaster from chipping. *(Hint: If the tape is clear, you may find that it's easier to just leave it up there on the wall when you're ready to move out than to peel it off and risk removing paint.)*

MAKING THE MOST OF YOUR SPACE

Imagine a library with no bookshelves, just endless, dusty piles of books. Even if there's some orderly system, it's still going to be a nightmare if the book you need is on the bottom of the pile. (Even worse, the librarian has had trouble keeping these piles clean, and there's probably something living inside the pile you need.) Now imagine bookshelves—lots of lovely, floor-to-ceiling shelves. What space is created! Now there's order, and breathing room, and cleanliness.

Shelves work wonders in even the smallest room. So do stackable boxes, crates, and hanging racks.

Like the librarian, you, too, can create order out of chaos. Just figure out what you have a lot of—books, shoes, cosmetics, tapes—then find a good, cheap way to store them.

One of the most (literally) eye-opening features of the new system: Students can use their telephones to activate a high-tech alarm clock. The program, which uses interactive voice-response software, is called "Wake Up, Little Snoozy," says Heacock.

The university also is wiring dorms (called "data dorms") so students can plug their computers directly into the university's computer network. Class registration is done mostly on computer, too, with something called the Maryland Automated Registration System, so students can register for classes over the phone.

More advances are on University of Maryland's technological horizon, Heacock promises. "We're getting ready to add cable TV to the dorms," he says. "But we don't want to just put in plain cable TV; we want something high-tech and interactive, with 500 channels. We want to make sure it will not only provide entertainment, but also high-level educational and interactive opportunities for students."

An example: "We envision that a student who may have missed a Chemistry 101 lecture can call up our Nonprint Media Library and have them replay the tape of that lecture on a certain channel at a certain time in the evening. We can actually do that right now. In 600 classrooms and lecture halls, we can play any kind of entertainment or lecture tape on demand, but we want it to be available in the dorms, too."

PLUGGING HOLES THAT AREN'T SUPPOSED TO BE THERE

It is not our policy to break school rules or encourage anyone else to break them. Obviously, if a college sees fit to enact a rule—say, about hanging things on the wall—then there must be some deep significance, some unseen force behind this rule that will shape your mind and morality to the good and that will make you a better person for following this important edict.

But sometimes things happen.

One of those unexpected events was that your prized velvet Elvis picture didn't stick to the concrete block wall with the masking tape you were advised to use. The gummy wads of stickum, which also were deemed acceptable for you to use, didn't work either. Now there are four holes in the wall where the nails—which worked great—used to be. And there's a big divot in the acoustic tile over your bed, which happened when you took down your big brother's Grateful Dead poster.

Now, you could go to a building supply or hardware store and get some spackle, and do this job right. In fact, you probably should. Or, there's a new product called "Patch Stick," made by Dap, that fills small holes and cracks within seconds and doesn't require sanding (as ordinary spackle does).

But, as some pragmatists would argue: Let's face it. This is a dorm, and you're one

Here are a few tips:

- **For shoes:** It's not easy to store shoes in dorm rooms. A hanging shoe rack, one that fits over a door or hangs in a closet (some hold up to twelve pairs of shoes), is good. So are shoe boxes. Though they may be more trouble, the boxes are neater, and they'll probably help you save time by enabling you to locate the right shoes in a hurry.
- **For important papers**: Take a shoe box and label it something appropriate, like "Important Business." Use this for storing receipts (from the bookstore, for instance), canceled checks, your housing contract, and anything else you can't afford to lose. Put this someplace secure, like a drawer in your desk or on the shelf in your closet.
- **For books**: It's a shame to take up all your desk space with books. Then you're in the time-wasting position of either clearing your desk every time you want to use it or finding someplace else to work—like your bed, which just makes you sleepy. So where can you keep your books? Crates are good—the stackable kind, wood or plastic. Two of them can serve as your bedside table; put a lamp on top and it's downright cozy. Tip: Get to know the crate. You'll probably be using these crates, or a scaled-up version of them, for at least the next decade or so to hold everything—books, sweaters, boxes, and cans of food, even your small TV set.
- **For cosmetics, contact lens paraphernalia, and other toiletries:** Some people like to store things of this nature in fairly small, specialized baskets or boxes. The problem with putting stuff like this in one huge container is that often you're not much better off than you were before—things are still hard to find. On the other hand, having too many little compartments for your stuff can also be annoying. Find a balance that works for you.

A few decorating hints

We've already talked about the main decorating hurdle—the walls—and the essential need for at least one lamp. The room's almost made. Now, what else? A plant always helps (if you're going to water it; if not, don't bother—a dead plant is pretty depressing and worse than nothing at all). A small rug by your bed is decorative; it's also nice for cold feet in winter. If you need to cover more space, consider buying a carpet remnant at a flooring or home improvement store. They're not too expensive, and nothing beats the "cold, institutional tile floor blues" better than a nice piece of carpet.

Some creative people also buy cheap but attractive sheets and make quick, easy curtains from them.

The key here is an important rule of economics: The Point of Diminishing Returns. Don't invest more money or time into something than you'll get out of it. Remember, this is a temporary home. Next year, you'll be someplace else, and you may want to give that new place a completely different look.

TOOLS EVERY STUDENT SHOULD HAVE

This isn't "Home Improvement," and you're not Tim Allen, but still—it's good to have the right tools. You don't need anything fancy, like a router or miter box. Your needs are few and basic (your first order of business should be to install a smoke detector, if your room or apartment doesn't have one). So really, we're just talking about a couple of tools, including:

- A hammer (although, in a pinch, the wooden heel of a boot or clog will do)
- Two screwdrivers, a Phillips and a flat blade.

That's it. You should also have a few nails of various lengths.

KEEPING HOUSE

Yeah, you're really grown up now. At last, nobody can make you clean your room, pick up your clothes, wash your plate and utensils after you eat, and generally tidy up after yourself. Except you. Face it, you're not a slob—really, deep down, you're not. You need a baseline of orderliness as, to varying degrees, we all do. Hint: Don't expect your roommate to clean your half of the room or do your chores. This could lead to resentment and unpleasantness.

of hundreds of students who, like so many cattle, will pass through here over the years. (As Mark, who went to Arizona State University, points out, "You're not looking for a permanent solution. You just want to fool that RA (resident adviser) who has to check you out of the room before you can go home.")

Sometimes you need a quick fix. Here are a few options that some freshmen who have gone before you have found useful:

- Toothpaste (to fill the hole). We live in a wonderful, market-oriented society that offers many choices, and no product is a better example of this than toothpaste. For example, we have Crest (green-tinted walls), Aim (blue-tinted walls), Pepsodent (white-tinted walls), and Aquafresh (rose-tinted walls).
- White-out (to cover over a small hole, or to hide a plug of toothpaste or another substance in a bigger hole).
- Oxy-5 or Oxy-10. For white walls.
- The inadequate, gummy adhesive wads that failed to hold up your art. (Use a nail to shove this adhesive into the hole. In fact, this may be the best use for the stuff.)

*Don't expect your room-
mate to clean your half of
the room or do your
chores. This could lead to
resentment and
unpleasantness.*

And let's be reasonable here: Nobody expects you to keep your room spotless, just reasonably neat. To do this, you will need a few basic cleaning supplies:

- A broom. Either a full-sized one, or a whisk broom.
- A dustpan. If you don't have one, you can sweep a mess onto anything flat, like a piece of cardboard or newspaper.
- A piece of cloth (about the size of a kitchen towel) to dust with.
- Some multi-purpose, spray-on cleaner that works on almost any surface—glass windows, tile floors, stainless steel sinks, chrome bathroom fixtures, etc.
- Paper towels. Some people's cleaning preferences lean toward the cheap reusable towel—the kind you keep washing until it disintegrates. But sometimes it's much nicer to clean up a yucky mess and then throw away everything even remotely associated with it. Thus the paper towel. (You can use paper napkins, but they're not as absorbent and therefore not as cost-effective.)
- Some liquid dish-washing soap. You don't need much of this at a time; a tiny dab is all it takes to wash a dish. Some people prefer to wash a whole sinkload of dishes at once. Others, including us, don't. For one thing, unless you're lucky enough to have a kitchen or bath in your room, you don't know where that sink has been. Do you want to add even more time to the cleaning chores by scouring out the sink before you even wash a single dish? We thought not.

*Your prized velvet Elvis
didn't stick to the concrete
block wall with the mask-
ing tape you were advised
to use. But the nails
worked great.*

Therefore, we recommend the "wash one dish at a time" method. Here's how to do it: Hold the dish under warm running water. Squirt a tiny amount of dish-washing soap on it. Use a washcloth or paper towel, rub it over the dish until you can't feel the soap anymore and the dish seems to be clean. (Tip: It's not necessary to actually scrub every bit of food off the plate; let the running water do the job for you. If you have a baked-on, caked-on situation, it might behoove you to let the dish soak in really hot, soapy water for a few minutes. Again, the idea here is to let the water work for you.) For silverware, put a little soap on the washcloth, and rub it over your knives, forks and spoons. One soapy washcloth can take care of all of your utensils in one fell swoop.

To dry: You can either put the dishes on a clean towel and let them air-dry (this could be a problem if you're using a public rest room), or you can dry them yourself, using paper towels or a clean towel. (Any towel that is not really clean—i.e., that has a little lint, or a funny, not-very-clean smell, is not a good choice here.)

Another household tip: Spray Endust or Pledge in the air. It won't do anything, but if you don't have time to dust or clean and you have company coming over, just the smell of these products may contribute to that indefinable atmosphere of cleanliness that so many of us would like to attain, even if we don't have time to actually do the work. It's a pride thing.

Other Necessities

- Dishes: You should have at least one plate, a bowl, two glasses, and two spoons, knives and forks. It's also nice to have a bigger spoon for dishing up such things as chili.
- Your high school yearbook. Believe it or not, you *will* want to look at it.
- A wastebasket. Even if your room already has one, you can always use another.
- An umbrella. At least one, and you might want to bring a spare, in case yours gets lost or stolen (desperate weather brings on desperate behavior). Also, high winds are murder on umbrellas, and every campus with high-rises has at least one area between buildings that's literally a wind tunnel, where the wind crashes through with enough force to power Holland.
- Your old pillow. You'll need the comfort and security of your favorite, plumped-just-right pillow.
- Some type of insecticide. (See below.)

Optional:

- A big, unattractive vertical pillow with arms. Many people think such pillows are a necessity, something intrinsic to the collegiate experience. We, however, feel they're vastly overrated. In our experience, they are NOT ONLY not very comfortable, but they take up much more space

HOW TO MAKE CURTAINS FROM SHEETS

This is so easy, it's ridiculous. Really! Here's what you do: First, get a twin bed-sized top sheet, the color and pattern of your choice. Note: Since you don't really need the complete set (in other words, the fitted bottom sheet), you might get a great deal at a linen outlet store that has a grab-bag of assorted sheets for individual sale.

You know that end of the sheet with the big hem, the part that's supposed to go up by your face when you sleep? That is now the bottom of your curtain. It's already hemmed, and ready to go. See, we're halfway there already—the bottom's already done! Now, take the bottom of the sheet (which will be the top of your curtain), fold it over a curtain rod (any basic rod will do), measure a generous amount of space for the rod to go through, and stick pins in every few feet to mark this (presumably straight) line, connecting the folded-over sides together.

Okay, here's where you sticklers for detail will depart from the crowd. To be perfectly honest here, you could have a decent curtain right now, just using this pinned-together sheet. But it's probably better if you go ahead and sew the top hem, instead of relying on the pins. Use a sewing machine if you have one.

For those of you who don't, and who doubt whether you

could sew a straight line the full length of the sheet, let's cheat: Just spot-sew. Start at one end; every two or three inches, make a few stitches, tie a knot, cut the thread (this is important), and move on until you've reached the other end. Or, even better, maybe now's the time to try out double-sided, iron-on hem tape.

Voila! You're done. Hang it up, tie it back on one side (a string or even an electrical cord will do; however, for a dollar or two at a fabric or craft store you can get a nice-looking, braided silken cord for this purpose), and you're in business. (Note: You may want to put a small hook in the wall at an appropriate spot. You can hang one end of the tie-back on this hook, wrap the cord around the curtain, and lash the other to the hook to keep the curtain open at a fixed angle.)

Now, what do we have here? Frankly, we have something that may not look that wonderful to a perfectionist. HOWEVER, for a temporary fix, it's great. You have a splash of color at your window that you can coordinate with the rest of your room decor. You've also got privacy—very important. You can have two sheets per window, tying back each side, or just the one, tying it back on one side as directed above.

than would seem possible at the time of purchase, and they make inadequate headboards that take every opportunity to fall behind the bed. Also, on most of these pillows, the arms are too short. So there.

One Student's Quest for a Bug-Free Life

Janet, a recent Vanderbilt graduate, is a little jumpy about bugs. She traces this back to her college experience. "Until I went to school, I'd never really encountered bugs," and by this she means ROACHES. But the student suites she lived in (which had their own kitchens) were real eye-openers. "I got so paranoid about roaches. I hate to think about how many there must have been that we never even saw. My friends who lived in other buildings had the same problem. Roaches everywhere. Once, I killed a roach just by opening up the cabinet—I got him with the door." The problem, Janet believes, is that "even if you personally are clean and don't leave food and crumbs lying around, your neighbors in other suites could be living in filth."

One of Janet's roommates "tried to solve the problem by leaving this nasty powder all over the kitchen," she says. "But it got on our glassware and dishes, and I didn't like the idea that those chemicals could get in our food." Spray insecticides like Raid or Black Flag, she found, worked best "on a case-by-case basis," killing individual roaches. Roach Hotels, boxes with sticky sides and bottoms that allowed roaches to "check in, but never check out," also worked on a limited basis—they did the job until they filled up. "Then roaches could actually crawl through the box, over the dead bodies of their friends." The other drawbacks of these boxes, for those who are squeamish, include listening to the roaches' sometimes feverish attempts to unstick themselves from the glue; the slightly sweet odor of the glue itself (particularly when the box was placed near a radiator or wall heater); and the fact that one eventually must dispose of the box, "which is gross," Janet comments.

Janet's quest for long-term pest control finally ended happily, when she found a product called Combat (there are other products on the market that work similarly), which she highly recommends. The idea here is that roaches are enticed into these small, disc-shaped units; "they come in contact with poison, then take it back to their nests, where other roaches come in contact with it, too. It wipes out a bunch of roaches at once, instead of just one at a time."

PREPARE FOR THE WORST: WHAT IF SOMETHING HAPPENS TO YOUR STUFF?

Mark, our friend at Arizona State University, was spending the weekend at home in Tempe. Early Sunday morning, he got a call from the campus police. It seems there had been a small fire in his dorm room. In one sense, Mark was lucky; the fire was confined to his desk; only one of his possessions, a lamp, was badly scorched. In another sense, however, Mark was in trouble. On the desk had been every single paper he'd written that semester for his English literature class. He was supposed to turn them all in at the end of the semester; his grade depended on it.

It turned out that the fire had been started by Mark's unsavory roommate, Greg, who had a drug problem and had fallen asleep while using a bong. Greg summed up his feelings about the incident, and his responsibility for it, succinctly: "Sorry, man."

What's the take-home message here? One lesson is to prepare for the worst: Store vital notes and papers in a safe place—a desk drawer, for instance, would have been a better option for Mark. If you do a lot of work on computers, make backup disks (more than one if it's something really crucial, like a 65-page thesis) and keep them somewhere safe. Melissa, a senior at Baltimore's Villa Julie College, keeps a backup disk with all her notes and projects in her backpack, which is almost always with her. Leara, a graduate student at Stanford, keeps backup disks in her refrigerator and freezer. ("For one thing," she says, "a thief generally doesn't take a big refrigerator, and for another, in case of fire, they might have a better chance of surviving.") *Tip: If you're using small, 3½-inch disks, it's easy to store one or two of these in an envelope inside your student mailbox.*

It's better to be a little paranoid now than a lot sorry later.

Another point, which we've already discussed (see page 15), is to leave at home anything you can't afford to lose. Mark was lucky that the fire (or Greg) didn't damage the expensive stereo system he had just bought.

THE INSURANCE OPTION

An option you may want to consider is insurance; some schools offer extra coverage for personal belongings. This may be a good idea. But first, check out your parents' insurance policy. There's an excellent chance that your belongings—because they're only temporarily away from home—will still be covered under your parents' homeowners policy. (Off-campus apartments are a different story, says a representative of State Farm Insurance in Maryland. If you live in an apartment near school, you should strongly consider getting renter's insurance.) *Note: In any case, talk to your insurance agent. It may be that if you're going to an out-of-state school, you'll need to buy the insurance from a representative and company based in that state, not in your home state!*

CHAPTER 2

Living With a Stranger

If you're a little apprehensive about living with a stranger, you're not alone. In fact, as one writer, Constance L. Hays, said in a *New York Times* essay, the roommate "is at once the most keenly anticipated and deeply feared aspect of the freshman collegiate experience."

You could become best friends. You could hate each other's guts. Or, you could just share a room. There are endless shades of indifference between being "Best Buddies" and "Roommates from Hell."

Here's the situation: You are about to move into a tiny cubicle of a room, where you will actually live for the next nine months of your life—with a person you may never have laid eyes on. A total stranger. Someone you couldn't pick out of a police lineup if your life depended on it. This is a scary thing.

Even more scary is that you may have had absolutely no say in this decision if it was made for you by some housing official or, worse, by the computer sitting on that official's desk.

What if she's a klepto who borrows your clothes and then sneaks them back into your closet, soiled with too-dark foundation and smelling of obnoxious perfume?

What if his socks are so foul that they can stand alone, and every night he props them (with feet inside) on the end of your bed as he watches "American Gladiator" reruns on TV?

What if he listens only to Metallica, while you're offended by anything that isn't country and western?

What if she plasters the wall with Hanson memorabilia? Or he asks, "Who's your favorite Spice Girl?"

What if she has passionate liaisons with her boyfriend in your room, leaving a note on the locked door telling you to go someplace else for 2 hours?

What if he smokes pot in the room, and you get blamed for it?

Well, our advice is to go ahead and imagine the worst. Get it out of your system. Then, after you've imagined sharing quarters with serial killer Ted Bundy (or TV sitcom shoe salesman/slob Al Bundy), one of two things will happen: Your roommate will be either a pleasant surprise, much nicer than you ever imagined, or a nightmare beyond belief, in which case you can generally get reassigned.

What happens most of the time is that some adjustments on both sides end up being made. Most of the time, people aren't instantly compatible, but they're not oil and water, either. Most of the time, roommates come to an understanding; they work out an acceptable arrangement. They compromise, and that's not necessarily a bad thing. Actually, it's pretty good.

What if she has passionate liaisons with her boyfriend in your room, leaving a note on the locked door telling you to go someplace else for 2 hours?

PICKING ROOMMATES: RANDOM CHANCE VERSUS ATTEMPTED MATCHMAKING

Some colleges and universities go to great lengths in an attempt to pick compatible roommates. At Duke, for example, all incoming freshmen must complete an extensive questionnaire providing information about majors, extracurricular interests, sports, entertainment, musical preferences, and so on. Many colleges also attempt to develop lifestyle profiles, asking entering freshmen to place themselves on a scale in several areas. For example:

I consider myself __neat __messy

I function best __ early morning __late at night

At other institutions, such as Harvard, the parents of incoming freshmen are asked to write a candid letter explaining their children's personality in some detail; the freshmen, who may see themselves differently, fill out separate questionnaires.

Stanford University used to put a heavy emphasis on course schedules in assigning roommates, with the idea that common intellectual interests would stimulate lively discussions and perhaps encourage friendships. They don't do that anymore. Now, says a representative of Stanford's New Undergraduate Student Information Project, "we don't necessarily pair students according to academic or intellectual interests."

Indeed, freshmen may find themselves paired with roommates who seem to be total opposites—an engineering major with a social science major, for example—so

One new trend at a grow-ing number of schools is for students to sign "roommate contracts" covering a range of issues including TV habits, study time, hobbies, and guests. These contracts also fea-ture hypothetical situa-tions, asking students how they'd handle poten-tially explosive matters.

that they might learn from each other. The idea now is to discourage a narrow intellectual focus and to foster a more open-minded environment.

When freshmen are admitted to Stanford, they fill out questionnaires that cover their likes and dislikes, plus any special needs (such as a physical disability) or other considerations. The goal, ultimately, is to "try to get, based on the information we receive from the student, a living situation as close to comfortable as we can make it."

One new trend at a small but growing number of schools is for students to sign "roommate contracts" covering a range of issues, including TV habits, study time, hobbies, and guests. These contracts also feature hypothetical situations, asking students how they'd handle potentially explosive matters, such as a room-mate's drug problem.

When the computer pulls the strings. Other colleges and universities, including many of the larger state institutions, follow a pattern of random assignment. Even here, at least a couple of questions probably will be asked, such as "Do you prefer a roommate who does not smoke?" and "Do you have a preferred roommate?" If so (and the preference is mutual), the institution will usually attempt to pair you up.

But, basically, random assignment means they take very few factors into account, and once that's done, they simply put two students together (or three or four, depending on the arrangement) and see what happens.

You may be given some choices. These might include location—which can matter a lot, especially on sprawl-ing campuses—and costs. The typical college or university may have anything from drafty but elegant antebellum residence houses to modern high-rises and a range of prices to choose from.

Other points of choice may be whether you want a coed dorm or not or whether you favor "open visitation," which means members of the opposite sex are permitted to visit some or all of the time; some housing may limit or forbid this. (Obviously, many students like the idea of open visitation; it lets them socialize without having to spend a lot of money. But other students regard this as an invasion of their privacy and would prefer not to have it as a round-the-clock option.)

Beyond such few things, however, there's a good chance that your roomie will be assigned more or less at random. Basically, you will be cast on the winds of Fate, scattered like a piece of birdseed by some bureaucrat sitting on the park bench of life, playing God.

There is, however, an irony here: In terms of percentages of roommate changes, random assignment—the crap-shoot approach—seems to work about as well as the most careful, pre-enrollment screening process.

"We look upon random assignment as a positive thing," says one housing director at a large state university. (He could add that for large universities, it's also a lot easier and less time-consuming and therefore probably cheaper than careful matchmaking. But we won't focus on that.) He goes on to make a valid point: "There probably won't be much screening done for you in the real world ahead. Getting to know a new roommate is a good opportunity for practice in learning to adjust, to get along." True. In that crazy, wacky road called real life, there's generally not somebody running ahead to smooth out all the bumps and potholes.

Besides, the housing director argues, it would be almost impossible to develop any kind of questionnaire so comprehensive as to identify all of the personality characteristics necessary to ensure a perfect matchup.

A word on tolerance: The audience on "Oprah" was in an uproar. The topic was Ellen Degeneres and the most famous "coming out" episode ever to hit TV. One woman objected to this. Strenuously. She was shaking, angry, frustrated, scared, and tearful. Homosexuality is against the Bible, she said. It's wrong.

We can't answer that. But here's another idea for you to consider: That's Ellen's business. How she runs her life is her problem. How we deal with it is ours. Our advice for you is to work on tolerance.

Why? Oh, millions of reasons: Look at the history of the world. Just about all of the most heinous tragedies we've ever inflicted on each other have been done in the name of religion. The Crusades—children's heads impaled on sticks in the name of Christianity? That's a positive statement. The Holocaust. Bosnia. Rwanda. Even the infamous "Heaven's Gate" cult, most of whose members committed mass suicide in California—the leader may have been unable to deal with his own homosexuality, and the cult may have been his way of reshaping reality.

There's a good chance that your roomie will be assigned more or less at random. Basically, you will be cast on the winds of Fate, scattered like a piece of birdseed by some bureaucrat sitting on the park bench of life, playing God.

ROOMMATE HELL: A CASE FOR THE COURTS

Once upon a time, a quiet, studious, scholarship student filled out a roommate request form before moving into a dormitory at a small, private college in the northeastern United States.

He thought the college would use the information in the form to find him a compatible roommate.

Instead, this student says, he got a polar opposite—a "party animal" who (with help from some unsavory friends) threatened and humiliated him, stayed up all hours of the night and, against dorm regulations, used drugs and alcohol in the room.

This student says he was driven to quit school for a year and seek psychiatric help. (According to newspaper accounts of the story, the student now is enrolled at a university in another state.)

He got a lawyer and is suing the college in federal court. His grounds for suit: He believes the college was negligent by failing to find him a more suitable roommate and by not giving him more protection.

Is this guy just a whiny extremist who couldn't cope and wants to blame someone else for it? Was the college hardhearted and even delinquent in its handling of his grievance? Just what are a dormitory resident's rights?

To what lengths should colleges go to make sure their students are happy—and safe—in their living arrangements? No answers have been

Do it for yourself. It's stressful, carrying around hate and fear. Tolerance doesn't mean you have to embrace—or even accept—ideas that you find personally abhorrent. Nobody's asking you to march in a Gay Pride parade. Just make the effort to put up with people whose ideas aren't the same as yours—just as they should make the effort to put up with you.

So there you are. You may not have much choice about your roommate. But you do have other choices: In fact, a lot of what goes on in this relationship will depend on your attitude, from the minute you walk through the door. (For tips on getting along, see page 30.) It's inevitable that you will be influenced at least a little by your roommate and that your adjustment to college life will, to at least some degree, be connected to the relationship you develop with this person.

But think about it: Chances are, your future roommate is not a total boor and is just as concerned about getting along as you are. This is why most roommate assignments, random or not, ultimately seem to work out.

WHEN IT DOESN'T WORK

It's easy for us to say that things will work out. But what if they don't?

For starters, it's wise to remember that when people expect the worst, it often turns into a self-fulfilling prophecy. People who look for the good in a situation tend to find some. But you probably know that already.

So let's assume that, indeed, the worst has happened, and you hate your roommate, there are irreconcilable differences, and it's an awful situation. What do you do next?

All is not lost; you are not helpless. (Remember that you're paying good money to attend this institution, and this entitles you to some rights.) There are options, including the following:

First, talk to your RA. In most residence halls, there is one RA, or resident adviser (or dorm counselor, or whatever they're called at your school), for about every 25 students. Their rooms are nearby, their doors are open, and their counsel is free.

For best results, think of your RA as a resource—as someone with training and expertise to consult when you have a question. Don't wait until you develop a major problem to take advantage of this valuable resource. (Remember—these people had to want this job, apply for it, and get picked to be resident advisers. Universities don't just give an RA-ship to any moron who comes down the pike; there is a screening process. Also remember that they're getting compensated, either in pay or housing, for their services, so it's their job to help you!)

Generally, RAs are chosen for their patience, maturity, leadership skills, and, most importantly, for their knowledge of how the system works. A savvy RA can help you slice through institutional red tape with the ease of a Ginsu knife and can save you hours by revealing shortcuts around the maze of academic bureaucracy.

But here's the catch: You have to make the effort. Seek out your RA. You aren't going to get much help by sitting around like a morose lump in your room, waiting passively for someone to "feel your pain" and trying to solve your problems alone.

"I'm amazed at how few students throughout the country really utilize their resident advisers fully," grumbles one administrator at the University of Kentucky. "It's as if they pulled into a gas station, gave the attendant $10, then drove off after getting only $5 worth of gas. They're only getting half of what they've already paid for."

Find out your school's policy on changing roommates. Many campuses have a deadline—usually within the first two weeks after school starts—for changing roommates. (At some schools, changes still may be allowed after this period.) Change, however, may not be automatic: Sometimes, housing officials try to mediate problems and resolve disputes between roommates if they can.

"If we can't," says the University of Kentucky housing administrator, "if there is just no way the problem can be worked out—if the two people are obviously going to kill each other if they stay in the same room—then we make every effort to let them change. But much depends on the availability of space and whether another person is willing to switch." (In other words, if there's even a vacancy someplace else!) "Sometimes," the administrator continues, "we just may not have a choice. Usually, the requests drop significantly after those first two weeks when no changes are allowed. That gives them

provided yet, at the writing of this book. But you can bet a lot of colleges and universities will be very interested in the outcome of this case.

A savvy RA can help you slice through institutional red tape with the ease of a Ginsu knife.

WHAT IF YOUR ROOMMATE IS GAY?

It's possible that your roommate may be gay. It makes sense that the incidence of homosexuality on college campuses would be about the same as throughout society generally. Actually, it's probably a bit higher, because campuses tend to be fairly tolerant places and also because this is the age when people begin experimenting on many different levels. A number of students may explore gay or lesbian relationships briefly, then choose not to stay with them.

Sexual orientation is just one part of someone's personality. If you can get past that, you can probably find much about that person to make him or her interesting, worth knowing, and liking. (You can't get AIDS from casual contact or from living in the same room; see page 190.)

Believe it or not, other students probably won't assume you're gay just because you're rooming together. And your roomie's most likely not going to put the moves on you. (Although if this is a concern you have, you should discuss it when you start talking early; see "Tips for Getting Along," at right.)

We can't tell you how to react; this issue is about as personal as it gets. Some students never manage to deal with this situation, and their solution has been simply to find a new roommate. But others work through their differences, find some common ground, and become friends.

time to let the dust settle." By the end of the semester, he adds, "they might say, 'Well, she (or he) is not so bad after all.' "

What does this mean? Well, on one hand, it may turn out to be a good thing that universities don't let you change roommates at the drop of a hat. You may accidentally end up making the relationship work. (Remember, one reason you're going to college is to meet, and try to get along with, different types of people.) So give your roommate and yourself every chance before you split up.

On the other hand, this also may mean that if you try in all good conscience to "give peace a chance," and you make a real, good-faith effort to work things out, you could miss your deadline and get stuck with your roommate for at least the rest of the semester.

If your situation is truly intolerable, don't give up. Be a polite but annoying squeaky wheel. Camp out on the Housing Office's doorstep until you get action. If all else fails, it may help if you try finding someone else who's willing to share a room with you. (It's even better if you can find somebody willing to move in with your present roommate.) Anything you can do ahead of time to help streamline the bureaucratic mechanics of the transfer will almost certainly help your request get approved.

TIPS FOR GETTING ALONG

Prevention is the best medicine. This is something you already know—you practice it every day (when, for example, you brush your teeth to prevent tooth decay or wash your hands before you eat to get rid of germs).

Now, apply this knowledge that you already have to your domestic life. Remember the Golden Rule? (No? Shame on you! It's "Do unto others as you would have them do unto you.") The bottom line here is, be a decent human being. Other secrets of "successful dorming" include the following:

- **Communication.** Start talking early about anything that could be a potentially troublesome issue. There are diplomatic ways of doing this. For example, if you notice that your roommate not only has a boyfriend but also that he seems to be a permanent fixture, you might open the subject with an inoffensive beginning such as: "I hope this isn't a stupid question" or "I don't mean to be rude in any way, but . . ." or "Please forgive me for asking this, but . . ." You can probably think of even better openings. The point is, be polite, but get your question out there in the open so it can be addressed.

- **Space**. Yes, it really is "the final frontier." Nothing will get your relationship off on the wrong foot—literally—quite like smashing your big toe in the middle of the night against the set of barbells he forgot to put away. Or always having to remove her hair dryer and curling iron (which seems to be permanently switched on) before you can plug in your hot pot. Reach an agreement with your roommate as to which territory belongs to whom, and be considerate in the living space you both share.

- **Neither a borrower . . .** That's right, nor a lender be. The best policy on borrowing is "just say no." This should be one of the ground rules you set up when you start talking early—before you even get to know each other very well.

This rule is harder to enforce than you might think.

We know, you don't want to be "mean." You want to be "nice." And nice people let their roommates borrow their stuff, right?

Sure. If, that is, your definition of nice people is that they're DOORMATS who exist only to be walked all over. Doormats aren't happy. The people doing the walking—now, they're the happy ones.

Think of it this way: What's worse? Your saying "no" up front or letting your roommate borrow the sweater you want to wear tomorrow—and then hating yourself for being such a weenie, feeling angry and helpless, making nasty remarks, and jabbing at her with your words like some pesky gnat?

If she's wearing something—or has just worn it and hasn't washed it yet—that you had planned for your big date tonight, whose fault is that? It's yours.

"CAN I BORROW YOUR CAR?"

What did you say? You "guess it's okay" if he borrows your car? WHAT ARE YOU, NUTS?

Borrowing someone else's car can cause horrible problems—everything from a collision (with another driver, who is not insured) to your own insurance liability (your family's policy may not apply to your use of a borrowed vehicle) to your managing to get the seat stuck permanently in a position where your roommate (who is eight inches shorter) can't reach the floor pedals, to disagreements as to how much gas the borrower used but did not replenish.

People can get unexpectedly cheap and downright nasty about funny little things like gas money and wear-and-tear on the car. While moments like these can reveal a lot about a person (more, perhaps, than you ever wanted to know), save yourself this aggravation.

What's worse? Your saying "no" up front or letting your roommate borrow the sweater you want to wear tomorrow—and then hating yourself for being such a weenie, feeling angry and helpless, making nasty remarks and jabbing at her with your words like some pesky gnat?

So grab a little courage, be very nice, and make your statement.

You could explain, for instance, that you want to avoid grief and misunderstandings, so you think it would be best if you don't borrow each other's stuff. Or, failing that, make it clear which things are absolutely off limits. You don't have to be stingy or obnoxious about this. Be diplomatic by explaining that you know he or she must feel the same way about a favorite sweater or pair of shoes.

- **Responsibility.** Your share of it ranges all the way from always remembering to lock the door to your room when you leave to taking and delivering messages accurately and promptly when your roommate is out. It also includes the little things, such as doing your fair share when it's time to clean up the place for guests or restocking what you take out of the refrigerator if it's joint property.

  Picture your roommate, studying diligently for 3 hours, planning ahead for that little reward she brought back from the Italian bakery, only to find it's gone (or worse, that it's there—all except for the huge bite you took out of it) when she opens the refrigerator door. People have been murdered for less.

- **Grow up.** When it comes to responsibility, you're pretty much on your own here. Nobody's going to roll you out of bed in the morning for breakfast and class or gently remind you to turn out the lights and go to sleep. Freedom is nice, but remember that your roommate and others on your floor have some freedoms too—like the freedom not to have to endure the ear-splitting sounds of your stereo at 2:30 a.m.

- **Sensitivity.** Your roommate just flunked a test, found out his girlfriend from high school is cheating on him, and had his car—which was parked where it shouldn't be because he couldn't find any other spot and had 5 minutes to make it to accounting class—towed. Now it's going to cost him $115.75 to get it back, and he can't even charge it—he maxed out his Visa card when he bought that leather jacket last week.

  So now he's got to work up the nerve to tell his

parents, who never wanted him to take the car to school in the first place, and beg them to lend him the money to retrieve his car. And, if all that weren't enough, he's having a bad hair day, he thinks he's getting a zit, and his nightly snack of Buffalo wings has just taken its toll. This morning he actually split his favorite pair of pants when he bent over to pick up a notebook he dropped—while he was walking down sorority row. There were many witnesses.

If ever anybody needed a little "down time" alone, it's now. If you can't get lost for a while, get quiet. Leave the poor guy in peace.

In addition to physical space, people need mental space, too. You never know, you may need him to return this courtesy one day.

Even when it's not such a rotten day, you can show that same sensitivity in other potentially explosive issues, such as when to turn off the overhead light, TV, radio, or stereo for the night; when to have your friends around and when to move the party to somebody else's room.

If you can be considerate of each other's moods and needs most of the time, you can work out almost any other problem.

MAKE YOUR OWN PRIVACY

How much privacy you have in the dorm depends, as you might expect, on whether your roomie is gone a lot. (Actually, this is often the case, particularly if your roommate has a job or an active social life.) If your roomie is always there and you feel a little crowded, juggle your own hours a bit: get up an hour before she does, or stay up later at night, or spend more time studying someplace else, like the library (where you may actually get more done).

A tip: Get to know the earplug. The little foam earplug is your friend, particularly when you're trying to study or sleep amid noise.

ROOMING WITH YOUR BEST FRIEND FROM HIGH SCHOOL

Should you or shouldn't you?

Our answer is probably not, and there are several reasons why:

One: Why mess up a beautiful friendship? We've seen it happen. Just because you've confided every secret since grade one, there's no guarantee that being together full-time won't get old real fast. On the one hand, it's great that you know she developed a crush on Peter Brady as you two sat in your living room, eating potato chips and watching endless reruns after school. But on the other hand, she knows you had a thing for "the Professor" on "Gilligan's Island," and we don't want that getting out in a moment of anger, now do we?

Two: There is such a thing as getting to know somebody too well. When this happens, the qualities you've admired most about your best friend can soon be

Just because you've confided every secret since grade one, there's no guarantee that being together full-time won't get old real fast.

CHEAP WAYS TO HAVE FUN

For the fun-loving and socially minded, the possibilities for instant, informal get-togethers in dorms are endless. You don't have to have a lot of money or go to a lot of trouble. In fact, it often seems that events that are a big pain to plan never live up to all the effort and that the most fun times often are the most spontaneous.

Here are a few ideas to get you started:

Chip in for pizza, Buffalo wings, or burgers to celebrate a particularly exciting episode of the soap opera you've all been watching. Ditto for "Monday Night Football" or "Melrose Place" or "Seinfeld."

In honor of Cinco de Mayo, have a taco party (with different people bringing various items such as meat, cheese, sour cream, black olives). Have brie and a baguette in honor of Bastille Day. Send out for egg rolls to commemorate the Chinese New Year.

Rent or borrow a VCR and some movies and have a movie marathon.

Hold a film festival in honor of an actor, such as John Wayne, John Candy, Bruce Lee, Sidney Poitier, Michelle Pfeiffer, Tom Cruise, Judy Garland, Michael Keaton, Whoopi Goldberg, or Jack Nicholson. Or a director, such as Alfred Hitchcock, Frank Capra, Woody Allen, Spike Lee, or John Waters. Or characters, such as Nick and Nora Charles, James Bond, Jack

eclipsed by annoying mannerisms or habits that make you feel you're about to lose your mind if you have to see them one more time.

Who knew, for instance, that she gets her teeth so shiny by brushing for 10 noisy minutes at a time, four times a day, while standing in front of the TV screen? And then the flossing begins, usually during the "Top Ten" list on Letterman. And goes on, and on, and on . . .

Who knew that every night after he turns out the light, he methodically cracks each knuckle—all twenty of them. You've memorized his routine. Oops, he forgot the right pinky. Go back and do it, get that pinky—there. Whew. You can't take this anymore. Murder plots worthy of Alfred Hitchcock begin running through your head by the time he's reached number twelve in the countdown.

Three: Rooming together could hinder one or both of you from making other friends. Perhaps, for fear of the unknown in your new surroundings, you stick together like Siamese twins every time you leave your room. You meet for each meal, go to parties together, even go to the movies on weekends. You're a couple of bookends. How are you going to make new friends?

Remember, this is your big chance—your freshman year! This is the best opportunity you'll ever have to meet other new people on your campus before they make other friends, form other social groups, and establish routines that don't include you. Don't miss this boat!

Four: You and your best friend may not grow and change and accept college life at the same tempo. It could be awkward to be in the position of one holding the other back socially in a sad attempt to cling to the past—those "Glory Days" of high school: "Remember when I made that basket in overtime and won the game?" "Remember when you mooned Sister Mary Agnes?"

Think about it: Aren't you a little young for "Remember when?" Isn't this something your grandparents do?

Now's the time to make memories, not rehash them.

Also, wouldn't it be nice to know that, in addition to your new roommate and his new friends, you could have your old buddy and his new friends just one floor up? It could be the best of both worlds.

Now, obviously, many best friends from high school have become college roommates and adjusted quite nicely together, keeping both the friendship and the roommate relationship intact.

But keep in mind that roommates don't always have to be best friends. As we've already talked about (see "Tips for Getting Along," page 30), it is possible to be on good terms without sharing the same interests—or the same high school history.

TIPS ON MAKING FRIENDS

You're basically shy. Should you worry about making new friends?

Not at all, if you can just see the bigger picture for a minute.

Many people who are basically shy get stuck focusing on themselves: how other people will think of them, what they look like to other people, whether they're perceived as cool or as a jerk.

Stop this thinking right now! It's hard to believe, but most people in this world aren't focusing on you. They're not evaluating or judging you. Most likely, we're sad to report, they're not even thinking about you one way or the other. They're thinking about their own problems. They're getting on with the business of living.

So you need to get on with it, too. Just keep telling yourself that you're not the only one feeling a little uneasy about moving into a new room with a total stranger.

Picture this scenario: There you are with all your earthly goods. Not only do you not know your roommate, you also don't know the dozens of people lugging stereos and suitcases up the stairs and creating general confusion outside your strange new room. It's chaos.

But this situation will soon settle down, and so will you. It may help to think of yourself as a foreigner in a country whose language you don't speak. What would you do? You'd smile a lot.

It's hard not to like someone with a friendly smile.

Be friendly. Believe that it's going to be okay. Make an effort, early on, to get acquainted. Don't blow this excellent chance! Don't let this window of opportunity close while you hole up like a hermit in your room, waiting for people to drop in and introduce themselves. Because that's probably not going to happen. People

Ryan, Sherlock Holmes, Charlie Chan, or John Shaft. Or a holiday—"The Quiet Man" and "The Commitments" make a nice double feature in honor of St. Patrick's Day. Get the picture? Now go out and get the picture(s)!

DORM LIFE FOSTERS TOGETHERNESS

For those who want it (and those who don't), the nature of dorm life fosters togetherness. Each floor has its community meeting places—the john, the lounge, the vending machine center, TV room, laundry room.

At most schools, an upperclass student or two (your Resident Adviser) will be on hand to arrange floor meetings, recruit for intramurals, and initiate a variety of other projects designed to encourage participation and a sense of community.

probably aren't going to come to you; they'll probably misread your signal. (Actually, signals that we think are clear as a bell are often misunderstood by their intended audience. It's a lot easier to just tell people what you think, rather than rely on intuitive powers that they may not have.)

Instead of thinking, "Oh, she's shy, I'll go ahead and introduce myself—and all the cute guys I know—to her," your dorm neighbors will probably think, "Oh, Miss Stuck Up, too good to get down off her high horse and mingle with the rest of us!" Or they may simply think you want to be left alone, and they'll respect your privacy.

It's a lot easier to meet people when everyone is new, during those first few days of the school year. If you hold off until patterns and relationships have already begun to form, you may find things more difficult. Ask questions, even when you think you already know the answers. Or be neighborly. "I'm going to the Seven-Eleven. Can I get you anything?" Or, better yet, "Do you want to go with me?"

Get a second opinion. "Does this outfit look stupid?"

Break the ice. "My mom made some cookies for my first week here. Want one?"

For those who want it (and those who don't), the nature of dorm life itself fosters togetherness. Each floor has its community meeting places—the john, the lounge, the vending machine center, TV room, laundry room. At most schools, an upperclass student or two (your Resident Adviser—see page 28) will be on hand to arrange floor meetings, recruit for intramurals, and initiate a variety of other projects designed to encourage participation and a sense of community.

Remember, thousands of entering freshmen would describe themselves as "basically shy." Most of them don't stay that way long.

A final tip: Avoid the "Angry Young Man" (or Woman) syndrome. Attitude gets old, fast. Strike your poses on your own time. While you're out in society—which means, in class, in the cafeteria, even your own dorm room—try to play the game. Be courteous. Save contrived rants for another time—like, maybe when somebody who actually cares is listening. Frankly, nobody gives a hoot about why "the system sucks," or "the faculty's out to get me," or "the students here are bogus..."

LIVING OFF CAMPUS

To dorm, or not to dorm? For many freshmen, particularly at small private schools, this is not even a debatable question; they pretty much have to live on campus.

But other students, for a variety of reasons, live elsewhere—at home, in an off-campus apartment, or even in someone else's house (see Melissa's story, page 40). Why is this, you may wonder, when the college dorm room—despite its homely image—has so much going for it? Think about it.

Living on campus is efficient. Classroom buildings and the library are usually within easy walking distance. Campus eateries may not be elegant or exciting, but they're convenient. The meals they serve may be on the drab side, but they're nourishing and relatively cheap. And, for the most part, dorm living is where the action is. There are plenty of people to hang around with, and there's usually something going on (whether you want it to or not) most hours of the day or night.

Yet, every year, many students choose to live someplace else. One big reason for this, particularly for students who live at home, is financial. Cut out the cost of room and board, and college is a lot more affordable for many families.

Another reason may be emotional. Many graduating seniors just aren't ready to leave home yet (or their parents aren't ready for them to go). In a year, or even a semester, the case may be different; but for now, they'd rather live with family.

Or, your choice may be for moral reasons: recently, a handful of students at Yale protested the university's policy requiring freshmen and sophomores live in campus dorms, because they objected to what they found to be a pervasive immorality there. One of them, Elisha Dov Hack, wrote in an opinion piece that appeared in the *New York Times* that life in the dorms, "even on the floors Yale calls 'single sex,' is contrary to the fundamental principles we have been taught as long as we can remember—the principles of Judaism lived according to the Torah and 3,000-year-old rabbinic teachings. Unless Yale waives its residence requirement, we may have no choice but to sue the university to protect our religious way of life." In touring one of the dorms during an orientation tour, Hack writes, "I literally saw the handwriting on the wall. A sign titled 'Safe Sex' told me where to pick up condoms on campus. Another sign touted 100 ways to make love without having sex, like 'take a nap together' and 'take a steamy shower together.' The 'freshperson' issue of the *Yale Daily News* sent to entering students contained a 'Yale lexicon' defining 'sexile' as 'banishment from your dorm room because your roommate is having more fun than you.' If you live in the dorms, you're expected to be part of the crowd, to accept these standards as the framework for your life."

Now obviously, not everybody at Yale is having rampant sex. Some people probably make it to class occasionally; some even manage to maintain their moral code and personal integrity. And besides, when you graduate from college, you probably won't be living in a single-sex apartment building. However, if, like Hack and his friends, you feel extremely uncomfortable in a campus environment (and there are no single-sex dorms or one-person apartments), then off-campus may be a better choice for you.

Still another reason, for those who choose to rent a room or apartment, may be the desire for more freedom and independence than a dorm allows. Many students have fun poring over the want ads and campus bulletin boards for the apartment of their dreams and can't wait to begin life on their own.

This is our advice: If you can afford it, start out in the dorm—at least for a semester. Dorm life offers a unique, hard-to-beat opportunity to make friends and get involved. It's hard to become part of the scene when everybody else goes back to one dorm to crash and bond after class, and you turn and walk a mile in the other direction to the commuter lot where you parked your car.

As a sophomore, perhaps, and even more so as a junior and senior—once you've established yourself—an apartment may come to represent independence more than isolation, and it may be a good option for you. But for now, if you can, try the dorm.

This doesn't mean that students who live off campus can't become an integral part of school life. They definitely can and very often do. It just means that, if

Dorm life offers a hard-to-beat opportunity to make friends and get involved.

It's hard to become part of the scene when everybody else goes back to one dorm to crash and bond after class, and you turn and walk to the commuter parking lot where you parked your car.

they want to make friends and get involved in campus activities, they may have to make more of an effort than other students who live on campus, particularly if they're from out of town and don't know very many people.

One Alternative: Work for Your Room and Board

Melissa is a student at Villa Julie College in Baltimore. It is a commuter college, which made her options a lot simpler: There just isn't any student housing. So all students live off campus.

Melissa wanted to try living away from home. But during her freshman year, renting an apartment was a financial strain. So she found an alternative: A job as a nanny that provided room and board. Her situation was great: Plenty of time off, free meals and snacks, use of the family's car, and her own telephone. No rent, no utilities, no fee for parking, and relatively few other expenses (mainly books and clothes). In return, she spent many of her out-of-class hours providing child care for a family that quickly came to look upon her as a second daughter. They benefited, and so did she.

Melissa also took part in several extracurricular activities, such as the college's theater group, which enabled her to become involved on campus and introduced her to many new friends.

Many of Melissa's buddies from high school who went to other colleges chose the dorm life. As she kept up with them and their experiences, Melissa (whose family and many high school friends were also in Baltimore) began to see living off campus as the best of both worlds: "If you prefer to be alone, it's ideal," she says, "because you can choose the time and place and people you want to socialize with. If you're into rollerblading and it's a great Sunday, you can just call up some people and arrange a time and place where you can rollerblade. And if you choose to become involved (with a club or other group that convenes regularly), you know there are designated times and places where you'll be meeting other people."

Living off campus, Melissa continues, "you have more control in deciding who you want to be with and when—as opposed to a dorm situation, where you don't have as much control because your roommate has just

Melissa's situation as a live-in nanny was great: Plenty of time off, free meals and snacks, use of the family's car, and her own telephone. No rent, no utilities, no fee for parking.

as much priority for visitors—and sometimes those visitors may not be your most preferred company."

How to Pursue This Option: If you're interested in pursuing an alternative arrangement like Melissa's, check the "Help Wanted" section in the local paper. Or place your own ad.

Also, look for ads for an "au pair" —which basically means a live-in nanny—on bulletin boards in local grocery stores, particularly those in the well-to-do areas of town. Roger, also from Baltimore, and a student at Loyola College of Baltimore, learned about his current job as a live-in groundskeeper from a sign on a bulletin board in a veterinarian's office (again, the office was in a well-heeled neighborhood).

Such arrangements often are mutually beneficial for employer and employee: For families with young children, it's great to have the help. For older people whose children have left home, it's nice to have young folks around the house. It's also a relief for them to know that the house, Fluffy the cat and the prize roses will be looked after while they're visiting their grandchildren or taking that world cruise. Or, on a more serious note, that someone will be around in case there's a health emergency and they need help getting to the doctor.

Note: Responsibilities in these positions vary. Some jobs may require light housekeeping and some cooking; some may require more or less than that.

Find out exactly what they want, up front. Nail down not only what's expected of you, but what you expect in return. Try to get the job description in writing. If you can't, then it's up to YOU to protect yourself from any misunderstanding down the road. Before you start, write the family a nice letter, and keep a copy for yourself, saying something like, "I look forward to working for you. I'm not quite clear about my duties, so I'd like to get them down on paper and see if my list matches your expectations. It is my understanding that these are my duties . . . In return, it is my understanding that you will provide me with room, board, and $20 a week . . .If this is not the case, please let me know by Wednesday, August 15. If I don't hear from you, I'll assume that I've stated the situation correctly. I look forward to seeing you next month . . ." It's better to put a specific deadline, rather than the ambiguous, "as soon as possible." That way, there's less room for misinterpretation on either side.

INTERVIEW POTENTIAL ROOMMATES

Carol Anne, a graduate of Syracuse University in New York, survived several apartments and a variety of roommates. She offers this tip: "Interview your roommates. Think of it as a job interview." During her junior year, Carol Anne and a friend found a great apartment. "I knew I could live with my friend because I had lived with her over the summer. But it was a three-bedroom apartment, so we had to find somebody else to share the rent. We interviewed potential roommates."

During the interview, Carol Anne and her friend asked such questions as "What are your hours? Are you a day person or a night person? What do you like to do, what are your dislikes?" Especially important, she notes, was " 'How clean do you like to keep the bathroom?' Because if you've got one person who likes an immaculate bathroom and one person who doesn't care if there's soap scum all over, you're not going to get along." One roommate, Carol Anne comments, lied about smoking. "She said she didn't, and she did. We kicked her out."

Carol Anne's other off-campus living adventure, before finding the three-bedroom apartment, "was a disaster," she recalls. "It was with two boys and another girl. The problem was that one of the boys and the other girl became romantically involved. Enough said! Also, every time they had a fight, we were expected to mediate." But

Why bother with such specifics? You may as well learn how to protect yourself now. Not that the worst always happens, but sometimes people have radically different ideas of the same situation. For example: You don't want to find out, a week after school starts, that your new employers/landlords are penny-pinching slavedrivers who also expect you to do all the grocery shopping, wash and fold the clothes, empty the trash, cook dinner three nights a week, dust, vacuum, mow the yard AND scoop after the family's two large Rottweilers, Rolf and Adolf—oh yeah, you're supposed to feed them, too.

SELECTING AN APARTMENT: FACTORS TO CONSIDER

You've decided to go for it. You're taking the big plunge. You're getting an apartment.

Hold it! Before you buy that cool-looking, oak-veneered stereo case and a big potted fern for your new living room, ask yourself the following questions:

Can you afford it? This is the biggie. Residence hall costs are constant and predictable; so are meals, if you buy tickets at the beginning of the semester or each month. But apartment expenses won't be predictable, particularly if you live in an older building with radiators that give you no control over the heat and where you simply get assessed your portion of the building's monthly heating bill. This can be as much as $250. Which seems particularly unfair because you were sweating—even with all the windows open—in November, and you weren't even there for half of December and January.

Also, can you truly estimate your grocery costs each month? And live within that budget?

How will you get around? How will you get back and forth to classes (and work, if you have a job) and the supermarket? If your answer is "by car," can you afford the upkeep? Gas money is just part of it, along with oil changes, tune-ups, and other aspects of basic auto maintenance. There's also the issue of being able to park on campus (see page 51).

Speaking of parking, is it free at your apartment? Is there a parking lot or a garage that you have to pay extra for? Or will you just take your chances on the street? If

How will you get around? If your answer is "by car," can you afford the upkeep? Gas money is just part of it, along with oil changes, tune-ups, and other aspects of basic auto maintenance.

this is your plan, look at the street signs. Will you have to get up and move your car before 6 a.m.? Will you get a ticket or be towed if you leave your car in one spot for a few days? It's a good idea to check the street, too. Are there tickets fluttering under the windshield wipers of some of the cars you see? Does one car have that telltale, dreaded iron "boot" clamped on a tire? (For those of you who aren't city dwellers, this nasty device effectively immobilizes a car and is designed to force the car's owner to settle up with the city for a bunch of unpaid parking tickets before it's removed.)

(See "Parking: The nightmare that doesn't end" later in this chapter for more on parking a car around campus.)

If your answer is "by bicycle," what provisions are you making for rotten weather? Also, where will you keep your bike? Will you have to carry it up and down three flights of stairs? (For fire safety reasons, you probably won't be able to leave it under the staircase or chained up outside your door.) *Note: Bring along a sturdy lock for your bike. Also, check with campus police; you may need to register your bicycle with them.*

If your answer is "by public transportation," have you figured out how much bus, train, or subway fare you'll need every month? (Add this plus food to the cost of your rent to get an idea of your monthly grand total.) At large schools, there's usually some type of shuttle bus to take students from one part of the campus to another; if your apartment is near a stop, you might be able to catch a ride on one. These shuttles are sometimes slow, often crowded, and not too glamorous. (At Johns Hopkins University in Baltimore, for instance, the shuttle is a fleet of creaky, un-air-conditioned yellow, white, and blue schoolbuses.) But they're generally reliable, and the service is free or provided at a minimal cost. They get you where you need to go.

What about location? This is often closely tied to affordability. Apartments and rooms within easy walking distance of the campus may be more expensive; cheaper housing may be miles away. The downside here will be a longer commuting time and a certain remoteness from friends and campus activities.

Is it quiet? Bradley, a recent graduate of the University of South Carolina who lived in an off-campus apartment, has this advice: "Definitely check out the neighborhood, because if you want to do any studying,

If your answer is "by bicycle," what provisions are you making for rotten weather? Also, where will you keep your bike? Will you have to carry it up and down three flights of stairs?

HITCHHIKING? NOT!

We shouldn't even have to put this in, considering you were smart enough to get into college, but don't even think about hitchhiking as your main mode of travel. In the 1950s, when the world was a more innocent and benign place, this was an acceptable transportation option for college students. Today, in a world full of psychos and handgun violence, this practice is not only illegal in many parts of the country, it's also dangerous.

GETTING HELP IN YOUR APARTMENT HUNT

The housing office at school may have a list of some good apartment buildings, particularly if, as on the Johns Hopkins University campus, there isn't enough housing on campus for students.

Failing that, ask around until you find other students (or even professors) who live off campus. Find out where they live, and see what they recommend.

At the University of Maryland in College Park, the housing office has a helpful file, where students who have had problems with particular landlords or leasing companies can leave notes of warning or appreciation. "You could go to this file and check to see if there were good or bad comments," says Elizabeth, a University of Maryland graduate. "It was pretty much all negative comments—I guess the people who had good experiences weren't motivated to write—but it was one way of checking up on a potential place."

that's important. Check out your immediate neighbors in the apartment, too, although they'll probably change from semester to semester, or even month to month. You may think, 'This will be great; I'll study on that nice little screened-in balcony.' The reality is that the guy below you is in his seventh year as an undergraduate, he likes to crank up his stereo, he's playing the same MegaDeath song for a record 2,000th time, and you can't get any studying done.

What about security? Is there a doorman? A security system? A 24-hour answering service for emergencies? You may not need such things, but then again, you might. Look at the cars in the parking lot. Do they all have "The Club"? This could be a bad sign.

Here's a tip: If you can, drive by your building at night. You may find that a building looks sleepy and benign during the day only because the drug dealers who hang out and do business there didn't get to bed until 4 a.m. A nighttime visit may give you more information.

Is it in good repair? This is an often-overlooked consideration, says one college housing director, "particularly (in) the older places close to the campuses. Landlords don't always keep the rooms and apartments in good repair, and some students, especially those from nice homes, have trouble adjusting."

What this guy is saying diplomatically is that your apartment may turn out to be a dump. A little dust and the occasional spider is one thing; peeling paint or plaster, a leaky ceiling, rusted-out tub, and more roaches than a flamenco dancer could stomp on is another.

Security deposits

The condition of the apartment is one reason students may find themselves embroiled in disputes over damage or security deposits. This is a chunk of money the renter must put up ahead of time to cover any harm to the apartment during the rental period. Some deposits amount to the equivalent of a full month's rent or more; others may be a flat fee of $100 or $200. Frequently, a landlord will insist on keeping the deposit, alleging that the student damaged the apartment. The student, meanwhile, will claim that the damage was done before he or she ever set foot inside. The landlord is a pro at this; the student—especially the freshman student—is an amateur. Who is most likely to win?

How not to get burned. Often, it's just a little too easy to intimidate new college students. So let's make it a little tougher. How can you even the odds? Our advice—corroborated by the lawyer whose counsel appears on page 46—is to write up a list of the damage you find when you move in. Sign it, date it, send it to the landlord, and keep a copy for your records.

"Make sure you note everything you think is wrong when you move in," the attorney advises. "List every little 'ding' you see. Err on the side of listing too much, so they can't come back later and say, 'Here's this chip in the wall that you didn't tell us about. That'll be $75 for the repairs.' This way, you can whip out your list and say, 'Excuse me, please turn to page two, item two, of my damage report. Look, here it is, chip on the lower right corner of the east wall.' "

Such a list isn't a full guarantee that there won't be problems later, but it should help significantly. If nothing else, it will send the landlord a clue that you're not as naive as you may look. For more on this and on signing the lease, see page 46.

What does the lease say?

Oops. You signed a 12-month lease, and you're only going to be in town nine months; you've already lined up a summer job back home. Your rent's $500 a month—that's $1,500 more than you bargained for! What are you going to do?

Students tend to trip themselves up by not reading or fully understanding the lease agreement. (It doesn't help that there's enough fine print in most of these to give you a headache!) If you sign a 12-month lease and didn't plan to stay around that long, you could be nailed for the full amount. But there may be options: One possibility is that you pay a penalty fee for breaking the lease, which, though it might hurt, still would cost less than the three months' rent.

To sublet or not to sublet? Another possibility is that you find somebody who wants to sublet the place for the summer. But this could be a mixed blessing if the person you lease it to isn't as responsible as you are.

Marion, a graduate of Muhlenberg College in Allentown, Pennsylvania, and a veteran of numerous apartment situations, thinks subletting is a bad idea. "I would discourage anyone from subletting," she says. "It puts you in the position of being an absentee landlord, so

"List every little 'ding' you see. Err on the side of listing too much, so they can't come back later and say, 'Here's this chip in the wall. That'll be $75.' "

you're still responsible, even though you're not on site. God knows what could happen to the place! One party, and it could look like *Animal House*—and you could end up paying for the cleanup! Even though you may feel like you're just a kid going to school, in the eyes of the law, you're an adult, and you're the one they're going to come after for the damages."

Free legal advice about apartments and leases

An attorney we know in Columbia, South Carolina—a man who has read a lot of contracts—isn't too optimistic about college students' savvy when it comes to finding an apartment and signing a lease. As he puts it: "Most of them might as well walk into the leasing office with a sign on their back that says 'kick me.'"

"The typical undergraduate student is going to go in there with some vague intention of checking out the contract," but many leasing agents do their best to discourage an exhaustive study of the lease, he continues.

Picture the scene, the attorney continues: You go into an office, you get seated in an uncomfortable chair, "and basically, they hand you a contract that may be ten pages long, with very, very small type.

"Pretty soon, the typical student—who may have an attention span about as long as a 3-minute video—begins to glaze over. You may spend 5 minutes going over the first two paragraphs, then you quickly tire of reading the thing."

The leasee—that's you—may be told to initial every paragraph to show that it has been read and understood (even though, quite often, this is merely a tactic of intimidation, without any particular legal merit). "What often happens is that you start racing from checkmark to checkmark, because you want to get out of there as fast as you can; you might read the paragraph that immediately precedes the signature block. Then you get your roommate or roommates to co-sign. At this point, you generally have signed away all your rights."

Many leases aren't even entirely legal. How can this be? "Look," explains the attorney, "anybody who prepares a document is obviously going to tailor everything to suit his or her own needs. What are the main issues that are likely to come up in an apartment situation? Somebody could get injured on the premises

"What often happens is that you start racing from checkmark to checkmark, because you want to get out of there as fast as you can; you might read the paragraph that immediately precedes the signature block. Then you get your roommate or roommates to co-sign. At this point, you generally have signed away all your rights."

or damage the premises. So the landlord is obviously going to do his best to shift the liability, saying, in effect, 'If anything happens, you're to blame, not me, and therefore you're going to have to pay the cost.' "

"It doesn't matter if it's legal or not. They put it in the lease, and then sort it out later," if any legal action is taken. The intention with such leases is for you to be browbeaten into accepting everything without question.

Don't be intimidated. Most college students, the attorney adds, don't think to say, "Can I take this home and go over it?" However, if they do attempt such a thing, the landlord may have a song-and-dance spiel all ready, "saying something like 'We scheduled this time for you to sign the lease. If we can't enter into the lease today, the apartment might not be here tomorrow.' " This is probably a bluff; but there's a slight chance that it might be true.

One point in negotiation: You have to be willing to walk away. If you want to take the lease home for an attorney or your parents to look at, for instance, and someone attempts to bully you, one choice is very easy: You can say "Thank you very much" and leave. There's probably an equally good or better apartment out there. You can always go back if you don't find anything else.

But even if you could take the lease home to pore over it at your leisure, "very few undergraduates are even going to know what they're looking for," the attorney says. "You may go in there with a cocky attitude like 'I'm prelaw' and try to bluff your way through it, but you really can't." Many states have a residential landlord-tenant act that spells out what your rights are. But too many college students don't have either the time or the inclination to investigate such legalities. That's why so many of them get burned on the security deposit.

"A real goal for college students ought to be to try and recover as much of the security deposit as possible. That's a good measure that you have been a good tenant."

SHARING AN APARTMENT WITH A ROOMMATE

Many of the concerns here are the same ones that come up when you share a dorm room—basic situations that, for the most part, can be prevented easily with a healthy dose of common courtesy and communication.

ARE PETS ALLOWED?

This is awful. You bought the cutest black Lab puppy, a nice crate, $50 worth of rawhide, and 40 pounds of puppy food. Not only that, but you've bonded with this little guy so deeply that you can't imagine life, or school, without him. But the lease specifically forbids pets. Or dogs. Or dogs over 25 pounds—and judging by your puppy's big feet, he's not going to stay within the weight limit very long. What do you do?

Some of us have been in this position and, with a lot of luck (and anxiety), managed to hide the dog and brazen it out for a few months; this involved finding out ahead of time when the apartment was going to be sprayed each month with pesticide and when the meter was going to be read, so that the dog could be kept hidden at such times.

We hope you'll be as lucky. We also hope that you're lucky enough to have a calm dog, one who doesn't howl desperately when you leave, or bark—as, let's face it, a dog is supposed to do—when somebody comes to the door. If not, you may be put in the position of having to give up either the apartment or the dog. (Or you could plead your case with Mom and Dad and beg them to give Rover a temporary home.)

EVERYTHING IS NEGOTIABLE

People are intimidated by contracts. They see the legal writing, the small print, and think it must be the law. That's the general idea.

"Usually what happens is that the rental company will control every aspect of the negotiation and of the landlord-tenant relationship," says our attorney friend. "Nobody ever thinks about negotiating any point of that lease. Everything's negotiable. You are free to negotiate. They may say, 'Forget it!' but you never know 'til you try."

Here's an example: Say you're trying to snag an apartment for the fall semester. It's May. You won't be moving in until August. The apartment you have in mind won't be vacant until June 30. They probably won't find anybody to rent it in July—apartment buildings near college campuses generally are dead in July and most of August.

So what the heck? See if you could start rent payments in mid-August, instead of July 1. What have you got to lose—except six weeks—and several hundred dollars—in wasted rent money?

There are other points, however, that may be unique to apartment living. For example, there are questions of logistics. In whose name is the lease? The phone? The cable, if you have it? If it's your name on all of these things, will your roommate voluntarily, and responsibly, cough up his or her share of the money every month?

Or will you be put in the unpleasant, time-consuming, and annoying position of having to nag him or her every single month to pay what he or she rightfully owes you?

That's what happened to our friend Marion, the Muhlenberg graduate. "The utilities and the phone bill were both in my name, so I was legally responsible to make sure they were paid. One of my roommates, Jane, was not very good about giving the money over in a timely manner. Her boyfriend was a missionary in Peru, so she made a lot of very expensive phone calls. I would get these $300 phone bills that had to be paid." Jane wasn't a cheerful giver, either. She would hang on to the money until the last possible minute, Marion continues. "She would say she was going to pay me, then she wouldn't. She didn't forget—she knew exactly what she was doing; she was a tightwad. It was an awkward situation."

There is an advantage to having your name on the lease, points out Marion. "It gives you more weight if you want to get rid of somebody—if it's your lease, it's your apartment." On the other hand, if you give somebody notice, she cautions, "you may have a hard time getting them to pay you the rent they owe."

Melissa, a Villa Julie student, had a much better experience when she shared a condo with a good friend. "My reason for leaving that situation was the money; I was working so much that I was only using it as a place to sleep and eat so, basically, I was paying rent for a pitstop. But we had a good experience."

Melissa and her roommate shared many of the same interests, and both had the same major. "We had the same goals as far as education. Also, she was really interested in physical fitness, and so was I. We're both very organized and neat and pretty much clutter-free. We were just compatible all the way around. We never really were aggravated by one another's living habits, and we were both very conscious about keeping our living space neat, so at any time, a visitor could walk in and we wouldn't be embarrassed.

"It was wonderful; we were able to help each other with our classes. Sometimes after an evening class, we would go out for dinner or a drink and discuss that class or other assignments."

Melissa and her roommate did discuss some issues, such as use of the telephone and overnight visitors, ahead of time. "If it was an overnight situation, we discussed where they would sleep and where we would sleep, since we just had a one-bedroom apartment. We bought a sofa bed for visitors who were coming from far away and wanted to spend the night."

In retrospect, Melissa (who moved back home for financial reasons) is glad she tried apartment life. "Our friendship in many ways was strengthened by living together. And we were made aware of many new aspects of each other—you think you know someone, but once you've lived with them, you know a world more about them. Some things you like even more, and other things you share different opinions about. You just grow in living with another person. And if you like them, it's a pleasant experience. If not—well, fortunately, we liked each other. We're still good friends."

In conclusion

There's a lot to think about here, including many negative aspects of apartment living. But if this is what you really want, don't be discouraged. Just make sure you give these factors some thought. Know what you're up against, and anticipate potential hassles before you get broadsided.

Thousands of students do this every semester, and they manage just fine. They cherish the privacy, the freedom, and the big step into adulthood they see embodied in their student apartments. For them, apartment life opens up a whole new world—one where they set up housekeeping, cook the kinds of meals they want when they want them, arrange furniture (and have fun buying it at yard sales, flea markets, and second-hand stores), and manage a home of their own. Living on your own is a maturing experience; for thousands of students, it's a joyous one as well. On the other hand, it could be argued that you'll be on your own the rest of your life, and that the relative lack of responsibility involved in dorm living may suit your needs better for now.

"She would say she was going to pay me, then she wouldn't. She didn't forget—she knew exactly what she was doing; she was a tightwad. It was an awkward situation."

LIVING AT HOME: PROS AND CONS

Freshmen who live at home tend to make better grades and spend less money. Freshmen who live on campus tend to have more fun and grow up faster.

You're going to college in your home town. Should you live at home or on campus?

This is a tough call, and a lot depends on your financial situation. We can offer a broad generalization, for what it's worth: Freshmen who live at home tend to make better grades and spend less money. Freshmen who live on campus tend to have more fun and grow up faster.

On the plus side, living at home allows you to stay in comfortable, familiar surroundings while easing yourself gradually into college life. Because you aren't trying to concentrate on everything at once, you can concentrate more on your studies. There won't be the distractions—a noisy dorm floor, a roommate whose lifestyle may be wildly different from your own, the logistical problems (like doing your laundry)—that can drain your energies away from academics.

Even with commuting costs, living at home is almost certainly going to be cheaper than living on campus. In many cases, this is the deciding factor. The fun you might have had living in the dorm could be clouded by guilt if you feel you're placing too great a financial strain on the rest of the family. This is an important consideration.

An alternative solution may be for you to rent a room in someone's house near the campus. This can be a very thrifty housing move; the cost is much lower than an apartment, and it probably already includes the utilities. It may also (but won't always) include house and kitchen privileges as well. You may even be able to reduce the rent by mowing the lawn or doing household chores and babysitting.

But, as with any housing arrangement, there are trade-offs: By renting a room in a house, you may miss out on some socializing in the dorm. On the other hand, the privacy may be a blessing to the serious scholar. (*Note: Check out the security arrangements. Can you lock the door to your room? Is it a good, strong lock with a deadbolt or a cheesy lock inside the doorknob that you can open with a credit card? Who else will have a key to your room?*)

By the same token, moving onto the campus has distinct advantages, too. You'll probably learn as much simply by living with all those assorted characters in your dorm as you will in any academic subject. Personal development—the kind that comes from coping with new surroundings and managing on your own—is part of your education, too. There's a good chance that the people you live with in your dorm (or, later, a fraternity or sorority house) will be significant parts of your life for many years to come. Now is a big time in your life for developing deep friendships and good memories.

Here's an idea: Can you move onto the campus for half a year? Living on campus for even a semester will give you the experience of "going off to college."

Get involved. If you just can't afford to live away from home right now, find other ways to involve yourself in campus life. Work on the campus newspaper, yearbook, or radio station. You don't have to be a writer or photographer or have a great radio voice to get involved here (you could sell ads, for example, or just volunteer your time); they'll be glad to have the extra help. Try a service or academic club as a way of establishing a base of operations on campus. Or see if there's an association of commuting students at your college or university.

Joining a club will give you a foothold in other arenas—intramural sports, parties, and an opportunity to run on the club's slate of candidates in student election campaigns. Before you know it, they'll be wondering how they ever got along without you! (For more on getting involved, see Chapter Ten.)

There's a good chance that the people you live with in your dorm (or, later, a fraternity or sorority house) will be significant parts of your life for many years to come. Now is a big time in your life for developing deep friendships and good memories.

PARKING: THE NIGHTMARE THAT DOESN'T END

Thinking of taking your car to college? Before you make too many more plans, find out whether it's even legal at your school. At many colleges, it's not, and freshmen are prohibited from having (and, therefore, parking) cars on campus. On other campuses, freshmen may grudgingly be allowed to have cars. But parking spaces are hard to come by, and freshmen are at the bottom of the food chain—the better lots may be among the perks of being an upperclass student.

What this means is that the only parking spaces open to you may be at the football stadium parking lot (unless, of course, there's a game that weekend). So even though you have a parking space, you still might end up having to walk or ride a shuttle bus to and from a distant part of the campus each time you want to use your car. (This also means that you probably aren't going to keep as close an eye on it as you might like. Let's hope there's a vigilant security guard patrolling that 10-acre lot.)

Or—and this can be a major pain—you may end up scrambling for one of the few spaces available on the city streets, where you are subject to local police regulations.

In other words, your car may be more trouble than it's worth.

Likely scenarios

Picture this. You get up at 5:55 a.m., throw on a baseball cap and sweats, and dash outside to move your car from the street directly in front of your building. That witch of a cop starts writing tickets at 6:01, and she knows your car. You drive around the block, hoping there will be a space one street over. There isn't. You keep circling, widening your radius, darting in and out of traffic like the seasoned pro you have become. There it is—a spot! It's a tight fit, but it's just big enough for your car. It's 6:35. You jog back to your apartment and snooze until 8:30.

When you return to your car in the late afternoon, there's a nasty note under the windshield wiper from someone you apparently blocked in. Among other things, it says (this is from an actual note received by a street parker), "Perhaps someday you will learn how to: (A) park, and (B) do it in consideration of your neighbors where parking is at a premium." You fight, and successfully resist, the urge to etch a response on the side of her car with your key. You get in your car and the circling begins again, as you try to move it to a better spot.

At last! You get a great spot, one without meters or signs telling you when it's okay to park there. But now the spot owns you—it's so great that you can't bear to leave it. You avoid driving your car for the next three days!

Or picture this. It's a crisp January morning. You sleep in because it's bitter cold outside, and your bed is just too warm and cozy. Finally, you're up and ready to go. But where's your car? You can't see it because it snowed last night. Eight inches. Fortunately, the street's clear because the Chicago city crews were up all night plowing and salting.

But where's your car? There it is. Oh, no! The street is clear because your car is buried! When they plowed the street, they pushed the snow to either side, creating huge, 4-foot snow mounds on either side of the road. You can't drive out. You have to dig. You actually do have a snow shovel—your parents saw to that—but you don't have the time. The snooze alarm took care of that. You try to hail a cab so you don't miss your first class. You'll dig out when you get back.

If you decide to take your car anyway. You will probably be required to register it with campus security. *A tip: Never let an upperclass student register your car so you can get a higher priority parking sticker.* For one thing, that student is going to be responsible for any parking violations you incur. For another, such subterfuges are often found out, and many campus security guards, we've noticed, have just a little too much fun enforcing their authority—so the resulting punishment could be severe. You may be the one they decide to use as an example.

At last! You get a great spot, one without meters or signs telling you when it's okay to park there. But now the spot owns you—it's so great that you can't bear to leave it. You avoid driving your car for the next three days!

CHAPTER 4

PERSONAL BUSINESS

Pepperoni, mushroom, and black olive. Your favorite pizza. You want it. Now. You've ordered a large one—you're planning to save some for later, already looking forward to the midnight snack and applauding yourself for your remarkable foresight. And now it's here. It smells so good, you can taste it already. You're short on cash, so you whip out your checkbook, scribble a check, and reach out for the pizza box.

"What is this?" cries Bub, the pizza man.

Obviously, it's a check. What does he mean, you wonder? Did you forget to sign it?

"This is for a bank in Ohio." Yeah, you know. "It's where I live."

"We're in Chicago." Again, no surprise.

"So?" you say, with a slight attitude.

"So, we don't take out-of-state checks. Got any cash?"

This is terrible. It's five o'clock and your roommate's at dinner with about half of the students in your dormitory.

"Wait one second," you say, starting to panic. You race up and down the floor, looking for an open door. Nobody's here. You dart up to the next floor, where you know some guys. Finally! Thank God! You've found somebody, and miracle of miracles, he's got some cash! You sprint downstairs and arrive at your door, panting.

And he's gone. Faster than you can say "extra cheese," Bub is outta there. You start to crumble in a sad heap on the floor—but then, you rise up. You're not going down without a fight. Following the lingering trail of pepperoni, you stride down the hall after Bub, with a glint of determination in your eye that would have made your tough pioneer ancestors proud.

Good luck—hope you catch him.

OPENING A LOCAL CHECKING ACCOUNT

The scene you have just witnessed could have been avoided, and you could be blissfully munching on your third slice of pizza already, if you had done one thing: opened a local checking account.

Like Bub, many local merchants just won't cash an out-of-state check; they've been burned too many times. Check policies vary from state to state. For instance, in Tempe, Arizona, home of Arizona State University, many merchants require a check-cashing card issued by the bank. (Annoyingly, there can be a wait of several months between the time the account is opened and the time the card is issued. So talk with your bank and find out if there is anything you can do—like establishing your account during the summer—to speed up the process.)

There are probably places on campus where you can cash a check from your hometown bank—perhaps the bursar's office and a place in the student union—but these won't be open nights and weekends.

It's a good idea to establish an account with a bank in your college community—preferably a bank with a 24-hour automatic teller, so you can get money any time you need it.

Look for interstate banks. If you're going to an out-of-town school, look around for a bank that sounds familiar; you may find that your home-town bank has a branch near school. That could mean the best of both worlds: keeping your account in your hometown bank and using the bank machines around your college campus without having to pay the service charge.

Another option: Get a local job. Truman, a student at Wittenberg University in Ohio, kept his account at his hometown bank in Lexington, Kentucky, and cashed his out-of-state checks at the student union whenever he needed extra money. But this didn't happen often, because he had a job on campus. It didn't pay much—about $40 a week—but that was usually more than adequate for his needs; Truman had a meal plan, and lived in a dorm, so his main expenses were laundry and late-night pizza. This arrangement worked fine. "But in retrospect," says Truman, "I probably should have opened a local checking account. It would have been convenient to deposit the money from my pay checks, and then just get out what I needed, when I needed it."

Guard Your PIN Number With Your Life

Allison, born and raised in Manhattan, is a student at Johns Hopkins University in Baltimore. "I thought, being from New York, that I was pretty street-wise, and able to take care of myself." And, out on the street, Allison is very crime-conscious. She takes excellent safety precau-

Interstate banks may let you have the best of both worlds—you get to keep your hometown bank account AND use the bank machines around college without having to pay the service charge.

tions such as walking briskly, with an air of purpose, and wearing her purse across her body (around her neck and shoulder), instead of just draped loosely over one shoulder, in an attempt to make a would-be purse-snatcher's job more difficult.

But sadly, Allison was more gullible than she realized. At school, in classes and the library, she let down her guard—in fact, she had a bad habit of leaving her purse unattended. One day on campus, unbeknownst to Allison, someone stole the wallet out of her purse. A few hours later, Allison got a phone call at her apartment. The caller identified himself as an employee of Allison's bank. "We've been having some problems with our mainframe computer, and we've lost some data," he said, sounding professional, bored and just a bit harried (as Allison put it, "very believable"). "Would you mind giving us your PIN for verification? Or, if you'd rather, you can come to our downtown location and do it today." This was an extremely shrewd thing for the thief to say—he gambled that Allison, a busy college student, would have better things to do with her time than truck downtown to give some guy her personal identification number.

"No," Allison said, "I'll just go ahead and give it to you over the phone." And she did.

Within the hour, someone cleaned out Allison's checking account—all $482 of it.

And Allison spent the next few days talking to the police, who weren't very optimistic about catching this thief, and canceling her MasterCard, gas station and department store credit cards—what a hassle!

What should she have done? (Beside psychically knowing that her bank card had been stolen?) One thing, the police told her, would have been easy: *Don't ever, ever, give anyone your PIN number.* Or, Allison could have verified that this man was who he said he was. She could have said something like: "I can't talk to you right now. Could you give me your work number, and I'll call you back in a few minutes?" And then, if the guy had hedged, or handed her some line like, "No, I'm not at my desk right now, you'll just get put on hold and transferred all over the bank—it'll be easier for you to just let me call you back," she might have gotten suspicious. She could have insisted on returning the call, and then asked to speak to someone in charge of customer service or account information.

"A general rule," advises a lawyer we know, "is don't do any business over the phone unless you initiate it." (For instance, if you call J. Crew, or Crutchfield, or any mail-order company to place an order and they ask for your credit card number, it's okay—you called them at the number printed in the catalog. On the other hand, if someone saying she's from J. Crew calls you and asks for your credit card number, don't give it to her. Hang up, call the store's 800 number, and find out what's going on.)

But it would have been still easier for Allison if she had just kept an eye on her purse in the first place. "Believe me," she says disgustedly, "I'll never do that again." Too bad she had to learn this lesson the hard way.

Beware of Identity Theft

All somebody needs is your Social Security number. With that, a smart and/or computer-savvy thief can get your credit card numbers, driver's license number, and checking account number. Crooks can go after your telephone calling card numbers, and ATM pin codes, as well. At worst, you can wind up with a ruined credit rating, get turned down for loans, and be charged with straightening out the mess of debt that somebody else racked up. (Note: Federal law limits your liability for credit card fraud to $50.) What can you do? Here are a few ways you can protect yourself.

- Never leave your ATM receipts behind. "You should always tear them up," says the agent in charge for the U.S. Secret Service in Columbia, S.C. (The Secret Service is the agency in charge of investigating credit card fraud.) "They have your checking account number on them."
- Cancel any credit cards you're not using. Like the one for the department store in your hometown; how often are you going to be using that one, anyway? Even if you consider the account dead—even if you've cut up the card, it may still be "open," and this information will appear on your credit report.
- Leave any unnecessary credit cards, your Social Security card, and other vital papers (birth certificate, passport) somewhere safe, preferably locked up in your room at home. If you must have

RECORDS YOU SHOULD KEEP

What should you keep? Everything. Fee receipts, canceled checks, housing contracts, sales slips—especially from the bookstore, in case something comes up (like, you drop a class, or somebody loans you a copy of the same book you just bought and you want to get a refund)—grade reports, schedule cards, everything that looks official.

You don't need an elaborate filing system. A plain old shoebox is ideal. It won't take up much room, and it could save you much grief.

You should even keep a copy of the college catalog from your freshman year. In a way, the catalog serves as a contract between the institution and you, and if the college changes its rules or graduation requirements, you should have the option (it's called a grandfather clause) of following only the requirements that were in effect when you enrolled.

It's also a good idea to hold on to all the tests and corrected papers you get back from your professors. If you have a problem with a course or want to appeal a final grade, these earlier papers could be essential evidence. And your class notebooks, as unhelpful as they may seem now, also may prove useful at some point down the road.

WHAT TO LOOK FOR IN A BANK

If you opt to go with a local bank and have several to choose from, try to shop around. Some considerations are:

- Convenience. Is there a branch or bank machine near campus?
- The monthly checking fee. Is there a flat fee? Does it depend on your balance? For example, do you get charged 25 cents a check if you don't keep a certain amount in your account?
- How friendly are the clerks? This may not matter now, but if you bounce a check, it's nice to know that at least somewhere in the building there's a friendly face.

them while you're at school, put them in a lock box, or in a local bank's safety deposit box.

- Be secretive when you're punching in your PIN number or telephone calling card number. Block the numbers with your body, or your other hand. "We have had cases where people in vans using high-powered zoom lenses watch PINs being punched in," the Secret Service agent reports. "Also, there are all sorts of personal numbers taken out of trash bags and dumpsters. When people are caught at this type fraud and go to jail, some of them (continue to) run the operations out of prison."

Writing checks: A few tips

No matter where you bank, there are going to be times when you'll have trouble cashing a personal check, when you'll be asked to show valid identification. Don't take it personally. This is sometimes harder than it sounds, particularly if you've grown up in a small community or folksy neighborhood where everybody knows you. Some students are devastated by this kind of confrontation. But, to look at the bigger picture, it's not personal. The sales clerk is just playing it safe, doublechecking that you are, indeed, who you say you are.

Having said that, let us add that attitude is one thing, your rights are another.

It is not legal in many states for a store employee to request an additional credit card—like a MasterCard or Visa—and then write down that credit card number on the check. They may be doing this with the idea that, if the check bounces, they can charge your account. But—surprise—Visa and MasterCard don't let merchants bill your credit card to cover a bounced check.

If a sales clerk gives you a hard time, you have two good options: (1) you can argue your case with the store manager, or (2) you can walk away without buying anything. They won't get your credit card number; they won't get your business, either. It is also illegal for a merchant to request your Social Security number. That's nobody else's business. There is no good reason for any sales clerk to need such information.

What stores can do. They can request your driver's license and write down that number, and they can check one of your credit cards to see if the name matches the name on the check (they just can't jot down the number from the card). These things are okay. It's also reasonable for them to have your address and a telephone number. But nothing more! Protect your privacy. It is your right.

HOW TO BALANCE YOUR CHECKBOOK

Well, you've got the first part down—you're doing a great job writing checks. But there's a Part Two here: The checks go to the bank, and then they come back to you. What are you supposed to do now?

Now you're supposed to do something called "balancing your checkbook," and there are a couple of ways to go about it. First, if you're lucky enough to have a personal computer or access to one, use a specialized computer program. (We recommend "Quicken," by a company called Intuit.) These programs know all the questions to ask; all you have to do is type in the checks you've written and their amounts, and it balances the checkbook for you.

If you don't have this program or a personal accountant, you get to do it the old-fashioned way (ideally, with the help of a calculator).

You may be wondering why it's important that you do this fairly regularly—once a month or so. Certainly we've often wondered the same thing. "After all," we say, confidently holding up our monthly bank statements, "it looks like they've done all the work for us." Indeed, the bank has kindly noted all our withdrawals and deposits and given us a nice, helpful balance. "This is the bank's job, right? Isn't that what our interest money pays for—services like this? Don't they know best?"

Sadly, the answer to that last question is "not always." Sometimes the bank makes mistakes. Sometimes the balance on your sheet doesn't reflect everything.

The basic reason for balancing a checkbook is to know how much money you've got. This is important because you don't want to write checks for more money than you actually have in the bank. Doing this could lead to the embarrassment (and the hefty service charge) of a bounced check. Doing it regularly could even give you a bad credit rating.

Sometimes the bank makes mistakes. Sometimes the balance on your sheet doesn't reflect everything.

So, quick and dirty, here are a few tips from the experts on balancing your checkbook. Like flossing, it's not so bad once you get the hang of it. Really.

1. *At the exact moment you're writing a check—not the next day or even an hour afterward—record the number and amount of that check in your checkbook register.* If you wait to do this, you may forget the precise amount (or even the fact that you wrote the check at all!).

2. *Never write a check before your deposit has had time to get to the bank.* (That check your Dad sent you will probably take two to five business days to make it into your account; cash generally takes one day).

3. Say you do something unfortunate—you write a check to a store called The Purple Cookie before your deposit has had time to clear. This is what will probably happen: First, the check will bounce. Boing! Second, the bank will stiff you with a nasty little penalty—something like $25—to discourage this from happening again. Third, the bank will return the check to The Purple Cookie so fast it'll make your head spin. Zoom! This boomerang effect is why it's called "bouncing" a check. Fourth, The Purple Cookie also may stick you with an extra penalty fee. (Did you notice a sign over the cashier's counter that said something like "$25 fee for all returned checks"? This is what they meant.) Ouch!

4. *Note: Even if you have an option at your bank called something like "Overwrite Protection," which means the bank will actually cover your overdrawn check and not hang you out to dry, the bank will probably still slap you with a penalty fee.*

5. *Hang on to your deposit slips, at least until you see that your deposit has been recorded on your monthly statement.* Your receipt may be the only way for the bank to trace your deposit if there is a question or mistake.

6. *Compare your canceled checks and bank statement with your checkbook register.* Here's your first check in this month's pile, Number 102, to Kroger's, for $12.47. Now, look in your checkbook register. Find Number 102. Is it for $12.47? Good. Now mark this particular check off the list and move on to the next one.

7. *Next, go back through your checkbook and add up any checks you've written that haven't yet made it into the statement.* (Like the check for an even 30 bucks that you cashed last Friday for weekend spending money.) Deduct this total from the balance on your statement.

8. *Add up any deposits that haven't been recorded by the bank, and deduct any service charges* (whatever the bank charges for handling your account).

9. *Now you should have two sets of figures.* One is your checkbook balance. The other is the adjusted balance on your statement. They should be exactly the same. If they aren't, go back and check your math and reverify each entry in your checkbook register.

If your account still doesn't balance and you can't find any errors, the next step is for you to take your checkbook and statement to the bank. (No offense, but you may want to have a friend or two look over your calculations to see if they can figure out the problem first. Think of how embarrassed you'd be if you get to the bank and they find that you made a major, screaming error in your addition.)

The bank should give you a prompt explanation. *Note: Don't expect the bank to do your bookkeeping for you. As a way to nip this habit in the bud, some banks charge a fee for unraveling someone's tangled finances.*

Hang on to your checks and bank statements. All done? Don't pitch your canceled checks and receipts into the trash. They are your proof of payment. (You may need them when the dreaded tax season rolls around in the spring. And, according to tax experts, it's a good idea to keep important documents like bank statements and tax forms for at least six years.) Stow these papers in a safe place, along with all your other important business.

An option: Duplicate checks. The big advantage here is that you balance your checkbook every day or even more than once a day; you do it every time you write a check. The checks are printed on special paper, so when you write one check, you're really writing two—you're making an exact copy of it to keep for your own records. *(Note: Some banks don't return these canceled checks.)*

WHEN YOU ORDER YOUR CHECKS

Get your local address and telephone number printed on the check. If you don't, you'll probably end up reciting this information every time you make a purchase. (And, worst case scenario, some unsavory person could overhear, and learn your address and home phone number.)

Tip: Add a "one." Look at the number in the top right corner of your check. What does it say? Number 101? Number 102? Or are we up to 103 already? Whoo, big time—104! What a consumer you are! Local merchants may think you're less of a goober (and that your financial record is more established) if, when you order your checks from the bank, you add a "one" to the starting number. (No, we're not talking about pencilling in a number on your check—do it on the order form, when you're ordering your checks from the bank!) So in the space on the form marked, "beginning number," put in "1101." This isn't illegal, and most banks don't care—they're your checks. Although for record-keeping purposes it's traditional for checks to start at 101, many banks will let you start at any number you'd like.

CREDIT CARDS

If it hasn't started already, look out—it will. Soon, you are going to be deluged with attractive offers from a bunch of credit card companies. People you've never even met are going to want to give you credit.

For the credit card companies, this is great: You're young, you're going to college, therefore you obviously have income-generating potential, and you're probably a good credit risk. The companies probably aren't going to invest a lot of money checking out your credit history because they assume you haven't got one. (They may also assume that your parents will be involved in—i.e., that they'll cover—your credit card payments.)

Getting credit will probably never be easier in your life than it is right now.

So don't blow it. The flip side to all this is that it's easy to make some big mistakes now that can haunt you and ruin your credit rating for years to come. Say you take several of these companies up on their friendly offer to give you a credit card. You get a Visa, a MasterCard, a Discover, a Sears, a Macy's, and a JCPenney's. Your wallet now looks like you have a deck of playing cards in it. Feeling like a real grown-up, you start charging, to the point where you owe a couple hundred dollars on each card. You decide to pay the minimum payment—$10 to $20 a month.

You have a big problem.

You need to know that the minimum payment is designed so you pay mostly interest—which can be more than 20 percent—and not what you actually owe. You're scraping off the icing every month but not touching the cake. The cake is still there, and it's getting bigger. To take a big bite out of that cake—in other words, to reduce your debt—you need to pay more than the monthly payment. Ideally, you need to pay off what you owe every month.

The goal, then, for people who use credit cards should be: Don't charge more than you can afford to pay off every month.

Credit cards aren't supposed to let you buy things you otherwise couldn't afford, but they've become artificial income boosters for many people. Buy now, pay later. Figure it out for yourself: if you buy a watch

Soon, you owe a couple hundred dollars on each card. You decide to pay only the minimum payment—$10 to $20 a month. You have a big problem.

now for $100, and your interest is 18.9 percent, and you take a year to pay it off, how much will you actually end up spending?

It is very easy to keep charging to the point where your debt is so big that you might never pay it off. This has happened to millions of people in this country—millions who will undoubtedly go to their graves owing money. You, or your parents, probably know or are related to some of these people who got sucked into the credit trap. Look at Bill and Ginnie, in Iowa City, who got married after their senior year at the University of Iowa in 1979: They're in a big mess now because of credit. They feel frustrated, and helpless, and guilty—they believe they've failed themselves, their parents and their two children, ages 13 and 6. What went wrong? It was so easy for them to charge things, making only the minimum monthly payments, that before they knew it they didn't have much ready cash, because they were using their disposable income to pay on their credit card accounts. So, with less disposable income, they charged even more things—big, important things, like braces for their son's teeth, eye glasses, private music lessons for their kids. Now they owed even more money, and had even less to spend—and the needs were still there. The washing machine died. They charged a new one. The air conditioner had a meltdown. They opened a new charge account at a new department store, and bought a new one. They began rationalizing every purchase: "We owe so much, what difference is $300 (or $50, or even $20) going to make? It's just a drop in the bucket." Yes, but all those drops add up.

You know, if you wanted to, you could charge anything these days—even groceries. This is terrible—it's a bad sign if you don't have enough disposable income to pay for food, which is about the most basic necessity there is.

Think it couldn't happen to you? Watch TV during the day. There are an awful lot of commercials aimed at people who need special "consolidation loans." Ever wondered what those are? Or why some commercials offer money to people with "slow credit or no credit?" These ads are for the many decent people out there who have run into financial trouble.

Imagine owing so much that you need a loan from the bank—for tens of thousands of dollars, even—to pay off those credit cards. People get such loans because the

BANK MACHINES

Many colleges have automatic teller machines on campus. You may want to find out which bank owns these machines and open an account with this bank. That way, you won't have to pay a service charge every time you use these machines. (In other words, if you belong to Bank A, but it's Bank B's machine, you may be charged two dollars or so every time you get money out of Bank B's machine.)

It is possible, in these days of multibank networks, to use out-of-state bank machines to get money from your home-town bank and never open up a local checking account.

For example, Tom lives in Baltimore and is a customer of Maryland National Bank. On his automatic teller card are some logos, including one that says "Most" and one that says "Cirrus." Tom goes to college at Boston University. He doesn't have a bank account in Boston. He just looks for a bank machine with "Most" or "Cirrus" and uses his Maryland National Card, typing in his Personal Identification Number (or PIN number).

Tom doesn't worry about writing local checks; whenever he needs money, he just gets cash or uses his card—he can even use it to pay for groceries in some big supermarkets. In emergencies, he can also use his Visa credit card, which has its own PIN number, to get money out of these bank machines. (Note: This step should be reserved for true emergencies; many credit card companies have higher service charges for cash advances.)

For Tom, this is fine. Whenever he uses the machine, he always gets a lot of cash—$50 dollars instead of $10 or $20—because he has to pay a service charge every time. This way, by getting more money less often, he actually saves money on the service charges, which have been as much as $30 dollars a month.

"However," Tom comments, "it can be a pain to carry around a lot of money," especially when he's out at some place like a dance club. He worries about losing his wallet or getting robbed. Tom has a lock box in his dorm room, but he doesn't like to leave the money there, either. "Why tempt people?" he says.

bank may charge less interest than the credit cards. Some of these loans are huge, the kind of big money people borrow to buy a house or boat, or to do major home improvements. But the people who take out these loans have nothing tangible to show for them—no house, no nice boat, no new deck to add value to their home. All they get is a little less weight on their shoulders from the personal debt burden they've been carrying around. It's like paying money for air.

What does this mean to you? A chance to stop a problem before it begins. When things come too easily, be suspicious. As the old saying goes, If something sounds too good to be true, it probably is. So be smart. Ask yourself, what's the catch here? If you decide to get a credit card—and, believe it or not, we think you probably should have one for emergencies—shop around.

Some guidelines for getting a card

- **Find a credit card with low interest and no annual fee.** Some companies charge you a yearly fee—usually $50 or less—just for the privilege of using their card. But watch out: With some companies, the trade-off for having no annual fee is that there's no grace period before the interest starts adding up.
- **Find out when the interest starts adding up.** At some department stores and credit card companies, the interest clock starts ticking the day you make your purchase. Think of it as a "credit card tax." Say your purchases total $100 in one month. Your credit card company has no grace period, so interest starts building up immediately. You pay off your whole bill that same month—but your total comes to $101.50. Which may not seem like a lot. But trust us—these things add up fast. At other companies, you get a grace period, which is designed to encourage you to pay off your debt promptly, before the interest kicks in.
- **Pay more than your minimum payment every month if you start using your card regularly.** If you owe $200 and your payment's only $10, pay at least $15 or $20.

- **Show a little restraint.** Ask yourself, "Do I really have to have this CD? This new jacket? Can I do without it—at least until next month?" Look at it this way: These are your salad days—your lean years. It's kind of nice to look back fondly at your tiny apartment, your dinners of Campbell's soup, your brick-and-board bookshelves, your thrift-store-chic clothes. If you try to have it all now, what will be left for later?
- **And finally, think about the long haul.** At the writing of this book, one of us just finished paying monthly installments on two student loans; they're due to be paid off ten years after graduation date. The point here is that credit card debt is just the (largely preventable) tip of the iceberg. Unless you're in the military, on a tuition-free scholarship, or otherwise lucky enough to have your college education paid for, chances are you'll probably have some student loans waiting for you after you graduate.

Be smart. Ask yourself, what's the catch here?

Playing it smart: Tips for using your credit card

- **Don't give your card number or expiration date over the phone unless you initiated the transaction.** It's okay if you dial L.L. Bean's 800 number to buy a pair of shorts, for instance, or if you call FTD to send some flowers for your mom's birthday—because you called them.
- **Don't give out your birth date or Social Security number more often than you have to.** An unscrupulous person could use one or both of these to apply for a credit card in your name! *Note: If this does somehow happen to you and you get bills for things you didn't buy, all you can be made to pay—your maximum liability—is $50.*
- **Don't waste your money on credit card registries.** There are companies out there that, for a small fee (usually about $15), will get in touch with all your credit card companies if your cards are lost or stolen. But even if you pay one of these companies to handle this task for you, you still have to make a list of all your cards and their

Don't give your card number or expiration date over the phone unless you initiated the transaction.

CO-SIGNING: MONETARY MADNESS

A friend wants to get a credit card, and he wants you to co-sign.
DON'T DO IT!

Run, don't walk, away from this potential hell! Save yourself and your friendship, now. Slap yourself in the face. Wake up and smell the coffee! Go the bank, get some money and buy a clue!

Do you know what it really means to co-sign on somebody's loan, car, credit card, or apartment rent? It means if that person defaults—if he or she doesn't pay the bills—then the bank, car dealer, credit card company, or landlord is going to come after YOU! You are going to get stuck with your ex-friend's debt. That's what you promise when you sign your name on the dotted line next to your friend's.

numbers. So why not save the money and just make these calls yourself?

It's not that much trouble to make a list of all your credit cards and numbers; in fact, it's really easy. Just go to a Xerox machine, line up all your cards, and photocopy them onto one sheet of paper. Then stow this list somewhere safe; you might even want to send a copy of it to your home address just in case.

- **Watch out for offers on your monthly bill that let you skip a payment.** Be suspicious. Why would your credit card company want to give you a break? Well, it might be doing it out of the goodness of its heart. Or it might be making you this spectacular offer so you'll take longer to pay off what you owe—so it can make more money off the interest of your principal debt.
- **Beware of offers to lower your minimum payment.** Again, here's a chance for the credit card company to make more money off of you. If you stretch out your payments over more months or years, you could end up tripling the amount of interest you owe. (Again, to hammer home a point: If you pay off your balance in full every month, you'll avoid interest charges altogether.)
- **Watch out for "overlimit fees."** An overlimit fee means the credit card company will nail you with a penalty of about $10 or $15 if you go over your credit limit. So know your limit, and know your current balance. In the credit card world, the best surprise is no surprise.
- **Expect to pay extra for cash advances.** Many credit card companies charge interest immediately for cash advances, skipping the usual grace period. There may even be a special fee (a couple of dollars) just for the privilege of getting this cash advance, in addition to the interest you'll have to pay on it.
- **Don't get every new card that comes down the pike.** Here's a scary fact: Every time you apply for a card, this shows up on your credit history. Having too much available credit—even if you don't use it—may make it harder for you to qualify for a mortgage or other major loan because potential creditors will fear that you may become overextended.

IF YOU GET IN TROUBLE

First, look in your local phone book for the Consumer Credit Counseling Service. This is a nonprofit group that helps people plan budgets and manage their debt. Talking to somebody who does this for a living (your college may offer debt management counseling) can't possibly hurt. Plus, it's almost sure to make you feel better just knowing that there are some people out there who have messed up far worse than you.

Your job is to kick the debt habit, and get your life back. But looking at the mountain of debt makes you feel overwhelmed, helpless, and very depressed. How to begin? Here are a few tips from financial advisers:

- First, figure out what you're dealing with. Write down every single debt you owe—the totals on your credit cards, any outstanding loans, doctor bills, department store credit accounts, everything. Beside every entry, note the interest rate, which you'll probably find somewhere on the bill. (Example: MasterCard: 16.45 percent interest. How can this be? When you signed up for the card, it offered a 6.9 percent interest. Oh, yeah—that was just the introductory rate, good for the first six months only. After that, it ballooned.)

- Set your priorities. Which debts are most pressing? First, figure out which, if any, are past due. Then see which ones charge the highest interest rate. Then, look for debts that can be paid off fairly quickly—if you're less than five payments away from paying off a debt, even if the interest is low, make this one a priority.

- Don't try to pay them all off at once. Get to work on the top-priority debt. Make minimum payments on the rest. (It may be helpful to pay off a card with a low balance first, just for the boost in morale.)

- Once you pay off a debt, CANCEL THE CARD. And, needless to say, stop charging on your other cards. It won't be easy, and there are always emergencies, in which charging is absolutely unavoidable (like, getting someone to fix your car when it died in the middle of the freeway). But you're going to have to be tough with yourself: The urgent need to buy a new CD is not a legitimate emergency. Charging a meal at a

WANT TO SEE YOUR CREDIT REPORT?

The following companies can help you get a copy of your report. Before you initiate a report, find out if there's a fee, and if so, how much. (*Note: If you've been rejected for a credit card, you're supposed to get a copy of your credit report for free.*)

Equifax Credit Information Services, P.O. Box 740241, Atlanta, GA 30374-0241, Phone: 800-685-1111. To report fraud, call: 800-525-6285.

Experian. P.O. Box 1017, Allen, TX 75031. Phone: 800-682-7654. To report fraud, call: 800-301-7195.

Trans Union National Consumer Relations Disclosure Center. P.O. Box 390, Springfield, PA 19064. Phone: 800-916-8800. To report fraud, call: 800-680-7289.

IF YOUR FAMILY'S FINANCES CHANGE

Act promptly. Get in touch with your school's financial aid officers and let them know what's going on. Give them an updated reassessment of your family's ability to help pay for your college education as soon as you can.

Very often, a change in family circumstances—divorce, loss of a job, death, or illness of a breadwinner—in addition to being emotionally devastating, will alter your level of financial need.

So provide your school the information necessary to review and, if need be, upgrade your financial aid package immediately, without your having to wait for a new academic year to begin.

The goal is to avoid unpleasant monetary surprises. Figure out what your budget will need to cover and how far you can stretch it.

restaurant "just this once" will not help you get out of debt. Have a little self-control, for Pete's sake.

- Don't get a consolidation loan. Many people get these loans with the best of intentions, and then end up with even more debt. They still keep charging, and end up not only with a wallet full of maxed-out cards, but crippling monthly payments on the debt-consolidation loan. Hello, bankruptcy!

LOOK OUT FOR HIDDEN COLLEGE EXPENSES

Have you ever rented a car for some really cheap rate, like $19.99 a day, and wondered why it didn't feel like such a fantastic bargain when you paid the bill? Let's see . . . the basic price is $19.99 . . . plus 20 cents a mile, plus the optional insurance—that's $12.95 a day (that optional insurance isn't really optional for you because you don't have car insurance that will cover it).

We're talking hidden costs here. Sneaky things that lurk just around the corner, waiting to eat up part or all of your money.

We can't tell you how much money you're going to need for college; only you and your parents can figure this out. It would be foolish and unhelpful for us even to try for two reasons: (1) living costs differ throughout the country, and (2) everybody's situation is different.

Maybe you've already got it all figured out down to the penny—your living expenses for every week, month, or semester. Or maybe you don't have a clue but aren't too worried; maybe you're just going to wing it because you have a built-in safety net—the parental checkbook.

But maybe, like most college students, you're somewhere in the middle—you have a budget, and you need to stick to it. So now it's reckoning time. The goal is to try and anticipate every possible expense now so you can avoid unpleasant monetary surprises later. Figure out what your budget will need to cover and how far you can stretch it.

Learn how to manage your money. This is not as hard as it sounds. Just as with managing time and energy, good money management centers around planning—making the best use out of what you have.

Figure your true living expenses. If you're living on campus, the big-ticket items—housing and tuition—are easy. You know how much they cost and what they cover. Depending on when you read this, you may even have paid for them already. Now, take some time to figure out what's *not* covered.

Food

At most schools, freshmen who live on campus are required to buy at least a basic meal package. On a weekly basis, this could pay for as few as ten meals (in which case you'll have to buy, prepare, or skip at least a few other lunches or dinners in the week) or as many as 21 meals, with the difference in price being, probably, a couple hundred dollars. Actually, the 21-meal package, compared with the costs of eating off campus, is probably not a bad deal—if you'll be eating three meals a day, seven days a week, on campus. If you won't, frankly, this will be a waste of money, and you should consider a cheaper one.

Analyze your needs. Will you, for example, be needing an actual breakfast (or lunch, or dinner) every day? If breakfast to you means a bagel and juice, you could save money by stocking those items in your dorm room. (Just think—no more tiny shot glasses of orange juice! You can have as much as you want!)

Will you even be on campus every weekend? If you're planning to spend at least a few weekends at home or out of town, you won't be able to use those Saturday and Sunday meals you've paid for, and you probably won't be able to get your money back. *(Note: If your meal plan includes a cash card, it's probably only good for one semester.)*

Will you be eating out a lot? Be honest with yourself. If the thought of the fast food strip across the street is too tempting to resist and you know it now, just plan ahead. Otherwise, one day as you stand in the cafeteria line, you may crack—"I've got your balanced, nourishing, color-coordinated, tasteless meal right here, lady! Right here on the floor!"

With a backhand swipe, you send overcooked broccoli florets, a red jello/fruit cocktail combo, and a rubber biscuit flying across the room. As people scuttle out of your way, you, transfixed by an epiphany, now feel in complete oneness with the fed-up Michael Douglas character in the movie *Falling Down*. Eyes agleam, you stumble out of the cafeteria, lured ever onward by the beckoning whiff of real french fries (as opposed to those

Analyze your needs. If breakfast to you means a bagel and juice, you could save a lot of money just by stocking those items in your dorm room. Just think—no more tiny shot glasses of orange juice! You can have as much as you want!

IF YOU NEED EMERGENCY MONEY

Nearly every college reserves a number of revolving loan funds to help students through legitimate crises, like not having enough money for food or rent. (Something like, "Oh, my God! I don't have the plane fare to get to Florida for Spring Break!" is not a legitimate crisis.) These loans typically run to a maximum of 60 days and must be repaid at that time. Little or no interest is charged. These loans usually can't be used to pay tuition.

The financial aid office administers most of these funds, although the dean of your college may have access to short-term loan money that's been donated to assist students in a specific field of study. *Note: Don't wait until the last minute to apply because it may take four or five days to process your request.*

institutional tater nuggets you just threw in the direction of the cashier) that tantalizes and torments you.

But we digress.

More questions. Will you be able to show up every day during designated meal hours? What if something comes up and you don't make it to the cafeteria before it closes? (This is inevitable and shouldn't pose much of a problem if you're prepared with, for example, cans of soup you can heat up in your room or the cash to get some food elsewhere.)

Know yourself. Be realistic, and plan to eat out several times a month. Make a rough estimate: For example, you budget five meals, at a conservative six bucks apiece, per month. That's thirty dollars a month. So, for one semester, allowing for a hectic schedule during finals week that might lead you to eat out more often, you may want to budget at least $100 in meals that won't be covered by your cash card.

If your meal package doesn't cover weekend meals: Again, plan ahead. This may be a great opportunity to save money. For example, you could go to a grocery store, buy a head of lettuce for 99 cents, two cucumbers, and a big tomato for another dollar. Make a huge salad, keep it in your refrigerator. Have part of it for lunch Saturday and Sunday, and you will have spent less than two dollars (plus the cost of salad dressing and maybe some canned tuna to go on top) for several healthy meals.

Or, conversely, this could be a big opportunity to blow money. It all adds up: ten bucks for a pizza Friday night, ten more for burgers and fries Saturday, $7.99 for the all-you-can-eat, gut-bomber brunch at Joe Bob's Country Fixin's Buffet on Sunday, and a dollar more for the rolls of antacids you stopped to buy at the gas station on the way back to campus. Again, how (and what) you choose to eat is up to you (see "Fighting the Freshman 10" in Chapter Five)—just make sure you don't spend more than you can afford.

Other essentials. You will need some cash to cover the cost of other basic items, such as toothpaste, deodorant, shampoo, and laundry expenses. (See Chapter One for a list of these basic items, then go to a discount or warehouse store and stock up. *Remember: The farther away you get from campus, the cheaper the prices.*)

Another tip: Go grocery shopping with your mom on those weekend trips home—any food or toiletries she happens to buy for you mean money off your budget.

Transportation

If you're an out-of-state student who plans to visit home a few times a year from a distant campus, this lone budgetary line item could easily run you more than a $1,000 a year. What can you do? Seek ways to economize. Talk to a travel agent and investigate cheaper airline or train tickets. One easy way to save money on plane fare, if you can swing it, is to fly to an airline's "hub" city (like Pittsburgh, Atlanta, Nashville, Dallas, Baltimore, or Chicago) near your hometown and either have someone meet you there or take a train or bus the rest of the way. Also, look into other options, such as flying stand-by, and check the travel section of your local paper for special "fare wars" rates.

If going home means a big road trip, you could lower such costs as car rental, motel rooms, and gas by advertising in the campus newspaper or on bulletin boards for one or more passengers from your neck of the woods to split the bills. At Vanderbilt University in Nashville, for example, there are informal geographic networks—particularly among students from Texas, New York, Kentucky, Ohio, and Georgia—of people who routinely check in with each other when they're planning a trip home.

As Joy, whose home base is Lexington, Kentucky (a four-hour drive from Nashville), points out, "It makes the trip a lot shorter if you have someone to talk to. Also, I just like having somebody else in the car, especially when I'm driving at night." *(Important note: Take a half hour, several days before you go, to meet and informally interview the person you're thinking of giving a ride. If you're highly or even moderately uncomfortable with this person, you may want to find someone else or drive solo this trip.)*

For in-state students, obviously, the transportation costs home or elsewhere are less, but they can still add up—gas and wear-and-tear on your car or donated gas money if you're catching a ride with someone.

Long-distance phone bills

How can this be? A long-distance bill of $84? For just one month?? There's got to be a mistake!

How can this be? A long-distance bill of $84? For just one month?? There's got to be a mistake! All you made were a few reasonable and brief phone calls home, and most of those were at night. Well, some of them were.

There was that one hour-long call to your brother in Tucson, who just got engaged. And then there were the calls to the stereo company in Oregon to check on those parts you ordered (how that company stays in business without a toll-free number is a mystery to you). And the one call back to your high school to get that letter of recommendation from your German teacher, Herr Schmidt, for that honors program you're applying for next semester (who would have guessed the old wienerschnitzel would want to chat for so long?). And the call to your now-former girlfriend, when you decided to "just be friends." Geez! That was a hellish conversation—two and a half hours. But what could you do? She was crying. . . .

One by one, call by call, long-distance calls add up. No matter how disciplined you set out to be at the beginning of the month, the bill is almost always higher than you thought you'd have to pay.

You can minimize expenses by checking out the major services—Sprint, AT&T, MCI—and shopping around for the best deal, either for your own long-distance account or a phone card as part of your parents' account, or a "prepaid card," which is good for a preset amount of phone time. You can buy these prepaid cards in certain unit denominations at some office supply stores or from your long distance company. An advantage here is that there's no reckoning at the end of the month—you know the cost of every call and you pay as you go. HOWEVER: Some of these cards from cut-rate companies, offer far less than they lead you to believe. How much do they charge per minute? If it's 15 cents or lower, it's probably a good deal. Otherwise, a $5 card could conceivably offer only ten minutes' of talk time!

One by one, call by call, long-distance calls do add up.

Other options for toll-free (on your part) calling include dialing collect (there are now several cheaper ways to do it than simply dialing "0") or having a family "800" number. Another warning: If the operator asks you to select a long-distance carrier, PICK ONE. Don't mumble something like, "I don't care." Why? Because there's a special "I don't care" network, and your parents could end up paying through the nose for one lousy call. We're not making this up! Also, check your long-distance bills periodically to make sure you haven't been "slammed." "Slamming" is a way for a lowlife long-distance carrier to steal your business without your consent, and charge you exorbitant rates until you wise up and switch back to a cheaper network. If you suspect you've been "slammed," you can call (700) 555-4141 to find out for sure. (Note: Don't cash any checks from phone companies; most likely, somewhere amid all the fine print, there's a line of implicit consent—which says cashing the check means you agree to have your phone service switched.)

Another hint: Use e-mail whenever possible. As a college student, you'll probably have your own computer account, and if your family has an Internet account, you can "call" home as often as you want—and the university will pay for it! Is this a great country, or what?

WATCH OUT FOR OTHER ACADEMIC EXPENSES

Your tuition money probably won't take care of such loose ends as lab fees for specific courses, late registration charges, drop-and-add fees, library fines, motor vehicle registration and parking fees, and various other course-related hits your budget will have to absorb. Individually, these fees may seem manageable—$25 here, $10 there—but over the span of a year, they can add up fast.

Your best bet here may be the preemptive strike: Find out about the existence of such fees, particularly in lab classes, before you register or during the first week of school, so, if need be, you can drop the class and take it later, when you've budgeted for it. (The fee might be mentioned in the schedule of classes, or you could find out from your professor or the department.)

And then, there's book money

Books are expensive, even though, in the grand scheme, they generally account for only a tiny fraction (probably less than 5 percent) of a student's total college expenses. One state school, the University of South Carolina, estimates that students will spend about $495 a year on textbooks.

IF YOU PLAN TO HAVE ANY KIND OF SOCIAL LIFE AT ALL

Even a modest social life costs money. One movie a week, one half of a non-gourmet pizza a week, one soft drink and one candy bar a day—we're definitely not talking life in the fast lane here—and you're spending nearly $90 a month. Add a concert here and a football weekend there and, before you know it, you've dropped a couple hundred dollars (and perhaps made a big dent in your budget).

Note: If you join a sorority or fraternity, talk to some active members and find out about any extra expenses you'll be expected to cover—special assessments, for example, to pay for parties, dances, gifts, photos, and other memorabilia—in addition to your regular dues.

GETTING SCHOLARSHIPS AND GRANTS AS A SOPHOMORE

Don't be discouraged. It's not too late. Not having a grant or scholarship as you start your freshman year doesn't mean that you can't have one by the time you finish it.

The scholarships and grants awarded to incoming freshmen are usually given for academic promise (often based on SAT or ACT scores). But after the freshman year, thousands of scholarships and grants are given to reward actual performance—the work you've done since you arrived on campus. Earn an impressive GPA (of about 3.5 or better), and there's a good chance you'll be considered for a portion of whatever general scholarship or grant money your school has available.

Other financial awards may take into account campus leadership as well as academic achievement. Many departmental scholarships and grants are reserved for upperclass students who prove unusually well suited for a particular area of study. *(Note: These departmental awards carry prestige as well as dollar value, in that they single you out as a top prospect in your chosen career field.)*

"Our department has about $150,000 available every year available for upperclass scholarships," said the chairman of a large communications department at one midwestern state university. "Some years

Are you helpless? Is there no hope for saving money here? Don't be silly! Of course there's hope. First, you can shave a huge chunk off your total cost for books and supplies by buying the things you could get anywhere—notebooks, pens (see Chapter One)—at an off-campus discount or warehouse store.

Save even more by buying as many used books as you can and by being creative. For example, if you're assigned the Oxford edition of *Pride and Prejudice*, you could pick up a cheap used paperback at an off-campus bookstore and, assuming the basic text is the same in any edition, just read the Oxford edition's introduction (to note any important points of criticism your professor may discuss in class).

Borrowing. If you're lucky enough to find willing lenders, this is also a great way to save. Ask around—befriend and/or plead with older students in your major (or in your dorm, club, fraternity, or sorority) and see if they'll lend you their textbooks. (We know you already know this, but if you borrow somebody's book, treat it with kid gloves. Treat it better than you'd treat your own book. Cherish it. Nurture it. Protect it. Don't write in it, don't dog-ear pages, don't read it in the bathtub, don't mark your place by leaving it open, face-down, and ruining the binding, and don't abuse the goodwill of the person who lent you the book. And don't forget to return the book when you've finished with it.)

Buy used books whenever possible. As you can imagine, used books are gobbled up fast, so buy early. (This means that you should sign up for advising and preregistration as soon as possible, so you'll know what courses you'll be taking. If you register late, you probably won't find a huge selection of cheap used books to choose from.)

At the end of the semester, you can recoup some money by selling your own books either back to the bookstore or to other students. You won't get the full price back, but you can recover at least some of your costs. *(Note: If you think you might be selling the book one day, plan ahead. Take the steps mentioned above to care for the book; in particular, don't write in it—you'll lower the resale value.)*

Buy only what you really need. Finally, be sure to find out whether each book on your course list is required or recommended. If it's just recommended, you may be able to get by without buying it. (Bookstores are supposed to label these distinctions plainly, but they don't always do it. If you're not sure, ask a clerk to check the professor's ordering instructions.) *Tip: Some professors put copies of the books on their list on reserve at the library. Which means that you may be able to avoid buying some books altogether.* (But be aware that this could be risky if you count on getting access to the books in the reserve room just when you need them most—like a few days before a big test.)

TIPS FOR MANAGING YOUR MONEY

The real secret to money management is easy: Avoid unnecessary spending. Easy to say, that is; much harder to do. But you can do it! Here are a few tips to get you started:

- **Stay out of stores.** What you don't see can't tempt you. If you do get dragged along by a friend, ask yourself ruthless questions:

  "Can I live without this CD?" Or "Can I encourage someone else to purchase this CD and then make a tape of it for myself?" *Note: Of course, we can't advise you to do anything illegal—which, strictly speaking, making a cassette tape of somebody else's CD is. Use your own judgment. (And, for best sound quality, a metal tape.)*

  "How much would this funky T-shirt be worth after it's been washed a few times, if I saw it at somebody's yard sale?" Don't kid yourself; you'd probably pay a quarter for it. Make a list and don't deviate from it once you set foot in the store—no matter how hard the impulse-buying bug bites. (If you really needed it, it would be on your list, right?)

- **Lie to yourself.** Promise yourself that you'll come back tomorrow and get the item—and then get the heck out of the store.
- **Count yourself out when your dormmates order pizza.** Say—truthfully—that you don't need the extra calories. Reach into your private stock of Chef Boyardee products or Healthy Choice frozen

we can't give it away because not enough students apply. And I know this fund is small compared to scholarship monies available at some private schools."

So if you didn't win scholarship honors or grant money going in, don't give up: As the old song says, it's not where you start, it's where you finish.

dinners and let your friends envy your willpower while you save five bucks for your share of the pizza.

- **Don't reach out and touch someone via long distance unless you can reverse the charges.** As we said, be ruthless. If it's your parents, they'll probably just be glad to hear from you and won't mind the collect call. If it's a buddy you're dying to talk to, suck it up and be strong. Show some restraint. Walk away from the phone. Set it down, slowly. Now back away; easy does it. Sure, you miss your best friend from high school. We all do. You wonder how her big date went last night. But letters are cheaper. So's the Internet. Or, if you absolutely must make the call, do it when the rates are at rock bottom—after eleven at night and on weekends. (See page 72 for more tips for saving money on long-distance calls.)

- **Write as few checks for cash as possible.** Some stores charge 50 cents or more to cash a check, and your bank may take another quarter for processing it. This means that a check for, say, $2.50 could cost you $3.25—which is money down the drain. So, even though you don't want to carry a lot of cash around with you, be sure you have enough on hand to take care of small expenses without having those nasty finance charges levied on your personal checks. Finance charges—perhaps most insidious of all the hidden costs—can torpedo an unsuspecting budget and sink it into oblivion.

CHAPTER 5

Surviving, Even Thriving, On Your Own

If, at the end of your freshman year you're able to say smugly, "Gee, I guess I'm still the same person I was in high school. I haven't changed a bit!" here's what you should do: First, give yourself a good smack on the head. Then, try to get your money back because you've wasted it, along with your mind, for two whole semesters.

The whole point here is to change and grow. This is why you're continuing your education. If you fear change and revere sameness, you shouldn't go to college at all; you should lock yourself away in a safe room someplace and throw away the key to the outside world. Throw away the mirrors, too, because they'll tell you something else you don't want to know. They'll tell you that your body is changing imperceptibly, every hour, every day, and there's not one thing you can do to stop it.

You may not realize it, but just like your body, your mind changes every day. If it's challenged, nourished, and given room to breathe, it blossoms like a lovely flower in the gentle sun. If it's closed to new ideas, malnourished, or denied the opportunity to reach its potential, it stagnates. It slowly withers into something resembling a hard and dried-up old prune—something so unappealing that, if you inadvertently stepped on it, you would quickly try to scrape off your shoe. Not a pleasant image.

Either way, change is going to happen, and you're going to respond to it. What kind of change you experience this year, and how you react, is entirely up to you.

Don't Fear Conclusions

In an age where multicultural is good, just about any sexual preference is okay, and making people feel bad about themselves (presumably by judging their behavior) is bad, many college students forget to use plain old common sense when figuring out right and wrong. For example: Kay Haugaard, an instructor of creative writing at Pasadena City College, often uses Shirley Jackson's classic short story, "The Lottery," as a flashpoint for her students. (The story starts out with deceptive normalcy, but ends with a shocker: A nice, normal-seeming town holds a lottery for human sacrifice.) In years past, Haugaard wrote in a recent issue of *The Chronicle of Higher Education*, "the story always impressed the class with the insight that I felt the author had intended: the danger of just "going along" with something habitually, without examining its rationale and value. The power of public pressure was illustrated chillingly. Jackson's message about blind conformity always spoke to my students' sense of right and wrong. Jackson had made an important and powerful point, which I hoped my students would take to heart, becoming more analytical about why things are done as they are."

Well, her most recent students just don't get it. *They don't want to judge.* Maybe ritual murder of an innocent person is okay—if it supports an agricultural ritual, or a religion of long standing. Said one student, a nurse: "Well, I teach a course for our hospital personnel in multicultural understanding, and if it is part of a person's culture, we are taught not to judge, and if it has worked for them."

WAKE UP! No, of course it isn't okay, and the students shouldn't have been afraid to realize that. Maybe in college you can get away with a moral compass that has the physical integrity of a decomposed wiener. But Out There, one of the most important tools you're going to need is your own personal B.S. meter, to help you discern bull and nonsense from stuff that actually matters. Our advice to you: Start working on it. And every now and then, take a stand for something you believe in.

YOUR PERSONAL DEVELOPMENT

Very few freshmen—only one in five—in a study done at the University of Iowa ranked intellectual development

PREPARE TO CHANGE AND GROW

Believe it or not, the most significant things that happen to you this year probably won't be academic. No, the biggest lessons you learn this year will probably be social. They may also be moral and philosophical. (The academic stuff—taking mind-expanding classes and liking them, buckling down and applying yourself to your studies—is more likely to kick in when you become a sophomore. It will probably become even more important in your junior and senior years, as you select a major and sharpen your career focus.)

"I learned you shouldn't follow your boyfriend and go to college just because he's going there," comments Kathleen, a University of South Carolina junior. "That's what I did. I came here to be with my boyfriend from high school, who's a year older. When I got here, I found out that he had another girlfriend, and he wasn't interested in me anymore."

The discovery, Kathleen notes, was devastating. At first, she felt "like a loser." Then she got mad, and then she decided that if she wasted her college time, she was the one who would be hurt most, and, in a way, "that would mean he had won," that "he had taken something away from me." Kathleen decided the best way to get even was "to make the most of my time here. I figured, 'I'm here, why should I spend my time being depressed over that jerk?' "

She worked hard to make her own set of friends, decided to major in journalism, and joined the newspaper staff. She became her own person, not just, as she had defined herself in high school, somebody's girlfriend.

among their most important experiences of freshman year. Instead, reported the study's chief investigator, psychologist Patricia M. King, the other 80 percent cited their most important experiences as the following:

- Involvement with other people
- Development of their own sense of identity
- Formation of moral principles and practical skills to guide their lives.

Here's what a few of these freshmen said:

- "One of the most important experiences I . . . had was meeting a person who became my friend. It was important for me because I had never met someone who had such a different background from mine."
- "My first accident (I broke my toe) . . . showed me that my parents weren't around. And also that when bad things happen, you can depend on your roommates and neighbors."
- "This one is very personal, but very important to me—my first time truly falling in love. It gave me hope for the future, kept me going through rough times, taught me a lot about myself and my boyfriend, and made me give a little more love back to my parents and friends."
- For one student, the most significant experience of his freshman year was choosing to go to Mass on his own. "It proved to me that I did have faith, and it wasn't that my parents made me go to church. I felt a sense of pride—or more . . . I thought that my faith, which I had . . . doubted, was very real."
- For another student, realizing that she wasn't the smartest person in the school came as a cold splash of reality: "I've always been good in school and I got good grades, so I came here expecting to get very few B's. That's the only part I got right. I'm getting the rest of my grades as C's instead of the A's I had expected. For a while, I thought I would adjust and get perfect tests, but thought again and realized that I'm not a genius. That helped."

If closed to new ideas, the mind stagnates. It slowly withers into something resembling a hard and dried-up old prune.

All of these students are doing fine. They're right where they're supposed to be at the end of their freshman year—at a different place from where they

All of these students are doing fine. They're right where they're supposed to be at the end of their freshman year—at a dif-

started. They haven't stayed the same. They've learned something about themselves.

Some people, in fact, value the friendship of college more highly than any academic reward. A lifetime ago, in the pre–Beavis and Butthead days of good conversation and mellow cigars, a Canadian scholar named Stephan Butler Leacock put it like this: "If I were founding a university, I would first found a smoking room; then, when I had a little more money in hand, I would found a dormitory; then after that, or more probably with it, a decent reading room and a library. After that, if I still had more money that I couldn't use, I would hire a professor and get some textbooks."

Acknowledge fear and move past it

Every year at Vanderbilt University, a professor named Oakley Ray gives an inspiring talk to freshmen—words of wisdom so profound that *Vanderbilt Magazine* recently reprinted some of what he has to say, including these thoughts:

"How do you treat you? You need to demand the best of yourself. The greatest restraint on what you can become is what you think of yourself and your life, your goals and aspirations. . . . The only limitations on you and your experiences . . . are the ones you impose on yourself. I call them black holes of fear. Black holes are antimatter—they suck everything up. Our personal black holes—fears that we can't do or shouldn't try something—also affect everything in our lives. These fears disrupt and constrict our beliefs, our ideas, and our actions. No one is ever free of fear, but as you recognize your fears and your self-imposed limitations, you can learn to control them and overcome most of them.

"Do the best you can. If you fall on your face—*c'est la vie!* Don't be afraid to fail. We all do. When you do fail, do it reaching out, trying. If you never fail, you're not setting high enough standards. Remember . . . you can't learn anything from experiences you're not having."

The big message here is: Get out there and try. Go forth and, well, kick some butt. Get your money's worth. You can attend college—you can just show up—or you can DO college. It would be a shame to look back one day and think, "Gee, I just skimmed the surface." Wouldn't it be nicer to say, "*Carpe diem*? Yeah, I did that. I seized the day."

"Don't be afraid to fail. We all do. When you do fail, do it reaching out, trying. If you never fail, you're not setting high enough standards."

BEWARE OF NOSTALGIA ATTACKS.

Many freshmen have sudden and fierce longing to turn back the clock. Believe us, we know how you feel, but this is an impossible dream. It can't be done. Accept where you are now and move on from there.

Some of the most pathetic people on any campus are those college freshmen whose thoughts, wishes, and (endless) conversations are all focused on how great high school was. Those big moments of glory (both of them—just kidding, there were three), when they just ruled the place.

You may already have met someone who fits this description. Don't you just want to tell him or her to get over it? Sure you do. And that's probably similar to what your new friends may secretly be wishing to tell you.

The big message here is:

Get out there and try. Go

forth and kick some butt.

HOMESICKNESS HAPPENS

This is not to say that your freshman year will be one easy, fun-filled, and personally enriching ride. It probably won't be, because few things are and because freshman year is difficult for almost everybody. Everybody runs into some trouble. Sadly, some freshmen don't make it; they fall through the cracks; they crash and burn. At some colleges, the dropout rate for freshmen is 25 percent or higher.

(This doesn't mean that all of these students are out of college forever. Some enroll in other schools rather quickly—a college nearer home, maybe, or a junior college instead of an overwhelming university—others may do something else for months or even years before trying college again.)

While we're on the subject: If what you're experiencing is going beyond the usual "I miss my home and friends and family" and is leaning more toward "I hate this place, I've made a huge mistake, I wish I'd never come here" (or worse, "I wish I'd gotten into one of my first three choices instead of winding up here at this crummy place"), don't despair. This situation won't last forever; it can't.

One of several things will happen. It might be that you'll settle in, make some friends, enjoy your classes and professors, and actually learn to like the place, if not love it. You may even think back fondly on your freshman year one day. Or maybe a snapshot of the future will pop into your head, and it's a picture of you in a sweatshirt with some other school's name on it. Maybe a transfer to another school is your destiny.

The point here is that if you're not going to your dream school, several options are open to you:

1. **You can stay where you are and sulk.** It's certainly been done; thinking about what might have been is a time-honored tradition. (It's also a huge waste of time, but that's up to you.)
2. **You can make the best out of your situation.** We hate to admit it, but that self-righteous gym teacher with the big gut who always made you gag by saying, "You'll get out of this what you put into it" was right. It's trite, but it's true.
3. **You can do well during your first year or two here and then transfer someplace else.** This also has been done, often with great success.

Ever hear of the expression "Fish, or cut bait?" It means "stop being miserable and take action." Figure out what you need to make you happy and go after it.

If, however, you're feeling unusually depressed and just can't "snap out of it" after a week or two (see Chapter Twelve for some symptoms of depression), talk to somebody about it—a counselor, your RA, a professor, or the student health service. There is help available; all you have to do is ask for it.

Now, back to homesickness. If you're living away from home for the first time in your life and if your home situation is any good at all, it would be unusual—in fact, it would be downright strange and insulting to your family—if you didn't feel minor or even major homesickness. This is natural. Don't worry about it. You are not an oddball. Be glad you come from a home that's good enough to miss. Know that, like most things, this will get better over time as you adjust to your new surroundings.

How long your homesickness and/or nostalgia lasts depends on you and how determined you are to plunge into your new life at college. One good way to do this—to put down new roots and make new memories—is to pretend that you're going to be on campus for the rest of your life. Forget that you'll be leaving college in a few years. For now, this *is* your home. So learn about it. Adopt the campus and community as your own. You've made the physical move to college, now make the intellectual and emotional move as well.

This doesn't mean you won't miss your old friends or that you should cut them out of your life. *Au contraire!* From now on, some of the best times you'll ever have will be on visits home, when you see your friends again, catch up with them, and talk for hours about the new lives you're beginning to make for yourselves. Your friends are growing and changing, too—you hope!—and it will be fascinating for you to watch and see how they turn out.

But in the meantime, you've got your own new world to adjust to. Don't let it pass you by!

PARENTS' WEEKEND

Most schools have them. But if yours doesn't, make your own. Invite your parents for the weekend. They may not be able to come, but you'll win big points—think how pleased they'll be that you asked them.

What if they do come? Again, show some common courtesy. This isn't the Queen Elizabeth II, and you're no cruise director, but it would be pretty rude of you if they just sat around in their hotel room waiting for you to find time in your busy schedule to see them. (They'll be wondering, among other things, why you bothered to invite them, and why they bothered to come. They may also speculate, again, whether you were switched at birth with some sweet kid who would have appreciated them!) So, show them a good time. And be proud to introduce them to your friends.

There's nothing more stupid-looking than some teenager cringing in mortal embarrassment at being seen with his parents and mumbling mortified introductions to his new friends. What, they don't have parents? Their parents are movie stars? Grow up.

DEALING WITH YOUR PARENTS

The most important point to stress here is to maintain contact. As Nike says: "Just do it." You need to keep in touch with your parents while you're away, for many reasons.

One is a matter of common courtesy. It would be pretty rude to just show up for Thanksgiving after two months of not talking to each other and expect everything to be normal.

If you keep them roughly up to date on what's going on in your life—filter the news if you feel the need, but at least give them the headlines—they can still be there for you, even from far away. One basic example: It's exam time. If your parents know you're worried about a particular test, they may give you a much-needed boost by calling to wish you luck.

Another example. Galen, a freshman at Southern Methodist University in Dallas, Texas, caught a cold in November. She told her roommate she was fine, and her roommate, a very busy person, accepted her answer at face value. Galen said the same thing later that day in a telephone call to her mother. Her mom, however, who knows Galen much better than her roommate, called back the next day to make sure, and the day after that. She heard her daughter sound increasingly worse and nagged her to go see a doctor (she even called a family physician in Dallas—the friend of a friend—and made an appointment). Guess what? It turned out that Galen had strep throat, a condition that can lead to some nasty complications if left untreated.

Even though you're far away, you still can be there for your family. Matthew, a freshman at Western Kentucky University in Bowling Green, happened to mention to his younger brother, Morgan, that he would be taking a long weekend, fishing and camping with some friends at Cumberland State Park from a Thursday night to a Monday. That Friday, his grandfather died of a sudden stroke. His parents called his dorm room repeatedly and got no answer. They checked with the RA, who didn't know where Matt had gone. Then Morgan came home. Within 5 minutes, he had gotten in touch with officials at the park; 10 minutes later, a kindly park ranger knocked on the door of Matt's cabin and told him the news. A few hours later, Matt was home, where he needed to be.

Get the point? They need you, you need them. This doesn't mean you should write twice-weekly letters detailing all that you do or check in each night before bedtime. Your parents probably know you're busy. They know that it's hard for you to find the time to cover all your news in one letter or phone call when you have a major paper due Friday, a psych exam tomorrow, an oral report in English due Monday, and (very important) a date Saturday night.

Relax. You don't have to keep them up to date with everything. The funny thing is, most parents are notoriously easy to please, as long as they hear something from you regularly—preferably that you haven't joined a cult or been kidnapped by aliens, that you're in reasonably good health, and that you're thinking of them.

Send a postcard or a cute greeting card. Tell them you're fine in 25 words or less. Or write a note to yourself to call them, and do it. You won't believe how happy you can make someone. (One guy we know, who wanted to be cool and didn't want his roommates to kid him about calling his parents regularly, simply wrote "E.T." on his calendar once a week—for "Phone home.")

Or communicate with your folks and friends using e-mail. As a student, you should have access to the Internet; if your parents have a home computer, they can subscribe to America Online or a similar service as well. You can send messages to them, and they can send messages to you. (One advantage to this is that, if it's 3 in the morning and you feel the sudden urge to communicate, you can. You probably won't get an immediate answer, but at least you've sent a message to them.)

Be prepared to listen to their advice. Hear what they have to say, but don't feel that your private territory or new way of life is being invaded. Realize that a natural, if somewhat painful, development is bound to happen here—a weaning process, in which you want to be with your parents yet want to be independent of them at the same time. Try to sift through your feelings. For example, your frustration and uncertainty at seeing them may be compounded by guilt, especially if your parents are making great personal sacrifices to help pay for your college expenses.

And finally, try for some perspective. Realize that the first few weeks of college are usually the most

Keep your parents roughly up to date on what's going on in your life. Filter the news, if you feel the need, but at least give them the headlines.

Let's face it: That Diet Coke you ordered with the Meat-Lovers Pizza Special isn't going to "cancel out" the fat you're putting in your body. And your new diet isn't going to do great things for your skin, either—they don't call it "pizza face" for nothing!

dramatic for many freshmen. Your ideas, your emotions, your entire personality could swing pretty far in new directions. But don't tell your parents on their first visit that you have decided to change your religion or join Richard Gere in the fight to restore the Dalai Lama or adopt a revolutionary new lifestyle because of something your professor said in Philosophy 101. There's plenty of time for that. Besides, you may change your mind.

FIGHTING THE "FRESHMAN 10"

The Freshman 10 (or 15 or 20), or the Freshman Lard, is an unfortunate phenomenon that strikes many freshmen, male and female. What does it mean to you? For starters, it means your pants don't look that great anymore when you put them on. The zipper is feeling the strain, and if that waistband button pops off, some unlucky person in the line of fire could lose an eye.

We're talking hefty weight gain here, and it's a pretty common thing. The Freshman 10 (for the extra 10 pounds or so of fat accumulating on your hips, thighs, and midsection) happens when people who have been used to fairly sensible, balanced diets are left to their own dietary devices—late-night pizza, fries with every meal, ice cream sandwiches from the machine downstairs, and chips, chips, chips. (Or, we regret to say, beer, beer, beer.)

Let's face it: That Diet Coke you ordered with the Meat-Lovers Pizza Special from the place that delivers until 2 a.m. isn't going to "cancel out" the fat you're putting in your body. (On a related dermatological note, your new diet isn't going to do great things for your skin, either—they don't call it "pizza face" for nothing!) When your mom told you to eat vegetables, she probably didn't mean the "Awesome Blossom" of onion rings from Chili's or the fried zucchini and mushroom appetizers they have at T.G.I. Friday's. Fried mozzarella sticks are not the best way for you to meet your daily calcium requirement.

Yes, temptation is everywhere—even in the school cafeteria, with its "burrito night" fiestas and "make your own burger" bar. But you've got more willpower than you think.

Just use a little common sense. If you're buying food in a grocery store, for example, take about 10 seconds extra to check out the labels. Most packaged foods are now required by law to list such things as the fat content. You can do a lot just by consistently selecting low-fat—or, better yet, no-fat—products. You can get fat-free mayonnaise, cookies, salad dressing, tortilla chips and cheese. And it actually does taste good! Note: Beware of words like "Light" or "Lite." The phrase "light yogurt," for example, may just mean it's made with Nutrasweet instead of sugar—so, even though it has fewer calories, it may be just as high in fat as regular yogurt. *And fat is your biggest enemy, not sugar.*

You don't have to eat only lettuce and rice cakes to stay trim. Here are a few tips from students who have fought the "battle of the bulge" and won:

- **Don't reward yourself with junk food.** You've studied 4 solid hours for your economics test. It's nearly midnight, and somebody's sending out for pizza. "You've worked so hard," says your well-meaning roommate—who has the metabolism of a racehorse and couldn't gain weight if he mainlined Crisco. "You deserve some nourishment." That may be true. But what does pizza have to do with your economics effort? If you must order something, go light—get a grilled chicken sandwich or a Greek salad. Listen to the bathroom scales—they're screaming, "No! No! Get off me, Tubby!"

  Think of the already-snug dress pants you bought just two months ago. Envision your rear end, stretching those poor pants to the breaking point. Be strong—do it for the pants.

- **Stock your own snacks.** If you can, rent a small refrigerator; if you can't afford it, stockpile some snacks that don't have to be kept cold: little containers of low-calorie pudding or applesauce, low-fat granola bars or pretzels (most of which have no cholesterol), or boxes of fruit juice. Get a hot pot and fix yourself some soup or ramen.

  True, these things aren't as exciting as the burger, fries, and milkshake you had in mind. But you're hungry, and the main goal is to fill up your stomach, correct? These snacks are here right now, in your room, already paid for—no 30-minute wait to sit through and no tip to figure out.

When your mom told you to eat vegetables, she probably didn't mean the "Awesome Blossom" of onion rings from Chili's.

- **Check out the whole menu.** In the breakfast line, instead of reaching automatically for that custard-filled doughnut or the cheese Danish that has your name on it, see what else is out there. Look—over in the healthy lane—there's grapefruit and a hard-boiled egg! There's toast (and there's no fat in the fruit jelly, jam, or preserves that you can spread on it). There's whole-grain cereal (fiber is always nice), and with skim milk makes a low-fat meal. At lunch and dinner, check out the salad and fruit plates. If you have a choice, pick the entrees with pasta or rice.

- **Don't try to starve yourself.** For one thing, it's stupid. For another, it's not a great way to lose weight—your metabolism drops with your food intake. In other words, if you don't eat breakfast and lunch, your body shuts down and says, "Okay, we must be hibernating; we'll wait it out." Then, if you pig out for dinner, thinking you've earned it, you'll still probably gain weight.

- **Get some exercise.** Even if it's just taking the stairs instead of the elevator or jogging up and down the halls of your dorm (or around your room) for 20 minutes a night. Every little bit helps.

- **Drink a lot of water.** You're supposed to drink eight glasses a day. We don't know anyone who actually does, but we do know that water is good for the body and great for the skin, and it works wonders on the appetite—you don't get nearly so hungry if you're already sloshing around full of water.

- **Find a food buddy.** It's easier to go through anything if you know you're not alone. Seek out friends who are also trying to eat healthy. Mutual support and reinforcement can make a big difference.

- **Think of Christmas vacation.** Imagine how nice it'll be to go home and hear your old friends say, "Wow, you look great! *I* need to lose some weight!"

- **Think of Spring Break.** When she got back to school from Christmas break, Pam, a University of Kentucky student, nailed a tiny, lime-green bikini to the wall over her bed. She looked at it last thing at night and the first thing in the morning. Fitting into it became her goal. She lost 11 pounds

just by cutting out a lot of fat in her diet, eating
sensibly, and exercising a little (jogging a mile
three times a week). She looked great, dropped
from a size 12 to a size 10, and fit into that bikini
by March.

HITTING THE BOOKS

Let's see: We've covered doing laundry, making friends, getting along with your roommate, decorating your room. That should about do it—oh yeah, we forgot academics. There is still that little matter of higher education.

Here's an interesting point to ponder: The academic adjustment may be the easiest part of your freshman year. Let's face it, you already know how to be a student; you've been doing it for the last 12 years. College classes, despite new teachers to figure out and subject matter to cover, aren't that much different from what you've gotten used to in high school. The basics—showing up, absorbing material and spewing it back out, with your own spin on it, in tests and papers—are pretty much the same.

The intensity may be a little different, though, and this can take some getting used to. For example, in some classes (particularly huge ones held in amphitheaters and taught by professors with inadequate microphones, where you may be just a name in the grade book—not even a face in the crowd—to the professor) you may have just two shots at your grade, a midterm and a final exam, which can mean there's more pressure on each test. *(Note: If the professor doesn't know you from Adam or Eve at the beginning of class, be sure that this isn't the case at the end. Make an appointment and introduce yourself.)*

Or, there may be more emphasis on class participation—times when the spotlight's on you, and you're expected to perform.

Lawanda, who went to a large high school in Pittsburgh, Pennsylvania, found herself in a small honors class at Ohio State University with a professor who based the final grade on three factors—students' performance on tests and papers and class participation. This meant two things: (1) Lawanda needed to show up for every class, and (2) she needed to do her homework. Lawanda, who had been used to being swallowed up in large classes at her high school (there were 620 students in her graduating class alone), found herself a very visible member of a roundtable discussion group of 19 students.

Not preparing for class was a gamble; Lawanda wasn't very good at faking knowledge she didn't have, and the punishment for sitting there in safe, silent anonymity was that she couldn't rack up any participation points.

"At first, I did sit there, not saying much," she says. "But then I noticed that the people who tended to do most of the talking weren't any smarter than I was; in fact, I thought some of their points were dumb. That gave me the confidence to start speaking up." In the end, Lawanda's class points turned out to be the deciding factor that pushed her borderline B grade up to an A.

CHOOSING CLASSES: SOME FACTORS TO CONSIDER

At some schools, the course catalog looks like a phone book. You may be thinking "information overload!" as your eyes glaze over and you begin to feel a little panicky.

If the sheer volume of possibilities is more than you can handle all at once, shut the catalog. Sit down somewhere and think about a few key things, including the following:

- **The basic, common denominator list of courses that you must complete to graduate.** Even if you don't know what your major is going to be, there are some classes that nearly everybody ends up taking. You'll have to take them sometime, so you might as well get started. Our advice is to get them out of the way ASAP, so you can take fun stuff your senior year—or courses that enhance your major or your employment potential.
- **Your major. What's it going to be?** Do you have any clues yet? This is a very big decision, and you don't have to figure it out today, this semester, or even this year. But start thinking about it.
- **In this quest for a major, the course catalog is your friend.** You may decide to look for classes that are prerequisites for important courses you'll want to take later. (A prerequisite means that you must have completed a certain class, such as Economics 100, before you can move ahead to

DO YOURSELF A FAVOR: REGISTER EARLY IF YOU CAN

Some colleges process requests by students with the most credits (i.e., seniors) first, but others do it on a first-come, first-served basis. If this is the case, know that if you snooze, you lose.

Hustle in for your advising appointment as soon as possible—the quicker your schedule is approved, the sooner you'll be able to nail down your place in your top choice of classes.

related classes—Economics 200 and beyond. Call it reaching point A before you can get past point B.)

- **Particularly good classes to take.** Every school has them—professors whose courses are Standing Room Only. Classes you'll look back on as thought-provoking high points of your academic life. Get the scoop from upperclass students.
- **Particularly bad classes to avoid like the plague.** Now's as good a time as any to find out which professors are dynamic lecturers, which are drones, and which are psychos.

  Jed, a University of Kentucky student and a "definitely nonscientific" guy, decided to get his much-dreaded biology requirement out of the way his freshman year—much like a patient in a doctor's office who shuts his eyes and holds his breath until the shot's over. He picked an easy-sounding course from the catalog, "Biology for Nonmajors."

  What a surprise he had in store for him! "First of all, it was a Tuesday–Thursday class that met at night, 7:00–8:30, and I could tell right away that it was going to be a struggle just to stay alert. Then this professor came in, and he had a real attitude. He said, 'I don't know why biology for nonmajors should be any different from biology for majors.' The next thing I knew, we were looking at slides of tertiary-level DNA, whatever that is! I freaked." The next day, he dropped the class like a hot potato. (He later found one much more to his liking, called "Human Ecology.")

- **Classes that will expand your mental horizons.** Live it up. Again, get to know the course catalog. Pore over it; read about everything that intrigues you even a little. Look for courses in subjects you never studied in high school. For example, here's your chance to learn something about art and architecture, even if you can't foresee any use for this knowledge in later life. Learn to play a musical instrument or ride a horse, just because you've always wanted to.

What's the point of learning things you can't use to make money or further your career? A lot of goal-oriented, job-focused people want to know the answer to this question.

Let's answer it by looking at an imaginary student, Joe Tunnelvision. He wants to be a doctor; naturally, he wants to get into a good medical school, and he's well on his way. In high school, every elective course he took was in science—he even made up his own independent-study anatomy class after he had exhausted the school's scientific course repertoire.

Now, as a freshman and a molecular biology major, he doesn't want to "waste his time" on anything that won't help him reach his goal. Therefore, he has no time for art, music, languages, or literature beyond the minimal requirements. (Joe, a cynic, only signed up for intramural soccer because he knows he's supposed to appear "well rounded" when he applies to medical schools. He also did some volunteer work for the same reason—to carve another notch on the old resume. Joe's too narrowly focused to comprehend the greater benefits of those extracurricular activities. Which is his loss.)

Joe can't see four years down the road, but we can. He gets accepted at medical school, all right, but not by one of his top three choices. Johns Hopkins, Harvard, and Stanford all turn him down, and Joe can't figure out why. It turns out that it's because of his big void in the humanities. His academic career was so heavily tilted toward science that medical school admissions officers felt he didn't have enough depth—compassion, a sense of humor, and a breadth of understanding—to become a great doctor. (For more on real-life Joes, and on what medical schools really want, see "Making Plans for the Long Haul," Chapter 13.)

There probably won't be a formal professor information service such as the one at the University of South Carolina at your school, but you can bet that there's plenty of helpful word-of-mouth information floating around out there—all you have to do is find it by asking around. If the professor in question teaches English, for example, find an English major. If this person can't give you a first-hand evaluation of the teacher, maybe he or she can at least direct you to other English majors who can.

A word of warning: Take everything you hear with a grain of salt. Are you talking to an airhead who resents having to crack a book? Or some angry person who didn't get the grade he thought he deserved and

Joe, a molecular biology major, doesn't want to "waste his time" on anything that won't help him reach his goal—medical school.

You may not be able to register at your school until you can prove that you've been immunized against certain diseases such as the measles. (Or, until you prove that you've actually had the diseases and thus acquired what's called "clinical immunity").

Many schools require "immunization clearance" for rubeola (red measles) and rubella (German measles). Because more physicians are recommending that students get immunized against hepatitis B, this may be added to the immunization list soon.

therefore has an ax to grind? If so, you may not be getting the most objective picture of the professor or the course.

It's true, forewarned is forearmed. You may, however, decide not to take somebody else's word for it. Maybe, you'll want to enroll in the course despite what someone says because it sounds interesting. To which we say: Go for it!

Don't be afraid of hard work or hard classes. If you're looking to coast through school, you're going to miss out on some demanding but very rewarding course experiences.

YOUR FACULTY ADVISER

You will be assigned to a faculty adviser whose job is to help you decide which courses to take and to help plan your overall program.

The faculty adviser, however, is just an adviser, not someone who dictates your class schedule to you, which is good in that the actual selection of courses is up to you alone. But it's bad in that, if anything goes wrong—for example, it's the last semester of your senior year, and you realize you've missed one of your college requirements—guess whose fault it is?

Even though your adviser's signature may appear on all your schedule cards, it's up to you to make sure you dot all the i's and cross all the t's.

For example, say your college has a rule that all students must complete four courses in a foreign language. Each semester, for seemingly legitimate reasons, you put off taking a language class. Then, in the final weeks of your senior year, a records clerk discovers that you haven't completed the foreign language requirement. Therefore, you can't graduate.

You scream in protest (sounding, in truth, a little whiny and defensive, but the feeling is genuine): "But my faculty adviser never made me take a foreign language!" You picture yourself working up the courage to make that awful call to your parents and grandparents, who have already paid for plane tickets to come to Los Angeles all the way from Seattle, to tell them you won't be graduating this spring after all because you have messed up in a big way.

Your objections are overruled. ("If we made an exception for you, we'd have to make one for everybody else." "I won't tell anybody—honest!" "Sorry, dear. You're hosed.") No degree.

So, with this horror story in mind, look out for yourself. Make sure you read carefully, and understand fully, the requirements as spelled out in the catalog. Be sure you know how your particular major program defines credit hours and know every little hurdle you need to jump through to get your degree.

(As one of us found out in the last week of her senior year, these hurdles may be so petty as to include paying an overdue book fee of 35 cents at the university library. At some schools, you can't graduate with any outstanding fees or parking tickets.)

What you can expect from your faculty adviser. At a minimum, you should be able to count on your adviser to provide accurate, up-to-date information about college regulations and to explain various alternatives in course selection. Your faculty adviser should also be able to grasp, and spell out for you, the possible consequences of your decisions.

You should be able to count on your adviser to provide accurate, up-to-date information about college regulations and to explain various alternatives in course selection.

But most faculty advisers do more than this. Most of them take a personal interest in your career and try to help you meet your educational goals, and they monitor your progress from one term to the next. The better advisers go beyond the basic call of duty and work to get you any other help you may need along the way—with prompt referrals to the counseling center, placement office, a learning skills lab, or tutors. Your faculty adviser can write recommendations for you when you're applying for a job or a place in a graduate or professional school. And sometimes, if you're lucky, your faculty adviser can become a mentor and friend as well.

If you don't get along. If you're not lucky enough to have a helpful adviser or if you don't like your faculty adviser—or worse, don't trust the advice you're getting—what can you do? Well, you're probably not stuck with him or her, and you probably won't be the first student at your university ever to have a problem with an adviser. Let's face it, some faculty advisers are not as well-informed on course changes, new requirements, and alternative courses as they could be.

So, for whatever reason, if you don't feel comfortable with your adviser, you can request and usually get another one. We say "usually" because you never know, there could be politics involved here. It may be, for example, that the department chair or associate dean or whoever's in charge of assigning advisers wants to divide the load evenly among the faculty and may not want to do any shifting around. But hey, is that your problem? No. If your request for a change of adviser does get turned down, and you feel strongly about it, take your case directly to the dean of the college.

But we're dealing with a worst-case scenario. Faculty advising is designed to take place in a friendly and helpful atmosphere, and for the most part, it does.

REGISTRATION: ORGANIZED CHAOS

Using your Touch-Tone phone: To add a course, press one; to audit a course, press two; to drop a course, press three. . . .

Picture the opening credits to the old TV show "Rawhide" and Frankie Laine singing the classic theme song: "Rollin' rollin' rollin'. Movin' movin' movin'. Keep them dogies movin', Rawhide. Don't try to understand 'em, just rope and tie and brand 'em. . . ."

There are a lot of similarities between a cattle roundup and the way colleges have traditionally handled registration. Which is organized chaos: Somebody's cracking a (metaphorical, we hope!) whip, and if it's hot and you're in the un-air-conditioned gym, it probably doesn't smell too good, either.

The good news is that an increasing number of schools are cutting the confusion by letting students sign up for classes using Touch-Tone telephones. At the University of South Carolina, for instance, students use a sophisticated system called TIPS (Telephone Information Processing System). By using any Touch-Tone phone (and, for early registration, by calling at a designated appointment time), students can register, change their schedule, check their fees, apply financial aid to their bill, and even pay their fees with a Visa or MasterCard.

To make it easier, students are asked to fill out a registration worksheet and to have their Social Security and four-digit student personal identification numbers handy. (It goes like this: To add a course, press one; to audit a course, press two; to drop a course, press three. . . .)

At other campuses, even though registration may still take place in the student union ballroom or the gym, computers speed up the process dramatically, telling you how many openings remain in a class and processing your choices quickly and efficiently.

At smaller colleges, registration may still be done the old-fashioned way: In some large, crowded area such as the gym, each academic department (chemistry, engineering, English) has its own clearly identified table. You wait in line, then, when you get up to the table, the nice department clerk checks to see whether the class you want has any vacancies.

If you are able to enroll in the class, the clerk adds your name to the roster and initials your packet. But if the class is closed, guess what? You get to pick another one, while everyone in line behind you sighs impatiently and makes you anxious. (The process gets to be even more fun if the alternative course conflicts with another class you want to take, and you have to juggle your schedule to make everything fit.)

Have a "Plan B" in mind. However your school handles it, the basic business of registration is simple: Each semester or each quarter, thousands of students try to fit themselves into hundreds of courses. The specifics differ from school to school, but the bottom line for both sides—students and administrators—is that it can turn into a nightmare if you can't get into the right classes at the right times. To come through registration with the schedule you originally intended, you will probably need some careful planning, a sense of humor, and some luck.

Because it's a good bet that at least one of your choices will be filled already, do yourself a favor—have a "Plan B" in mind as a backup, just in case, before you begin.

(Note: If you're shut out of a class you really want to take, don't give up right away. Many schools have waiting lists for courses with limited enrollment. In some cases, you can get into a course by taking your case directly to the professor. Go to the first few class meetings and tell the professor you really want to take the course if space opens up. Even if space doesn't open up, the professor may be impressed by your motivation, and you may get a spot in the class anyway.)

The wonder is that registration works at all. But somehow, every semester, it does—students get placed into courses. The only real catch, again, is that course you get may not be your first pick.

Students are asked to fill out a registration worksheet and to have their Social Security and four-digit student personal identification numbers handy.

*The wonder is that regis-
tration works at all. But
somehow, every semester,
it does. The only real
catch is that course you
get may not be your first
pick.*

At many schools, registration officially begins with some sort of advising session, where you'll get a briefing on college requirements (which may sound eerily like a vacant-eyed stewardess you once saw explaining in a monotone how the underseat flotation device works) and some help in planning your course schedule. Unless it was mailed to you already, now is probably when you'll get a copy of the schedule of courses. (Unlike the course catalog, which describes every single course taught at the university—including some courses not offered every semester—the course schedule is more specific, with the days and times that classes are offered.)

Some official, such as your faculty adviser, will probably check over your proposed schedule (to make sure that you, in a daze, didn't do something moronic like sign up for two Monday-Wednesday-Friday classes at 11 a.m.), and then sign it.

Depending on your university, registration may also be the time when you pay your tuition, lab fees, and any other charges they can stick you for, so you might have to visit the cashier's office and pay up. Your financial aid check, if you have one coming, may also be collected at this time. Also, now is probably when you'll pose for your student ID photo and fill out additional forms for things such as the student directory.

DAY ONE

*Be resourceful when you
register. Have "Plan B"
courses ready, just in case
your first choices are
closed.*

Some professors give very general first-day lectures; others get right down to business, referring often to the textbook.

What to take. A notebook—either a big one with dividers, or several small notebooks, one for each class—and a couple of pencils or pens. (To be safe, stick the course textbook in a book bag and have it in case you need it.)

What to expect. Many professors don't explain things very well. We hate to say it, but it's true. Most have a lot of training in a particular subject area, such as the Civil War, galactic astronomy, or the prefrontal cortex of the brain, but very little training (if any) in the techniques of teaching. In other words, their heads may be full of useful information, but they may not know how to get this knowledge out and into your head. You may find that your high school teachers were much more organized and better skilled than your college professors in the plain old nuts and bolts of teaching.

What does this mean for you? It means that again, as in so many things, you need to take an active role in your courses right from the start. Be your own advocate. Nobody's going to spoonfeed you.

Note: This sink-or-swim attitude may be kind of a shock to students who come from school systems with a strong focus on self-esteem in addition to academic material. In college, whether or not you feel good about yourself probably isn't going to matter that much to your professor; it also won't have any effect on your grade. Most college professors see their students as adults who are there because they want to learn; to them, that's serious business.

On the first day of class, your professor will probably discuss the outline for the course. This introduction may cover everything you need to know. But if not, don't be afraid to ask the questions that will take care of loose ends. (If you're a little shy and don't want to ask in front of the whole class, try to snag the professor afterward or during office hours.)

Things you need to know as soon as possible

If a course is grossly different from your expectations, here are some things you'll need to know so that you can drop it without penalty (and sign up for another course) during the late registration period:

- **Costs.** Some subjects are expensive. You may have to buy a dozen or more paperbacks for a literature class or shell out hefty lab fees in some science courses. An introductory course in photography might mean an extra $350 in camera rental, darkroom fees, chemicals, film, and paper—which, if you're not expecting it, might cause a budgetary meltdown. Find out just what the additional costs will be. You may want to reschedule an expensive class for another semester, when your budget is in better shape.
- **Objectives.** What are the professor's goals for this course? What approach will be followed? Maybe your Spanish course is going to deal mostly with literature. Which is a surprise, since you signed

CLASS ATTENDANCE POLICIES

From your school's point of view, the simple fact that you paid your tuition doesn't mean you get to operate entirely on your own terms as a student. The institution has certain rules, which you agreed to, directly or indirectly, when you enrolled. A big one is that the professor is in charge of his or her class.

Therefore, as long as the professor behaves reasonably—and having an attendance policy is certainly not unreasonable—he or she can enforce a policy that says you must attend class or have your grade affected accordingly.

Obviously, attendance policies vary; to a large extent, they depend on the size of the class. In a huge lecture course, your professor will have a ton of material that needs to be covered during each session and probably won't spend precious minutes checking the roll.

In smaller classes—particularly those small discussion groups—a high premium is placed on student participation, and you'll probably be expected to carry your share of the discussion. (So will your fellow students; if you're absent, their chances of being called on are increased!)

Even though many professors are fairly relaxed about attendance—and most can even understand and excuse the occasional absence—some professors still impose harsh attendance policies.

And they're confident of the full backing of their deans and presidents if those attendance policies are challenged.

An example: One day Taylor, a senior at Tulane University, went up to her rather stuffy English professor a few minutes before her three o'clock class met. "I have to leave 15 minutes early," she explained politely, "I have a dentist appointment." (Actually, she had a job interview, but she didn't think that would go over too well.)

"This is an appointment, too," her professor said icily. "Not excused."

And Taylor just sat there, steaming, mad at the teacher and mad at herself for not having the courage to get up and leave. She was five minutes late for the interview. (She didn't get the job, either!)

up to learn conversational skills. Now's the time to find out, so you can switch to the class you thought you were getting.

- **Grading.** This is something you'll need to know early, so you can plan your study strategy accordingly. How will your progress be evaluated? How many exams will there be? Will the final exam be comprehensive—that is, will it cover the entire course content or just the material presented since the last test? How much weight will be attached to the final exam? What kinds of tests will there be: essay, true or false, multiple choice? Does the professor use a strict grading scale (93 to 100 is an A, for example), or will the grades be "curved"?

- **Outside work.** How many assignments, such as papers, book reviews, and case studies, will you be given? How much time are these things likely to require—are they one-page or twelve-page papers? How much of your grade depends on your performance in these outside assignments? Again, it's good to know this as soon as possible—so, for example, you don't blow off your only paper, wrongly thinking that it's one of many and therefore doesn't count for much of your grade.

- **Attendance.** Again, good to know from Day One. Many professors ignore classroom attendance, but some professors monitor it carefully and may reduce your grade for excessive absences (find out what "excessive" means—it might mean missing two classes!). There's usually not a general, campuswide rule on attendance, so you'll need to know each professor's policy.

Some profs like to give surprise "pop" quizzes, and students who are absent get a big doughnut in the grade book for that day. Be realistic enough to know that you're probably going to miss a class from time to time (sometimes just so you can prepare for some other class!). Make sure you know (1) whether those absences are going to hurt you, and if so, how much; and (2) if make-up quizzes are possible.

Office hours

When will the professor be available in his or her campus study? Professors are not always conveniently available when you need them; they may be holed up in the library doing research, home grading papers, or actually out having a life. If your professor doesn't tell you office hours on the first day, find out.

Remember, you're the consumer here, and you have every right to know what you're getting yourself into when you sign up for a class. Don't be bashful about asking questions. As one professor at the University of Missouri confides, "I usually have a little trouble getting back in the teaching groove the first day." Translation: Your professor may still be in the "hammock mode," so if some important point doesn't get explained to the class, it may be because your professor simply spaced out and forgot to tell you.

If you miss a class

It is going to happen. Unless you're unlucky enough to be absent on the one day your professor decides to give a "pop" quiz, you'll probably get away with it. Almost every university has some sort of attendance policy, written in lofty, generally unenforceable language, that says something like "Students are expected to be present throughout each term at all meetings of courses for which they are registered."

Right. But at most schools, each professor sets his or her own ground rules for attendance. Some professors check the roll without fail, every class. Most don't. This means, basically, that if you want to sleep through your 8 a.m. English class or catch a matinee during your biology lab, you can. Nobody's going to call your parents; in fact, if the class is fairly big, your professor may not even notice that you're not there.

The decision to go to class, like the decision to skip class, is yours. There are lots of good reasons to skip class: Tickets to a major-league baseball game. A gorgeous fall day and a picnic hamper. The long-awaited reunion of your favorite soap opera stars.

Why shouldn't you skip class? The main reason is that you may miss out on something important, and this could hurt you later. Terrence, a Washington State student, blew his A in American History because he failed one exam—he bombed it, in fact; got a 58. "Six of the questions came from the two lectures I missed all semester." Terrence thought he was covered because he borrowed two friends' notes. One guy, unfortunately, had such bad handwriting that "I didn't get much out of

IF YOU'RE RUNNING LATE FOR CLASS, GO ANYWAY

Tiptoe in. Yeah, you may be embarrassed by the slight interruption you cause, especially if the professor, a cantankerous geezer who thinks he's hilarious, stops his lecture so everyone can watch you get settled, waits for you to pick up the pencil you dropped in your haste, and then inquires, "Enjoyed your breakfast this morning, did you?" This is a small price to pay for catching at least a portion of what could be an important class. You may not get all the material that has been covered that day, but at a minimum, you'll pick up the emphasis, which is always useful to know when you're trying to study for the next exam.

If you're frequently late, you're probably going to tick off the professor; you probably won't win too many points with your classmates, either. Consistent lateness is rude. If, however, you actually have a good excuse—if it's a ten o'clock class and your nine o'clock class meets at the other end of campus and the teacher in that one, an old windbag, always tends to run overtime—then show some common courtesy. Tell your ten o'clock professor what's happening, so she doesn't get the idea that you can't be bothered to show up on time.

his notes, but I thought the other one had done an adequate job. I really studied those notes, too."

Another reason, particularly for smaller discussion classes, is that if you make a habit of not being present, you can't pull your weight. Even if your professor doesn't check the roll religiously, it's pretty clear who's coming regularly and who's not. And directly or indirectly, in these smaller classes, your attendance record is inevitably going to be reflected in the grade you get for the course.

If you are absent, make an effort to find out what you missed. Find out from somebody reliable in the class—preferably, remembering Terrence's story, someone who not only takes good notes but has decent penmanship. *Tip: Make a point early in the semester of getting the names and phone numbers of a couple of reliable-looking classmates who would let you borrow their notes in case you're absent. And be willing to return the favor for them someday.*

It's probably not the coolest move to ask the professor what you missed. From the prof's point of view, it's a waste of time to conduct one class for you and another for everybody else. (And don't be like one student we know, who won big points with his professor by calling him at home and saying, "Sorry I wasn't in class yesterday. Did I miss anything?" "No," the professor answered curtly, "I just did my usual B.S. and wasted everybody's time.")

The decision to go to class, like the decision to skip class, is yours.

But, if you miss several classes—if you had the flu, for instance—do talk to your prof. Don't just gamble that the professor didn't notice; make a point of saying *something*. It's not only common courtesy, it's good public relations on your part. In return, the professor might just volunteer a bit of useful information for you, like "We hit chapter three pretty hard on Friday. Be sure you understand those charts on page 79; you may be asked about them on the next quiz."

WHEN A CLASS IS NOT FOR YOU

There it is, that sinking feeling in the pit of your stomach. You have made an awful mistake. This class is going to be a living hell. Whatever made you sign up for it?

Are you stuck? No, not if you act fast. Trust your instincts. If you're already deeply miserable on the first day, chances are the class is not going to improve suddenly over time. (Even if it's a course you absolutely must take, maybe you'll be more prepared for it and able to handle it better—or maybe another professor will be teaching it—in a later semester.)

So GET OUT! Take advantage of the drop/add/change "window," and act now, while there's no penalty.

Your class schedule is not an ironclad contract—at least not in the beginning of the semester. You can make adjustments fairly easily during the drop/add/change period, which may last from days to a few weeks, depending on your college. That's what this grace period is for (at Yale, it's even called the "Shopping Period").

During this time, the paperwork (and hassle) involved is generally minimal. Later on, it gets more difficult to add a course; you'll need the professor's permission, which you probably can't get after a week or so of class (the professor may feel you've missed too much to catch up), plus the approval of your adviser and/or the dean. You have much more time—usually a month or so—to drop a course without being penalized for it.

At the University of South Carolina, for example, students who drop a course after the late registration period but within the first six weeks of classes get a "W," for "withdrawal," on their permanent record, but it doesn't have any effect on the grade point average. It just sits there on the transcript. After the first six weeks, South Carolina students who withdraw get something less pleasant, a "WF," for "withdrawal failing," unless they have a really good excuse that's acceptable to the professor and the dean. (At most schools, students who have to drop a course later in the semester because of a medical problem, death in the family, or other extenuating circumstance may still get a "W," with no effect on their grades.)

You've probably figured this one out already, but we'll just go ahead and say that if you just stop showing up for class but don't officially withdraw, you will almost certainly get a big fat "F" on your record.

The take-home message here: If you're having a problem that's going to result in prolonged absences from class, talk to your professor or faculty adviser. There may be a way to work it out—such as completing the course in

You have made an awful mistake. This class is going to be a living hell. Whatever made you sign up for it? Is it too late? Are you stuck?

independent study or getting a "W" instead of a "WF"—so your grades don't suffer any long-lasting effects.

A lot of students intentionally sign up for more courses than they ever intend to take—18 or 21 hours—go to the first meetings of each class, size up the profs and the requirements, drop the least appealing class or two, and trim their schedule down to a more manageable size.

Again, your professor is ethically obliged to explain at the outset how much work is expected of you, how you'll be evaluated, and so on. If what he or she is saying terrifies you (or puts you to sleep, or irritates the heck out of you, or all of the above), consider unloading that particular course and picking up another one.

Note: Before you withdraw from a class, check with your adviser to make sure this will not hurt your eligibility for financial aid (if, for example, your student loan specifies that you carry a 15-hour course load per semester).

A nice aspect of drop/add/change is that other people are doing the same thing, so maybe that class you wanted but couldn't get into now has a vacancy with your name on it.

An Incomplete

"An Incomplete is like selling your soul to the devil," states Trisha, an Emory University student. In the first semester of her freshman year, Trisha got the chicken pox, which can be much more severe in adults than in little children. "I was okay in all my classes but French literature," which required two rather lengthy papers. Trisha took an Incomplete for the course, and "it hung over my head throughout Christmas break and into the spring, until I got those stupid papers done. I wish I'd just gone ahead and done a bad job on them in the fall—at least I would have been finished!"

An Incomplete is normally granted to a student who is otherwise passing, but who, for some good reason, can't finish the work on time. Stuff happens—like Trisha, you could get sick. You could be in an auto accident or break a leg skiing and need to stay in traction for a month. There could be a family emergency.

On most campuses, to get an Incomplete, you need to show that circumstances beyond your control are preventing you from meeting your course deadlines. Your professor will determine, first, whether you can and should be awarded an Incomplete, and second, what you need to do to get the Incomplete off your transcript and receive a letter grade for the course. In any case, it's up to you to initiate the request for a grade of Incomplete.

The upside. The good thing about an Incomplete is that, in the short run, it takes some of the pressure off and lets you concentrate on getting well, or doing whatever it is you need to do so you can get on with your life. In a time of crisis, especially near the end of a semester, the Incomplete grade can be a godsend in averting what could otherwise be an academic disaster.

The downside. An Incomplete doesn't make the pressure go away; it just pushes it off to the side for a while. In other words, you can run but you can't hide. That term paper isn't going anywhere; you're still going to have to write it, and it's going to be a monkey on your back until you get it done.

Our advice: Avoid Incompletes if you can. It's far better to tough it out and finish a course—even if you don't do as well as you think you could have. Your work in the uncompleted course probably isn't going to be that much better over time—in fact, it will probably get worse as the material cools off. You probably don't need the extra burden in any semester of removing Incompletes from the semester before.

THE GPA

We've been dropping those pesky initials all over the place, so now it's about time we explained what the GPA is all about. The GPA is your grade point average. Basically, it's used to translate letter grades into numerical values, which gives you (and the university) a much more precise and uniform way of measuring your academic performance. On most campuses, grade points (some schools call them quality points) are awarded this way:

A = 4 grade points per semester hour
B = 3 grade points per semester hour
C = 2 grade points per semester hour
D = 1 grade point per semester hour
F = 0 grade points

As you probably know by now, each course is worth a specified number of college credits, called semester hours (or quarter hours if your school is on the quarter system). Your English 101 course, for example, is probably a three-hour course, which carries three

THE REPEAT OPTION

Take two! If you're bombing a course, you may opt to take it again in a later semester. Many schools offer the repeat option; some schools don't, so make sure this is a possibility for you before you try it.

Say you got a D in Economics 101. You're distressed about this and worried about the effect this grade might have on your cumulative GPA, a prospective employer, or a graduate school admissions officer. Or maybe you just feel that you didn't understand the course, and you really want or need to master this material for another course you're planning to take.

You take Econ 101 again and get a B, and your GPA improves. (At some schools, your final grade in this course would be the average of the two scores—a C. At other schools, the B would cancel out the D, and only the B would be used when your grade point average is computed.)

The repeat option can be a lifesaver for students who are desperate to reach a certain GPA—gunners shooting for Phi Beta Kappa or borderline students who must somehow pull up to a 2.0 to get off academic probation and stay enrolled in college.

Other students, like Derek at Arizona State University, use the repeat option simply to neutralize a disappointing performance and prove that they can earn a top grade in a particular subject.

Derek repeated three courses during his college

career, artificially boosting his grade point average. The price he paid for this was that it took him five years to get his degree. He also paid three times as much for those credit hours. (We can't help wondering how fast Derek, who is bright but often unmotivated, would have made it through college if he'd just pushed himself a little bit harder the first time around.)

Many schools limit the number of repeat options to a maximum of three or four. Also, you may be required to notify your dean in writing when you use one of your repeat options, so make sure your faculty adviser and dean know what you're doing.

semester hours of credit. This means if you made a C in it, multiply the grade points given for a C on our handy chart (two for each credit hour) times the number of credit hours (in this case, three). Do that for each course in your schedule, and you can figure out your semester GPA. Here's an example:

Course name	Credits	Grade	Grade Points
English	3	C	3 credits x 2 points = 6
French	3	B	3 credits x 3 points = 9
Biology	4	C	4 credits x 2 points = 8
Art History	2	A	2 credits x 4 points = 8
Sociology	3	B	3 credits x 3 points = 9
Archery	1	P	
	16		40

As you can see, no grade point is given for the Pass you got in archery. You earned 16 credit hours toward graduation, which is the main thing, but since the archery credit was not taken for a grade, we'll use only 15 here to compute your GPA.

Divide the 40 grade points by the 15 credit hours: 40 divided by 15 = 2.67 (grade point average).

This means you have an average of C plus or, as you will probably inform your parents, a B minus, for the semester. As the semesters roll by, you build a cumulative GPA (or "cume"). There are some students out there who know theirs down to the third or fourth decimal point.

IF YOU THINK YOU'VE GOTTEN AN UNFAIR GRADE

You put your heart and soul into this paper. You cried when you read it, it was that good. Secretly, you envisioned your professor using some of your points (crediting you, of course) in teaching this material to future students; you thought about entering it in an essay contest—it was that good.

Shock doesn't begin to cover what you're experiencing today. You nearly stumbled out of class, your face ashen, your belief in the basic decency of human nature—of the inevitable, ultimate triumph of right and goodness over evil—shaken to its core.

You got a C on this, your master work. Apparently, somebody didn't think it was that good. What do you do now?

Take a deep breath. Put the paper in your backpack. Go to the cafeteria and get a cold drink. Sit on a bench and watch the squirrels or the frisbee throwers behind the school. Take your mind off this heinous travesty, if only for a few minutes.

Don't even think about confronting your professor when you're this upset. You'll probably say things that are barely coherent and that you'll later regret. Also, you'll probably blow any chance you may have of getting this paper reviewed again.

A professor we know describes grading as "the hardest and dreariest part of my job." Furthermore, "we on the faculty are misleading our students and ourselves if we pretend that our grading methods are scientific, accurate, perfectly proportioned, and uniformly fair. They're not."

In other words, only an arrogant buffoon would claim that professors never make grading mistakes. Of course they do. Being human, or nearly so, every professor occasionally misjudges or miscalculates when attempting to arrive at a grade.

Even worse, your paper or test may not even have been graded by the professor. This hatchet job could have been done by a teaching assistant; it's entirely possible that the professor, if he or she took the time to read your paper, may disagree with the grade you've been given.

Give your professor a chance to review your work

Here's the bottom line: If you think you've been dealt with unfairly, you should speak up about it. Give the professor a chance to review your work and, if deserved, a chance to correct any injustice that may have been done.

Now, what's the best approach? When you get back to your room, read over the paper again. Try to absorb any comments and think objectively about them. Are any of them valid? Is the paper as good as you thought it was two weeks ago, at three in the morning, when you finished writing it?

If it is, and you believe in it enough to fight for it, your next step is to talk to the professor. A piece of advice: Don't pitch a fit about it in class, just before class, or just after class. Don't have a tantrum in front of an audience that may force your professor into a hurried

THE PASS-FAIL OPTION

Wouldn't it be great to take every class pass-fail? All you have to do is pass; you don't have to ace a test, or paper, or anything. You just have to get by! What a great idea!

Wait. . . . Before you start rolling out the kegs and Cheetos for a semester-long party of a lifetime, let's have a little talk about pass-fail and what it means to you.

First of all, you can only do it with electives, not required courses. Bummer! Second, the main goal of pass-fail is not to promote goofing off but to encourage students to explore unfamiliar areas of interest without fracturing their grade point average in the process. It's a relatively risk-free way to broaden your academic horizons and enrich your education.

Remember our friend the grind, Joe Tunnelvision, obsessed with getting into a good medical school? Let's say he has seen the light. Let's pretend Joe actually wants to learn something for the sake of learning it, not for what it can do for his resume. Joe is Mr. Science; his course schedule is usually loaded with biology and chemistry courses and labs. But for some unknown reason, in answer to a yearning he can't understand or resist, Joe is drawn to a course called "The Modern American Novel." It speaks to something buried deep within him, his long-repressed creative spirit. "Fitzgerald! Hemingway! Faulkner!" he whispers. "I must take this course!"

But the premed side of him, like the Dark Side of Luke Skywalker, is strong. "This could be dangerous territory," it whispers. "All you know, all you are and will ever be, is science! This class will be wall-to-wall English majors—literary sharks—and they'll snap up all the top grades. You may get in way over your head. How will that C minus—maybe that D—look on your pristine transcript?"

Joe is tormented. Then his old friend, the course catalog, comes to his aid. As if by magic, it opens up to the page describing the "pass-fail" option, and Joe realizes in a blinding flash of insight that he can earn credit hours for the course without having the grade figured into his overall average or even recorded on his transcript. Which means that Joe can take "The Modern American Novel" and no one will ever know what his grade was. It could range from an A plus to a D minus, just as long as he passes. He is free to learn.

Don't press too hard, and don't let the conversation get ugly or emotional because you'll lose.

public decision that almost definitely isn't going to be in your favor. (For example, an approach like, "Did it make you feel like a big man to put down a paper that obviously threatened your value system?" probably isn't going to go over well.) The professor may instead become defensive and increasingly closed-minded the more you protest.

Make an appointment to discuss your grade. Do it during the professor's office hours, when you're calm and can present your case fully—and, ideally, when you have the professor's undivided attention. Base your arguments on the merits of the work. Don't try to persuade the professor to raise your grade just because you "put so much time into it." Big deal, your professor will probably think. Factoring your lifestyle, study habits, or even what you intended to write but didn't (who cares what you meant to say?) is not part of the professor's job.

Your best approach is not to question the teacher's competence or judgment—presumably, these have been verified by others who are in a position to know—but instead to point out things that may have been overlooked or misunderstood. Tactfully.

A good approach is something like this: "Your comment said I should mention the bird imagery, and as you can see, I did on page 6; I admit, it might not be as specific as it should have been, but it is there. I didn't omit it." A bad approach would be something like this: "I've got your bird imagery right here! What are you, blind?"

Like most people, professors resent being leaned on. Therefore, don't press too hard, and don't let the conversation get ugly or emotional because you'll lose. You may lose anyway: Your professor may not budge, and this particular grade may stand unchanged.

Your office visit, however, can have great strategic value. For one thing, you'll probably learn a lot about how your professor grades, and that's valuable information to have. (Some professors have irrational pet peeves. One we know is notorious for hating adverbs; he irrationally takes off points when students use adverbs excessively.) Also, your presentation—assuming you handled yourself in an intelligent and mature way—may convince the professor that you're a serious, conscientious student. This is a favorable image that may prove extremely helpful if, say, you wind up the semester with a grade on the borderline between a B plus and an A minus.

Another point: Think how it looks to the professor if you don't make an appointment to discuss a bad grade. He or she may think you just couldn't care less about this class, and you can't be bothered to interrupt your social schedule to figure out how to solve this problem. Doing nothing might even affect your grade in a bad way, if your grade is on a borderline.

Your right to appeal

If you feel your grade for an entire course has been unfair, then you certainly have the right to appeal. Present as much supporting evidence as you can—all your previous tests, papers, and other documents. Recall the professor's own ground rules for determining grades (they should be in your syllabus from the first day of class), and argue your case accordingly.

Hint: A well-thought-out, unemotional, courteous presentation is the best way to go. Some arguments that probably won't work are as follows: "I need a good grade to get into law school," or "I'll lose my eligibility to try out for cheerleader," or "If I don't make at least a C in this course, I can't be initiated into my sorority." Again, your professor is paid to evaluate your work in a specific class, not to boost your career or social aspirations.

Also, don't demand an immediate decision; give the professor time to review your entire file and to rethink how your performance compared with that of the rest of the class.

If the professor refuses to change your grade, and you still feel strongly about it, you can carry your appeal up the line. Consult your student handbook for the specific procedures at your school. In most cases, your next step would be to arrange a meeting with the department chair, then the dean. On larger campuses, there may be an official ombudsman to handle student grievances. (See Chapter Twelve, "When You Need Help.")

But know this: Most grade appeals fail, no matter what procedure is involved. They ultimately come down to questions of judgment by the professor who was hired to teach the class. Department chairpeople, deans, and even college presidents are usually very reluctant to overturn a professor's decision when an individual student's grade is concerned.

If you feel your grade for an entire course has been unfair, then you certainly have the right to appeal.

Think about it from their point of view. This kind of interference can create severe morale problems throughout the faculty. The real value of your appeal, if your complaint is legitimate, is that it will draw attention to your professor's unfairness and/or incompetence and perhaps lead his or her superiors to wonder whether such a person should ultimately be kept on the faculty.

If a number of other students file similar appeals, and if these appeals are valid (if they don't come from a bunch of your friends, for example), the professor's career at the university will ultimately be affected. This won't do you any immediate good, obviously, but there are misfits in teaching, as in anything else, and they should be found out.

Basically, unless your professor is indeed an utter incompetent, a fanatic, or some other kind of goofball, you're probably better off accepting your grade, even through gritted teeth, and not making a federal case out of it. Commit your energies to a good showing next semester instead. Unless you have a compelling reason, don't waste your time and energies haggling over something that's already in the past.

Most probably, you and your professor had what's best described as an honest disagreement. You saw your performance one way and the prof saw it another. So you did get a C in a course where you feel you deserved a B. Next time, you may luck out with an A when you truly deserved a B or even a C. Life is like that.

KEEPING GRADES IN PERSPECTIVE

In one sense, grades are everything, either by themselves ("Yep, made the Dean's List for the fifth straight semester"), or as a ticket to bigger and better things ("Oh, my God, I got a B—I'll never get into law school at Harvard! My life is ruined!"). It's kind of a shame that grades are the main way of keeping score academically and that grades are so important to so many people.

A macho football coach with a big gut and a pin-head once said, as his masochistic team cowered in the locker room, eyes glazed over like the brainwashed robots they had become: "Some people will hand you this garbage about, 'it's not whether you win or lose, but how you play the game.' Well, boys, I'm tellin' you this: How you play the game determines whether you win or lose!" In other words: Win, no matter what. Make good grades, no matter what.

It's amazing how many people worship grades. A disturbing number of students believe they aren't "winning" at college unless they have a top GPA to prove it. They'll do a lot to get that GPA, too—seek out mediocre but easy professors; enroll in "gut" courses that are basically time-wasters but virtually guarantee high marks. They'll suck up to professors. Some of them will even cheat if necessary, so great is their fear of the substandard grade. Anything and everything to rack up that impressive GPA.

There are a lot fewer people at the other end of this spectrum—those relatively few cavalier students who ignore grades altogether. They may become well educated, but their transcripts can't convince anybody of it.

Our advice: Be a "prudent student." Sure, it's good to be conscientious about grades. But four years from now, you're going to need to get a life; even if you go to graduate or professional school. In the long run, your sense of perspective, and your personal values, are going to matter a lot more than the grade you made in "Spanish Women Poets of the 17th Century."

So pick a road you can live with. Expect to be asked about your grades—by parents, the financial aid office, employers, academic and professional societies, graduate and professional schools, scholarship committees, nosy neighbors, anxious aunts, and proud grandparents. But also know that no matter how well or poorly you do, college is not forever, and there's a lot more to living than grades. If you're lucky, what you actually learned in a class will stick with you and enrich your life much longer than whatever grade you finally made in it.

It's amazing how many people worship grades. A disturbing number of students believe they aren't "winning" at college unless they have a top GPA to prove it.

CHAPTER 7

THE PROFS

Picture a black-and-white Disney movie starring Fred MacMurray. The old absent-minded professor, beloved inventor of Flubber, wearing a shabby cardigan and dreaming up endless new, amusing contraptions in his garage out behind the house.

Or, picture the old MGM movie of your choice, featuring the classic professor—also beloved, he's easy to spot, with his horn-rimmed glasses and tweed jacket with the leather patches at the elbows. He's rather fussy, graying at the temples, and his favorite thing to do is hang out in his book-lined study (in coat and tie, of course), absorbed in *The Origin of Species* or some other light reading, as the grandfather clock slowly ticks the evening away.

Now get out the big magnet and erase this videotape. Today's professors defy typecasting. They may wear tweed jackets or spandex biking shorts. Their personalities may run the gamut from austere ("should have joined the family mortuary business") to fried ("the sixties were so cool") to wacky ("star of the karaoke lounge at the Ramada Inn on highway 50"). They may have Ollie North military buzz cuts, Richard Simmons perms, Shirley MacLaine pixie bangs, Gilligan bowl cuts, or Michael Jackson—well, that strings-over-the-face thing that he does. But there is one thing professors do have in common: They've all worked hard to win their position on the faculty.

You're probably going to respect most of your professors; some of them you may even adore and look back on one day with great nostalgia. A few of them, for one reason or another, you may come to dread.

But keep your eye on the ball; remember what you're here for. Your main concern shouldn't be whether you like the professor, but whether you can learn from him or her. Here's something you might hear: "Well, yes, I did get a D in calculus. I just didn't like my teacher." That is so feeble! Instead of a plausible explanation, it sounds more like a lame excuse coming from a whiny brat who bombed the course because he or she either couldn't cut it or just didn't try hard enough. You probably don't want (we hope!) to sound like that.

We actually witnessed the following scene: Chad's mother was at a family reunion when the subject of college grades came up. Some of her sisters and cousins bragged about their children's grades; but Chad's mother, who had absolutely no reason to brag on this subject, tried to put the best face on her son's dismal academic record. "Chad's so smart," she began. Family members sighed and rolled their eyes; they had heard about Chad's "brilliance" *ad nauseam* for the last seventeen years. "He just refuses to apply himself in a class unless he respects the professor," she insisted. "If he has no respect for the teacher, he won't lift a finger."

Is this something to brag about? That Chad is some misunderstood genius and not, in fact, just a misfit of barely mediocre intelligence who acts obnoxious and superior to camouflage what is probably a staggering inferiority complex? We think not.

Our point here is this: Your work in college will be easier and far more pleasant if you and your professors get along. Therefore, it's a wise move on your part, and good personal politics, to find out something about this diverse group of men and women you're going to be dealing with for the next four years.

You're probably going to respect most of your professors; some of them you may even adore and look back on one day with great nostalgia.

UNDERSTANDING THE HIERARCHY OF PROFESSORDOM

There's a hierarchy in academics, just like there is in the military. You can get a big clue as to the status of your professor in the college pecking order—length of service, scholarly and professional achievement—by his or her rank (it should be in the course catalog; it also could be in the school phone book).

On the lowest rung, like military privates, are instructors or lecturers (translation: no job security, a temporary position at best, they need to move up the ladder real quick).

Next are the lieutenants—assistant professors. This is where new Ph.D.s often begin (traditionally, it's a bigger vote of confidence to start someone out here than as an instructor); they still have a way to go to prove themselves, but they've got more time to do it.

After a typical "window" of about four to seven years, assistant professors who have done well (or who have

You can't go wrong by saying "professor." It's the proper form of address at all levels. (Don't call your teacher "Associate Professor Jones," even if that is her actual rank.) You're also safe in referring to Mr. Smith, your history teacher, as "Doctor Smith," even if you're not sure whether he has his Ph.D. You'll rarely be corrected, even if you're wrong, for conferring a doctorate on somebody. TAs frequently prefer to be called by their first names, but wait for them to say so; it's their call. Otherwise, address them as "Mr." or "Ms."

somehow convinced colleagues and deans that they've done well) may be promoted to the rank of associate professor.

Eventually, some of these, who now rank as the rough equivalent of majors in the army, will be promoted to full professor or, as it's officially called, professor. They're colonels, or even generals, now.

Some institutions honor their most distinguished faculty members with "super ranks," which signify an endowed position and a higher salary. If you see someone listed as "University Professor of Economics," or "Truman Langdon Professor of Chemistry," you can assume that this person is golden in the university's eyes; that he or she has brought the institution special prestige and is being rewarded for it. (Helpful translations for this could be "please don't leave our faculty and take your big grant with you." Or, "You're the only one on the faculty who's publishing anything. Please stay here and make us look good.")

At the other end of the scale (no benefits, slave labor) are part-time faculty called AIs (assistant instructors) or, more commonly, TAs (teaching assistants). For the most part, these are advanced graduate students who are getting classroom teaching experience and financial support while they're working on their doctorates. (Which means they're expected to do a lot of work grading and preparing lectures, while, at the same time, they're supposed to be taking classes and working on an awesome thesis that will get them a full-time, paying job on some faculty somewhere.)

Many undergraduate classes, especially at the freshman level, are taught by TAs, and if you attend a large university, you'll almost certainly encounter several of them during your first year or two. This is not necessarily bad; TAs are often effective and caring teachers, and many undergraduates actually prefer them to some of the full-time faculty, who are older and perhaps more remote.

THE SCOOP ON TENURE

Colleges think long and hard about granting tenure because it's not an easy thing to undo. A professor who's been granted tenure normally can't be fired unless flagrant personal or professional misconduct is proved (what does that mean—being arrested in an FBI sting operation, in a sleazy motel room, with an underaged sheep? Maybe. More likely, the professor would have to be caught plagiarizing research or falsifying data), or the institution falls into financial jeopardy. Basically, for all practical purposes, tenure equals a lifetime of job security.

Why do colleges do this? It's a fair question, one that gets asked often (especially by hard-working business people who don't get this luxury, who instead must continue to justify their own positions year after year in a highly competitive environment). To many people, academic tenure seems certain to stifle ambition and condone mediocrity. If a professor chooses to abuse the privilege, it means in the worst-case scenario that someone can just coast for the rest of his or her life, be totally unproductive, and not be punished for it.

Essentially, tenure is designed to protect professors from political pressure. A college or university is supposed to serve as an open forum for ideas, many of which might be unpopular, radical, or even hateful to some citizens. Not everybody understands this. "Are your political science professors still teaching communism?" an angry congressman once demanded of a university president. "Yes, I suppose we are," the president said, "just like we're still teaching cancer in the medical school." Tenure gives a professor true freedom to explore any intellectual avenue no matter how controversial (or, conversely, no matter how esoteric and boring).

Tenure is not given lightly

Because tenure is such a profound and expensive commitment, it's taken very seriously. The professor must first serve a period of probation—sometimes as long as six or seven years, during which time he or she can be readily dismissed (which means starting over someplace else). At the end of this probation period, most campuses force a decision—up or out. They either promote the individual and award tenure or give notice.

While the professor is being considered for tenure, a special committee spends several months scrutinizing his or her work. Basically, such committees look under a lot of rocks, consulting everybody they can think of—current and former colleagues and students, the

There's a hierarchy in academics, just like there is in the military. You can get a big clue as to the status of your professor in the college pecking order by his or her rank.

GETTING CAUGHT IN THE CROSSFIRE

Sometimes, we hate to say, the people who vote thumbs up or thumbs down play God.

Enrique, an instructor at the Johns Hopkins School of Medicine, recently had his research proposal turned down by a national grant committee. When he wanted to know why, he was told it was because Martin, the faculty member in whose lab (and under whose guidance) Enrique would be working, "was not felt to be a cutting-edge scientist pursuing any ideas worthy of note." Enrique was strongly encouraged to find another mentor and apply again.

Ouch! So what happened here was that a small group of people had decided that Martin was to be shut out of all future grants because they didn't consider his work valuable. Enrique just happened to get caught in the crossfire.

department chair, academic dean—for reasons why they should or should not give this person tenure.

Deciding factors generally relate to the individual's teaching, research and publications, and service to the profession or institution. At some schools, research counts heavily; at other institutions, teaching ability is the most important consideration.

Ideally, everything checks out, the professor's prayers are answered, and tenure is indeed granted (usually, the board of trustees, acting on the president's recommendation, makes the final decision). Then the professor is free—liberated—to do his or her best work without fear of undue external (or internal) influence. "This," one professor with tenure says simply, "is a marvelous privilege, one most of us cherish and are grateful for." Some faculty members abuse it. Most don't.

THE PUBLISH-OR-PERISH THING

It stinks. Not that we're biased. Well, we kind of are, because we've seen too many friends, teachers, and colleagues judged by their output alone; in other words, on a bottom-line basis of quantity, rather than quality. What a shame.

At some colleges and universities, young professors are awarded raises, promotions, and tenure on the basis of their ability to teach. What a concept! On many other campuses, the professors are expected to create new knowledge as well. They attempt to discover new findings that can widen the scope of the field or to reinterpret old knowledge in innovative and improved ways. Good teaching, to a large extent, is assumed (often mistakenly).

All this new research is written up and offered to scholarly journals or to the publishers of scholarly books. The best research studies, as determined by experts who serve as juries or referees, are published in these journals (often called refereed journals). When a professor has an article accepted for publication, it means that his or her research has been carefully studied and is now recommended as a genuine contribution to the scholarship of the field.

On the other hand, rejection of the professor's research (many more manuscripts are turned down than published) is generally interpreted to mean that he or she isn't saying anything new or worthwhile and thus isn't really contributing to knowledge and not developing as a scholar.

On some highly competitive, research-oriented campuses, a young faculty member may need to have published up to six or more articles or books to qualify for promotion and tenure. Without this minimum quota, the administration might decide to dismiss this person and find a replacement who might be more productive. Such a decision can be, at best, awkward; at worst, brutal.

That's why young professors frequently feel terrible pressure to publish or perish. (Or, for many women—because the tenure window often coincides with the baby window—to have children before they hit 45, or not at all. Imagine the agony of trying to pick one goal over the other, or the pressure of trying to do it all at once.)

Every university has its share of horror stories about splendid teachers who were fired because they didn't publish, while mediocre teachers were promoted and tenured because they had managed to publish meaningless research in obscure, and largely unread, scholarly journals. Some universities have their priorities for faculty all wrong, and it's often the students who get shortchanged in the process.

But ideally, teaching and research go together. Some of the most brilliant teachers are those who are also deeply immersed in research—people who continue to learn and who share their excitement with their students.

There are other fine teachers, too, who work well with students and love being in the classroom but are simply not interested in doing research. These faculty members (the best of them, anyway) are not lazy or inept; they just happen to prefer teaching to scholarship. There ought to be room in the system for them, too; but in a great many cases, there isn't.

So if that likeable young professor in your Economics 260 class sometimes seems preoccupied, it may be because his mind at that moment is on his research—in other words, on his ticket to academic survival.

For many women professors, the "publish-or-perish" window coincides with the "baby window."

SHOULD YOU PHONE THE PROFESSOR AT HOME?

Use your own good judgment; yes, if it's an emergency—something big, like a family crisis that prevents you from taking tomorrow's test. If not, it's probably not the brightest idea if you just want to chat. We know some professors who resent it when students track them down at home. They argue that professors have the right to a private life when they leave the campus. A surprising number have unlisted numbers, and a few have disconnected their telephones altogether.

"What happens if there's an emergency on campus?" a colleague who recently switched to an unlisted home number was asked. "In a well-run university," the colleague sniffed, "there are no emergencies."

There are some nights during the academic year when professors just know they're going to get a lot of calls, all from worried students. "After the fourth or fifth call," says one professor, "my husband will inquire: 'Giving an exam tomorrow, are you?' " Yes, and most of the students are calling with questions about the lectures and readings that should have been raised a month ago. There's nothing like an exam or a term paper deadline to blast open the channels of communication between student and professor.

Remember: Your professor probably hits the sack a lot

OFFICE HOURS

You need to talk to your professor, and you need more time than five minutes before or after class. What do you do?

Two words: Office hours. Two other words: Voice mailbox, if your school's phone system offers them. Two more words: electronic mail (e-mail) for campuses with networked computer systems. Your professors are expected, and probably even required, to keep office hours—a regular time each week when the office door is open and students are welcome to come in for conferences.

Don't be intimidated, advises one University of Missouri professor. "Most of us genuinely like our students; if we didn't, we wouldn't have gone into teaching in the first place." Most professors enjoy having informal conversations with students outside the classroom. (Look at it from their point of view—until they're able to pick out one or two of you, they're lecturing to a sea of unknowns. It's nice for them to know who's out there listening.)

However, points out one nice professor who often gets imposed upon, "this doesn't mean that we're always readily and casually available."

Most professors may be somewhat less than enthusiastic about a student conversation that begins this way: "Uh, what's up, Doc? Get it? I was in the building early today—they just restocked the vending machines downstairs. I have a class in 45 minutes and some time to kill, so I thought I'd just drop by and visit."

Hey. Now the professor's life is complete. As the nice professor says, "You wouldn't drop in on your physician or your dentist or lawyer that way; your teacher is a professional whose time is just as important, if not always as expensive." So respect it.

Now, on the other hand, students who have a reason to talk to their professors are always welcome. It doesn't have to be an earthshaking reason, either; maybe you need clarification on a paper that's coming due, or you didn't quite understand an idea that came up in yesterday's discussion. Or maybe you need advice about books to read or courses to take next semester, or pointers for finding a summer job. Let your professor help, if at all possible, and if the problem can't be handled during regular office hours, your prof can usually arrange the time for a specific appointment with you.

HOW TO GET BROWNIE POINTS

First, come to class. Second, appear interested in what the professor is saying. Third, ask intelligent questions. In other words, involve yourself in the course, and the brownie points will take care of themselves.

This is such an obvious statement, we shouldn't even have to make it: Professors appreciate enthusiastic students. Consciously or subconsciously, they find ways to show their appreciation when grades are handed out.

This does not mean you can blatantly suck up to a teacher and be rewarded with an A for your trouble. Professors may like to be appreciated, but they're not stupid—they're going to know what you're up to. In other words, you can't be Eddie Haskell on "Leave It to Beaver," saying, "What a lovely dress, Mrs. Cleaver," or "Your hair is looking particularly exquisite today, Mrs. Cleaver," and think you're going to snow the teacher.

Note: Don't even think about attempting to bribe him or her with variations on the "apple for the teacher" theme. Not only are such cheap stunts totally inappropriate, pathetic, and (we hope) beneath you, they could be violations of your school's honor code.

What we are suggesting to you is that professors are human, and they tend to treat people as they would like to be treated.

It may take you a while to notice this, but the attitude of students plays a major role in setting the tone of a class—no matter what the professor does. A teacher may love her 10 a.m. class and, as a result, become inspired to do a superlative job with it. At the same time, she may dislike or even come to dread the class she has at 11 a.m., because of the students in it—they're unprepared, dull, bored, and therefore boring. Each class has a distinct personality. If you can help set a positive tone for your class, through your genuine enthusiasm and active participation, you'll get better instruction and almost certainly a better grade.

On the other hand, if you cut class often, yawn visibly (very rude!) and/or audibly (extremely rude, this also indicates a lack of personal control) when you are there,

earlier than you do. Though midnight may be prime time to you, it's probably long past your professor's normal bedtime. Therefore, we strongly advise you to keep whatever academic problem you develop at such an hour to yourself until tomorrow.

Tip: Ask if your professor has a voice mailbox at home or the office. That way, if you have to get in touch with him or her, at least you can leave a detailed message and say what you need to say.

Involve yourself in the course, and the brownie points will take care of themselves.

doze off, read the student newspaper, or do fingernail maintenance while the professor is trying to teach, you'll help make the class a dreary one for everybody, including your fellow students, who probably aren't going to think your attitude is too cool.

Remember, unlike high school, most college students are there because they really want to be, not because some truant officer is forcing them to come. Therefore, although you may generate a few smirks by being rude, you'll also probably create a lot more ill-will. Also, you'll probably get a poor grade. Which you will deserve.

A few teachers are able to psych themselves up for each class meeting and deliver a top professional performance regardless of the circumstances. But most professors need positive feedback from students to bring out their best teaching efforts. Have you ever given a speech or gotten up in front of a class to say anything? Imagine yourself doing it now, and think how you'd feel if you saw some disrespectful jerk in the audience yawn loudly enough to distract attention, rummage through his backpack for his copy of *Deer Hunter* magazine, and begin to read—while you're still trying to talk.

Performers—and, let's face it, teachers are performers—need a live audience.

Good questions can work wonders, and don't feel bashful about asking them. *Again: Use good judgment, and don't repeatedly ask questions that call attention to yourself or belabor the obvious to your professor and your fellow students.* Everybody, including your professor, will think you're just trying to score points, and this could rebound if you become annoying. ("What an excellent point you just made, Mrs. Cleaver." "Shut up, Eddie!") The best questions are those that lead to a wider understanding of the material, clarify important issues, and nail down loose ends.

Good questions can work wonders; don't feel bashful about asking them.

The number and caliber of questions can serve as a barometer to the success of the lecture. Over the years, a journalism professor we know has invited a number of guest speakers to talk to his students; afterwards, he asks the visitors how they felt their talk went. "I'm pretty pleased with it," is a typical response. "Lots of bright questions. Who was that kid in the front row, the one who asked me about Watergate? Bright guy. Good student, I imagine." Well, if he wasn't in the "good student" category in the professor's mind before, he may be in there now simply because he made the effort to ask a good question.

MAKING THE GRADES: WHAT PROFESSORS LOOK FOR IN YOUR PAPERS

First, your professor will examine your work all by itself, and then look beyond it, seeking out comparative differences between your work and somebody else's. Paper X is fairly strong. Paper Y is somewhat weaker. Paper Z is clearly the best of the lot. Paper Z gets an A. Paper X a B, and Paper Y a C.

This is much easier said than done; professors may spend hefty chunks of time arriving at those distinctions. And what do such phrases as "weaker" and "fairly strong" really mean? They're judgment calls, arrived at in unique and highly personal ways.

Some professors look at grading as a positive thing. "Nice paragraph," they may mutter as they pore over an essay exam. "This was a key point . . . seemed to get the essence of the argument here . . . showed some understanding of this concept . . . fairly strong conclusion." Profs with this point of view tend to start the student out with zero, then award points for the admirable things they discover in the paper.

Other teachers take the opposite approach. They spot the student a full 100 points at the outset, then take away points for the faults they find. "This argument is only half-made . . . unpersuasive reasoning . . . lousy punctuation . . . three misspelled words in one paragraph! . . . the entire second page rambles . . . careless sense of organization . . . fairly weak conclusion." In each case, the grade on the paper may come out the same; it's just that the graders got there by different routes.

Beyond that, some teachers are favorably impressed or put off by some things more than others. Many professors are notorious pushovers for good writing. It doesn't seem to matter so much what you write, just as long as you write gracefully. Other professors are impressed when students correctly use technical terms that are a part of the vocabulary of the course; this suggests that they are immersing themselves in the

GRADE INFLATION

In recent years, there's been a sharp increase in the percentage of good grades awarded—a trend that even has its own name: "Grade inflation" or "grade-flation." Indeed, for many professors and students, the average grade now appears to be not a C but a B, and any student who does slightly above average work may feel entitled to an A.

(Some academicians think this upward trend began during the Vietnam war; many professors were reluctant to give anything but top grades because they knew any male student who flunked out of college faced a good chance of being drafted and sent into combat. Other observers trace the grade-flation phenomenon to the advent of student evaluations of teaching. Fearful of low evaluations, professors began freely awarding high grades in rather pathetic attempts to keep their students happy. For whatever reason, there are a lot of cheap A's and B's floating around out there.)

CRITERIA FOR EVALUATIONS

Despite the differences in grading styles—and there are as many of these as there are professors—each teacher will most likely evaluate your work according to three broad criteria:

Knowledge: your familiarity with the material. In other words, are you spewing total B.S. that you hope sounds good, or can you back it up with an impressive array of relevant facts?

Judgment: your ability to separate the important from the unimportant. Can you cut to the chase? Can you grasp the main points and convey them? If your thinking is muddled, it will show.

Skill: your ability to present your arguments with clarity, polish, and conviction. This is an area where there may be some leeway, and you can pick up some points; students who can write well always have the advantage.

subject matter. Still others place an unusually high premium on organization; students who carefully and emphatically outline their answers, listing and supporting key points one by one, invariably do well with these profs.

Shrewd students learn from what their professors say and write, and then prepare and present their work accordingly. Look for important clues early in the semester: The typical professor will assign a short paper or hour-long exam that seems important at the time but probably won't count for much in determining the final grade for the course. Carefully analyze the professor's comments on this paper and try to figure out what the professor's looking for.

HOW PROFESSORS MIGHT DETERMINE GRADES

Again, it's different for every professor, but there are two basic approaches:

The absolute system. Some professors have developed specific objectives for you, in the belief that your progress can be measured precisely. You'll find yourself evaluated not only in the context of the current semester but against the work of other students who have taken this course in the past.

This is the kind of grading you're probably used to from high school, where there's a predetermined scale that covers all possible performance levels. (A grade of 90 to 100, for example, might be an A, 80 to 89 a B, and so on.) Your class average, your point on the scale, determines your grade for the course. Under this absolute grading system, every member of the class could conceivably get an A in the course. Or, nobody could get an A.

The curve system. Other teachers take each class as its own entity. Grades are decided by how each student performs in relation to the other students in that class. Using this approach, the top students would get A's—even if their averages were, say, 89, which would be a B under the other system. After the top grades are determined, the professor then curves the grades downward: If the students in the first group get an A, then those in the runner-up group, not quite as good, should get a B, and so on.

In theory at least, professors using the curve system would award an equal number of F's and A's, and an equal number of B's and D's, and the largest group, the bell of the curve, would get C's. This rarely happens, by the way, because classes don't normally fall into such convenient patterns.

Professors who curve their grades—and many do, at least to some degree—begin with some basic assumptions about each class, including:

- Most students are average, so the largest percentage of grades should be in the C range
- In each class, at least one student should make an A
- Somebody should flunk

These are chancy propositions, and only the most literal-minded professors refuse to abandon or modify them during the semester as circumstances dictate. Students often resent the curve system because it places them in head-to-head competition with their classmates. And it is demoralizing, that first day of class, when a truly stellar student walks into the room, and somebody groans: "There goes the curve!"

CHAPTER 8

Managing Yourself

Managing yourself means more than keeping up good personal hygiene, although we certainly hope that ranks right up there on your list of priorities! No, what we mean by managing yourself is staying on the ball. Having a pretty good idea of where you're headed and what you need to do to get there.

In this case, where you're headed is easy; you're headed to the end of the semester. After that, you're headed to the end of the year, and eventually, to your college degree. Now, what do you need to do to get there? Well, you need to know what papers, assigned reading, and tests will be looming on the immediate horizon so you can be ready for them. You need to have—or brush up on—certain skills to do this work. You need to know where and how to get information and help, and you need to know a couple of basic academic ground rules.

Ready? Let's go.

TAKING GOOD LECTURE NOTES

Better nail down this skill right away, if you don't already have it, because you're going to need it soon. Picture this: You're studying for a test, anxious and kind of mad at yourself because you waited until the night before—again—after you vowed to change your procrastinating ways. You open your notebook and, for the first time, really look at your lecture notes. Something awful begins to dawn on you: "My God," you say out loud, "these are pitiful!" A split-second later, the grim realization hits: "Oh, no, I'm going to flunk!"

Then, assuming it's not too late, you start feverishly racking your brains, desperately trying to remember the name of that girl who sat next to you—yeah, yeah, you know, Nick's friend, the one from Kansas whose oldest sister knew your brother when he was in college. Maybe she took better notes, you tell yourself in a panic.

Forget it. You're doomed.

There's an obvious, easy way to avoid this nightmare: Take good notes.

You can't escape the lecture. You can't get around it; the lecture is still the most common form of instruction in college. It's a fact of your life right now—as inevitable, perhaps, as the need for Oxy 5 and caffeine.

The typical college student will sit through literally hundreds of hours of lectures during an undergraduate career. Most students actually stay awake throughout these lectures; many even listen hard and try to learn. And yet, only a relative few ever develop an adequate system for taking good lecture notes. Meanwhile, the many students who take terrible notes wonder why they don't do better on exams.

Fact: Good note-taking is essential to good academic progress

Of course, there's no one perfect system for taking good lecture notes, and nearly everybody develops some personal code of abbreviations, patterns, and outline forms. Nevertheless, there are some general guidelines that can help you get the most out of those long lectures and make your note-taking more productive.

- **Do your assigned reading beforehand.** Even if you don't have time to study the material, at least try to read over it the night before class. Otherwise, you may have no clue as to what the professor's talking about and your notes could make absolutely no sense whatsoever. If, for example, tomorrow's lecture in biology will deal with the circulatory system, do the reading assignment and become familiar with the terms and concepts your lecturer will be using, so you don't just sit there, stupefied and obviously lost by words such as "capillaries." *(Note: When you and your teacher are on grossly different wavelengths, it's bad for everybody, including your professor, who may become frustrated if it's clear you're just not getting it.)*
- **Get to class on time.** Often, the professor will tell you the objectives and even outline the lecture at the beginning of the hour. The professor may also start out by offering to answer questions and clear up any loose ends from last time. This is your big opportunity to clarify any points you didn't understand earlier. Make the most of it.

Something awful begins to dawn on you: "My God," you say out loud, "these notes are pitiful!" A split-second later, the grim realization hits: "Oh, no, I'm going to flunk!"

Throughout the lecture, try to figure out the bigger picture. Keep asking yourself: What makes this important?

Note: Be inspired by the character of Tonto in the old black-and-white "Lone Ranger" TV shows. Remember, he was always saying cryptic things such as, "White man speak with forked tongue." He didn't waste words, and neither should your notes.

- **Look for significance.** Throughout the lecture, try to figure out the bigger picture. Keep asking yourself: Why is my professor making this point? What makes this important? Realize that a lecture is not just an explanation of a subject; it's the professor's interpretation of why that subject is important. You may not always agree with this interpretation, but you need to know what it is (for your next exam, if nothing else), and you need to get it into your notes.

- **Listen for organizational cues.** Some professors write out their lectures word for word; others don't write anything but speak totally off the cuff. Most, however, speak from outline notes. With a little practice, you can quickly pick up how the professor has organized the lecture material. Listen for such phrases as "the second reason for the change is," or "a third important factor is," or "still another consideration is." These lead-in lines reveal something about the professor's own thought patterns and attitudes.

- **Don't try to write too much.** If you find yourself taking dictation instead of taking notes, you'll probably get bogged down in details and miss something really important. Avoid trying to recapture the professor's sentences word for word; unless you've taken shorthand, he or she can probably talk faster than you can write. Are you going to school to become a stenographer? No? Then leave out the little words and phrases and focus on the big points. Jot down specific figures that seem important and summarize the main points as tersely as you can while the lecturer is presenting them.

- **Be sure you understand terminology.** Each subject has its own jargon. In economics, for example, some essential terms include *GNP*, *cartel*, *marginal productivity*, and *equilibrium*; it's almost a whole new language. Make sure these terms are properly defined in your notes. If the professor uses an unfamiliar term during the lecture, ask a question early for clarification.

- **Don't let your notes cool off.** This may be the most important tip of all. When the lecture is over, take a couple minutes to look over what you've written to be sure it makes sense. Fill in the blank spaces, complete the fragmented ideas, and—this could be key—*write a one- or two-sentence summary of the main points.* The piddly amount of time this takes will pay off in a major way when you're studying for the next exam.

Cold notes—notes with isolated words or figures that mean absolutely nothing to you weeks later—aren't much help at all at exam time. You think you'll remember, four weeks from now, what you heard today? Trust us: You won't. Take the time today and save the torment tomorrow.

Classroom etiquette in a high-tech world

If you must go high-tech, here's the drill: Laptops and tape recorders, yes. Beepers and cell phones, no. We know a couple of professors who've actually confiscated beepers and cell phones from repeat offenders who are either too dumb or too boorish to remember to shut them off. (They gave them back at the end of class.) Maybe, if you're on an organ transplant waiting list and the donor could come through any minute—maybe—there would be an excuse. Otherwise, there isn't. Whatever business you've got can surely wait one lousy hour.

About laptops: Some, mainly graduate students, use them. Most don't. "I don't mind it," says one professor, "it's not offensive. But I wish the students using them would listen more and not try to take dictation. If you're just obsessed with working your laptop, you're going to miss a huge percentage of what's actually said." In his experience, the professor adds, the laptop users don't seem able to summarize as well as they should. "They just try to take it down word for word." Unless you're planning to be a court reporter, this is probably not the best use of your time. Remember: These machines are supposed to work for *you*, not the other way around.

And another thing: Is class over? No? Then why are you loading up your book bag or backpack? "This hacks me more than anything," grouses another professor. "It's just the rudest thing. Say you have a hundred people in a class: Even if only ten are throwing their books in the bag, this still makes a huge noise. That's really, really rude." The professor believes the paper-rustling, book-tossing students aren't trying to be disruptive: "They aren't even aware of the noise they're making. But it really creates a problem." In this prof's class, however,

GO FOR THE EXTRAS

If the professor offers any extracurricular workshop for students in the class, take it.

An English professor at Vanderbilt University, for example, offers an optional two-hour seminar for students in his Shakespeare class on how to extract meaning from lines and passages of various plays.

Even if you don't glean any new knowledge in such a session (but chances are, you'll probably learn something), your time won't be wasted.

For one thing, you'll get an idea of how the professor thinks and what he or she expects to see in your work.

For another, the professor will know that you cared enough to attend this session, and that's likely to count for something, too.

TAPE RECORDING LECTURES

Sure, do it if you want to—or have a friend do it if you miss the occasional class—but in the long run, this is not a good use of your time. Think about it: If you sit through a lecture, and then sit through that same lecture again on tape, you're doubling your class time, not your study time.

the problem doesn't last long: He stops talking until the interruption ceases—which usually happens in about five seconds.

IMPROVING READING SKILLS

In high school, learning comes largely through listening. But in college, the emphasis shifts to reading. It has to because there's just too much material to cover in lectures alone.

One: There's no shame in having this problem, only in doing nothing to fix it.

Two: You're not the first person to need help with reading skills, and you won't be the last.

Three: That's why almost every campus in this country has a learning skills center, operated by the counseling office or perhaps by the school of education, to offer remedial help free of charge to students who need it.

Four: Nobody else has to know. Nobody's going to call your professors or parents behind your back to reveal your "secret," and it certainly won't hurt your academic career to enroll in such a program—in fact, it might be the best thing you could do for yourself and your future.

"Fifty percent of effective reading comes in learning how to get organized for the reading task ahead," says the director of a college counseling center. "We can teach that. Twenty-five percent is in motivation. We can't teach that. The other 25 percent is what the student is born with."

Until now, your reading skills may never have been truly tested; in high school, learning comes largely through listening. But in college, the emphasis shifts to reading. It has to because there's just too much material to cover in lectures alone. During your first week of classes, your professors are going to say, "Start reading!" Some students aren't going to be able to do this without getting some help. Learning skills centers see students with a range of problems: A few students can barely read at all; many others lack the vocabulary and technique to read at the breakneck pace their college courses will require.

Whatever your particular problem, there's probably somebody at your school who can help. Qualified counselors use many approaches, including one-on-one sessions, reading workshops, and noncredit classes that may last several months.

You may not learn to be a speed reader; you may not become a wonder student capable of devouring hundreds of pages an hour and one Russian novel a day. But you can learn to change how you think about your assignments; you can be taught to develop a mindset for managing a reading assignment and tackling it with confidence.

Whether or not you take advantage of a learning skills center is up to you; participation at such places is purely voluntary. Also, how much you improve also depends, to an overwhelming extent, on how determined you are. But for most students who do decide to attack their reading problems, the improvement is usually dramatic.

Reading effectively

If you don't need remedial work—if you know how to read a book, but you're not great at absorbing the information it contains—then learning how to read effectively becomes a matter of sifting. Think of a miner in the Arizona hills, working day after day, using all kinds of sifters to filter out the junk—sand, dirt, and other minerals—and isolate the little, precious nuggets of gold. When you read for college classes, you're doing the same thing: You're sorting out the material and working on it until you understand it.

Here are a few tips that might help you find the nuggets of information your professor has in mind:

- **Begin with the overview**, by examining how the chapter is organized. Before you dig into the actual text, look over the titles and subheadings to see how the author has outlined the presentation. (Trust us, it has been outlined, by some editor if not by the author, with major points, supporting information, and conclusions.)
- **Look for insights**. Communication is normally a matter of getting two minds to share the same thought. In this situation, you're looking for a three-way communication, involving the author of the book you're reading, your professor, and you.
- **Ask yourself a few questions** after you've finished reading the assignment, such as why did the professor want us to read this material? What was the author trying to explain? What were the key points? Do I understand each of the main points (and each concept and term)? What test questions might the professor ask about this material? How

During your first week of classes, your professors are going to say, "Start reading!" And some students aren't going to be able to do this without getting some help.

WHY GOOD WRITING MATTERS

In college, writing is inevitable, and you're going to need to know how to do it fairly well, or your grades are going to suffer. Some professors even believe that writing is the most important factor in determining academic success. Top writers tend to get top grades, mediocre writers to get mediocre grades, and bad writers—those who are unable to achieve even a minimal level of competence—are likely to find themselves looking down the barrel of academic probation or suspension.

We're not talking literature here—nobody expects you to be the next Ernest Hemingway. But it is reasonable for your professors to expect you to be able to explain your ideas clearly and logically and in passable English. In college, your writing will be tested again and again, most commonly in essay exams and research papers. When grading these efforts, your professors are going to evaluate presentation as well as content; in other words, not only what you write, but how well you write it—the clarity and skill with which you made your point.

would I organize my answers to them? And perhaps most important, the big picture: How does this piece fit in with the other material covered in lectures and readings?

- **Finally, explain it back to yourself.** If you really want to nail down what you've just read, try explaining it—to yourself, your dog, a classmate. After all, as almost any professor will tell you, the best way to learn a subject is to teach it.

BECOMING A BETTER WRITER

"There's nothing to writing," said a famous newspaperman named Red Smith. "All you have to do is sit down at a typewriter and open up a vein."

Ouch! And yet, how true. Even those of us who do it for a living go to great lengths to put off writing. Some of us tend to wait until the last possible minute, until the pressure of a deadline reaches an exquisite level of torment (usually involving some form of headache and a few upper and lower digestive tract symptoms). We grasp eagerly at any distraction, no matter how insignificant or far-fetched. ("Hey, it's the classic pickle episode of 'The Andy Griffith Show'—can't miss that!" or, "It's such a pretty day, I think I'll just lie out here in the sun and work on my notes for the next chapter," or even, "Gee, my cuticles look bad.")

For many college students, writing is an incredibly painful experience—one so unpleasant that they try to avoid it whenever possible. Well, that's a mistake. Because you can run from writing, but you can't hide.

- **Make an outline.** It doesn't have to be formal. Don't make the mistake of assuming that a written outline is merely junior high school stuff; we've seen prize-winning professional journalists prepare an outline before writing a straight news story. Be like Abe Lincoln—write it on the back of an envelope, or a "yellow sticky," or your hand.

  An outline is essential for organizing your thoughts any time you need to write. You should crank out an outline before you tackle an essay exam. Even though it may take a few valuable minutes and you desperately need the time, it will be worth it: Your essay will be clearer, more persuasive, and certainly more polished if you outline it first. (It's bad to have an obvious afterthought on an essay exam, which you stick in the appropriate place with desperate-looking arrows or, worse, notes to your professor like "see insert B.")

- **Eliminate the mechanical errors.** This is an easy thing to do if you know what to look for (which, basically, is anything that will annoy your professor to have to correct, because he or she will feel—justifiably so—that you should know better). Catch and correct all mistakes in grammar, spelling, and punctuation before you turn in your paper. Many professors simply cannot bring themselves to award a high grade to a student whose writing is mechanically flawed. Some academic hardliners will even flunk an otherwise brilliant essay if it contains a number of misspelled words. If you have to, lug a pocket dictionary to class, and if you're not sure about how a word is spelled, look it up. Efforts to improve the mechanics of your writing will pay off handsomely.

- **Revise and rewrite.** Take a second look at what you've done. No matter how good you think your first draft is, it can probably be better if you go over it again. Many good writers do four or five revisions, polishing, fine tuning, and cutting out excess material, before they think a piece is ready to go. "That spontaneous wit I'm supposedly famous for," a noted author once admitted, "usually comes on about the fifth draft." The weakest student papers—and the ones most likely to suffer at the hands of a grader—are those that are obviously rough and hurried first drafts. Where you make the same point two times in a row, for example, because you didn't take the time and trouble to read it over.

- **Take time for neatness.** It really does count. Type (typewriter or computer) if you possibly can. (You may have no choice; some professors won't accept handwritten papers.) Teachers may not admit it, but they're favorably impressed with papers that are neat and legible. Think about the impression you're making: If you hand in some messy, disorganized-looking effort—no matter how

CHOOSING YOUR PRONOUNS

While we're on this subject, do us, your professors, yourself, and the world in general a favor: Learn how to use pronouns. Some pronouns—I, he, she, we, and they—were meant always to be used as subjects. Others—me, him, her, us, and them—were meant always to be used as objects. Therefore: "Hi, it's me" is wrong. "Let's keep this just between you and I" is wrong. And "as the doctor was saying to he and I" is wrong—but a lot of people use pronouns this way all the time, and maybe they even think they're sounding more educated. They don't.

There's an old saying that some professors don't really read the essay exams—they just weigh them, and the heaviest papers get the best grades.

good it may be—the professor isn't going to be impressed. Particularly if you had the whole semester to do it. If you don't take pride in your work, your professor probably won't think too much of it, either.

- **Use the terminology of the course.** Many teachers—jargon-loving nerds themselves—like it when you demonstrate a familiarity with the specialized language of the field. This suggests that you're beginning to involve yourself with the course—their chosen field of study—and it results in a sense of gratification on the part of the professor (and more points for you). *Note: Be sure you're able to use the term in the right way, or else don't bother.* (In the language of anatomy, for example, "hemorrhage," "hemorrhea," and "hemorrhoid" sound similar. They aren't!)

- **Go the distance.** Write as much as your professor permits. If the assignment calls for an eight-page paper, don't hand in three pages and say, "I thought you would respond better to three really good pages than eight pages filled with hot air." Yeah, right. Remember, your teacher has to have some basis for evaluation, and he or she can't give you a grade for work that isn't there. This rule works on essay tests as well: Don't expect a top grade on a brief, skimpy essay. This isn't a telegram, where you get punished if you go over a certain word length, and therefore, there's no good reason (in your professor's eyes) for you to be brief. Write until you have to quit.

Many professors will judge you on quantity as well as quality, so get your money's worth. Writing a lot on an essay test at least shows some effort, even if you aren't as familiar with the subject matter as you should be. Writing very little shows that not only did you not know the subject but you didn't even try to answer the question. There's an old saying that some professors don't really read the essay exams—they just weigh them, and the heaviest papers get the best grades.

WHAT YOU SHOULD KNOW ABOUT COMPUTERS

What can we say? They're here to stay. Even if you have no desire to ever do anything on the computer beyond point-and-click surfing the Net and playing Commander Keen, you should at least know some basics—like how to format a disk—and you should be familiar with at least one word-processing program. Since Microsoft seems poised to take over the world, it might be wise to familiarize yourself with Word; however, WordPerfect, by IBM, is also good. The nice thing about both of these programs is that, if you need extra help there are lots of easy-to-follow books out there (not manuals, but "how-to" books) written in plain English for regular people telling you, step by step, how to use them. Note: Both of these programs are popular in office systems everywhere, so it will be an added advantage when you're out there looking for a job to be able to say, "Sure, I know that program." (Once you've mastered one word processing program, it's not hard to adapt to another.)

On many campuses, at least one course in computer science is required of all students; most dorms are hard-wired for personal computer use, and many colleges provide students with their own PCs to use during the school year. Even if you somehow escaped high school without learning rudimentary computerese, don't worry—there's plenty of help out there. Check with your school's computer center—it may offer free lessons or classes in computer basics.

Most colleges now offer their students a free ticket to the information superhighway—your own password or account number that lets you get on the Internet (which, since the school pays for it, basically means you get to talk to your friends and family long-distance, via the computer, for free). Most students abuse this privilege, at least at first—even sending e-mails to their own roommates. Some professors grade essays, tests and term papers via e-mail. Whether you're forced to or not, you should make it your business to become computer-literate as soon as possible. If you can learn a little about programming, so much the better.

No matter what you do, develop your typing skills. When you're sitting in front of a computer keyboard (or worse, when you're sitting there in a computer lab trying to write and some annoying goober is waiting for you to hurry up and finish and leave, so he can use it next), you'll have enough on your mind without the added pain of figuring out where the letters and numbers are. Note: The keyboard is the same as on a

SAVE, SAVE, SAVE

Bettina, a University of Mississippi student, was on page eight of a 10-page paper on antebellum women, at 10 o'clock the night before it was due, when disaster struck: Her computer spontaneously "went down." Like the Titanic. And Bettina's paper was lost. "All I was able to save was what was right on the screen, because the screen froze," she says. "So I pulled out my notebook and copied everything down as fast as I could. They eventually rebooted the system, and I had to start over almost from scratch." The next day, Bettina went to the campus bookstore and bought a box of preformatted disks. Now, she says, "I save practically every sentence, I'm so paranoid." (Of course, since Bettina has started backing up everything she writes, the computer has never crashed. "But at least if it does happen," she says, "I'm ready.")

ONE MOM FIGHTS BACK

A 15-year-old boy named Cory saw some horrible pictures of his sister on the Internet. The head was hers, all right, but the body (to which it was electronically attached) wasn't—and the poses were pornographic. His sister is Alyssa Milano, who gained fame—and apparently, some unsavory fans—as Samantha on the ABC sitcom "Who's The Boss." Alyssa's mom, Lin Milano, decided to fight back. As she recently put it: "I told Alyssa that I was going to try to kick some butt and tell these people that this is not right." Mrs. Milano got tough, e-mailing the operators of the trashy web sites, and demanding that they remove the filth immediately. If they didn't cooperate, her lawyer followed up with a letter threatening a lawsuit—which usually worked.

typewriter; so if you get a chance, take a typing class while you're still in high school. (Another option, if you have a computer: For less than twenty dollars, you can buy a program that can help you learn how to type.)

One final tip: Buy a virus-checking program, and either install it in your computer or run it in the computer you're using. The last thing you need is a virus from someone else's computer killing your data, obliterating your papers, and generally messing up your life.

THE INTERNET

Okay, you've probably already gotten it out of your system, but if you absolutely must, do the immature things on the Internet. Look at the dirty web sites. Find Pamela Lee's home movies. Peep—but please, don't participate—in the chat rooms. Now, wash your hands, gargle, and spray your mind with Lysol. Cleansed? Good.

Prurient Web sites aside, the Internet is a marvel. It's great for a lot of things, and probably unsurpassed at covering fast-breaking news in a high-tech world. However:

It's no substitute for a library. Most magazines and scholarly journals, for example, keep only a limited stockpile of articles for your reference; their Web pages just couldn't hold a permanent backlog. Your professor can access the term paper Web sites, too—so DON'T EVEN THINK ABOUT downloading a paper written by somebody else and passing it off as your own. And don't be lazy. Get out of your chair, go to the library, and explore the world.

E-mail *is* great for venting. Sometimes, at the University of South Carolina for example, there are student servers, with bulletin boards and chat sites where students can vent freely—to which the professors have no access. This is probably a healthy thing. But:

Cyberspace is not secure. Everything you write on the computer stays there, somewhere, in MEMORY. There are dozens of companies throughout the country that specialize in retrieving, for a fee, deleted files from personal computers, and in tracking computer correspondence. Even on the Internet, what you say lingers out there in cyberspace, and it can come back to haunt you. So be cautious. Don't say anything in an e-mail that you wouldn't want your parents or the dean to find out. It could happen. Maybe you're just writing to a friend, and your friend decides to print your letter, or accidentally hits the "forward" button and sends your e-mail on to everybody in his computerized address book. Or—even in a well-meaning spirit—hits the "cc" button because she thinks some of your other friends should know about what a jerk your boyfriend is, so they can help you, too. Boom, you're immortalized. And maybe you're in trouble, too. The telephone is actually a lot safer.

Shopping on the Net: Many stores have customer passwords and encryption programs to protect the security of your credit card number. We still don't trust them. Our advice: Browse all you want, but don't buy over the computer. Instead, either call for a free catalog, or call their customer service department and talk to a real live human. Tell her what you want, and order it the "old-fashioned" way—over the telephone. By the way: NEVER give your Personal Identification Number (PIN) for your credit or bank card to anyone, even in a call you've initiated. Especially don't do it if someone calls you, claiming to be a bank or credit card official or a police officer. And NEVER do any business involving your credit card number over a cellular phone. Jerks with scanners can easily intercept such calls, can steal your number, and run up a huge tab before you can say, "Cancel my Visa card."

Stupid things you can do on the Internet: Besides saying something you'll live to regret, of course. Well, let's see, there's the case of Monica, a student at Columbia University, who in a fit of infatuation scanned a nude photo of herself into her computer and sent it to her boyfriend, Max. Guess what he did with it when they broke up? That's right. The "See Monica Naked" Web site (her name has been changed) was very popular, until Monica's father's lawyer called Max's parents and strongly suggested that they have their son take down the site. Still, Monica shudders to imagine how many creeps downloaded her picture. Note: An unscrupulous person could do horrible things by scanning your head over any naked person's picture. For help fighting back, see "If You're Being Hassled Online," below.

Chat at your own risk: Oh, yeah, another stupid thing you can do: Play around in a chat room, reveal a lot about yourself, and believe that your confidante is trustworthy and that he or she is not a pervert.

There's the case of Monica, a student at Columbia University, who in a fit of infatuation scanned a nude photo of herself into her computer and sent it to her boyfriend, Max. Guess what he did with it when they broke up? That's right. The "See Monica Naked" Web site.

Here's a quick sample of the kind of thing that could send you racing through the library as you work on essays and term papers in the years ahead. Your mission: Determine where to begin looking for answers to the following questions.

1. When Tom Clancy's novel *Debt of Honor* appeared in 1994, how did critics react to it?
2. What were the main points in President John F. Kennedy's inaugural address?
3. What articles have appeared in recent years on the subject of acid rain?
4. What are the names and locations of some restaurants in Rochester, New York?
5. W. O. McGeehan has been called "the greatest sportswriter of this century." What were the highlights of his illustrious career?
6. What is the average family income in Huntington, West Virginia? What are the major stores and shopping centers there?
7. What articles and books, if any, has your college president written? What teaching positions has he or she held?
8. What is the exact wording of your state's law regarding the minimum drinking age? What are the penalties for violations?

WARNING: "Heather" from Carmel, California, who says she's 5'10", 115 pounds, with long blonde hair, green eyes and a light tan, with whom you've just engaged in some suggestive or downright inappropriate banter, may actually be Chester from Milwaukee, typing with two grubby forefingers on a keyboard, clad in rumpled briefs and a tank-style undershirt with more hair on his back than Mr. Ed. And please, don't EVER make an appointment to meet someone you met on the 'net, particularly at a hotel or out-of-the-way location. Don't be naïve. If his computer name is "Love Tool," he's probably not going to want to take you to dinner and a Broadway show. Rapists and psycho killers can use the Internet, too.

If You're Being Hassled Online: "Spamming" happens when some unfunny prankster bombards your e-mail address with so much junk mail that nothing else can get through. It's a major hassle for you, the "spam-ee," who must download and wade through hundreds or even thousands of files, as well as for any friends who are trying to get in touch with you. The only thing to do there is report this—to the Student Affairs office, Computer Services, or the particular office that assigns your e-mail password and monitors your account, which may then attempt to track down the "spam" perpetrator—and change your address. Do the same if you're being stalked online—if you're receiving unwanted or threatening messages from anyone. Print the messages, and take them to campus security. Then get your e-mail address and password changed. (Note: If you are being stalked online, there's a chance you might be stalked in real life, as well. For tips on staying safe, see Chapter Eleven.)

MAKING (AND MISSING) DEADLINES

When one of us was in high school, his school's tennis coach insisted that his players always hit forehand drives precisely when the ball had bounced waist high. "But coach," one player asked, "what if the ball comes at us so we can't hit it waist high?" The coach was unimpressed. "Then all you have to do," he said, "is move your carcass to the spot where you can." So there.

What if you miss an assignment due date? Don't miss it, that's all.

Major class assignments are usually given well in advance. You have no immediate pressure to begin work on them, and the temptation to procrastinate is overwhelming. We know; we've been there and done that. We're sadder but wiser now. In college, assignments tend to hit the fan in clumps. So, not only is that English essay due tomorrow, but there's a major test in biology Wednesday afternoon, an in-class presentation in history on Thursday, and you suddenly realize you've fallen dangerously behind in economics. Boom, boom, boom.

Crises like these are how grade point averages are made and lost.

One cold winter morning, we visited a friend who works on the set of NBC's "Today" show. Knowing that this guy was regularly at work at 3:30 a.m., we couldn't help wondering how he was able to discipline himself to wake up and function at that unearthly hour every work day. "The discipline isn't in getting up early," he said. "The discipline comes in forcing yourself to go to bed early the night before."

That same reasoning applies to meeting assignment due dates. The virtue is not in the supreme, Herculean effort you put forth on that desperate, caffeine-a-thon night before the deadline. Big deal—you're driven by fear, and even a wild animal, when driven by fear, can do amazing things (chew off a leg to get out of a trap, for instance). No, the real virtue is in the steady, patient work you do on the project days and weeks ahead of time, long before the paper is due.

If you turn a paper in late, expect at the very least to have your grade lowered as a penalty. Some professors refuse to accept late papers at all; they will return them to you ungraded or toss them in the wastebasket and record a big, fat doughnut for you in the grade book instead. Unless there is a legitimate emergency—one that can be verified—don't ask the professor for special treatment. He or she doesn't want to be put in the position of having one set of rules for everybody else and a separate one for you. If everybody else can get it together, you should be able to, too.

Bear this in mind: The deadlines you face in college are nothing compared to those you'll face in the real world.

THE LIBRARY

Learn to love it. It's there for you.

9. What books does your college library have about Winston Churchill?
10. Name the films that John Huston directed after *The Maltese Falcon.*

Answers. (Note: Information is packaged in many ways, as intrepid librarians know, and the answers to these questions could be found in various places. In each case, we list just one or two sources that will get the job done. There are undoubtedly others.)

1. First, try the *Book Review Digest,* an annual publication that summarizes reviews of important books.
2. *The New York Times* will have carried the full text. Use the *Times Index* for 1961 to pinpoint the edition date and page number, then locate the speech in the *Times* file, which your library probably has on microfilm. President Kennedy's speeches are also printed in the *Public Papers of the President* series, which the documents librarian can make available to you.
3. The *Reader's Guide to Periodical Literature*—get to know it—is an excellent place to start. The Public Affairs Information Service is also useful for researching this kind of subject.
4. The maps department of the library should have several current U.S. travel/vacation guides on hand. Also, there's probably a collection of telephone directories, which may include Rochester's

yellow pages, in the library someplace—maybe in or near the reference department.

5. A brief but authoritative profile of McGeehan is included in the *Dictionary of American Biography*.

6. *Sales and Marketing Management* magazine publishes an annual survey of buying power that describes in detail local economic situations throughout the country. *Editor & Publisher Market Guide* lists principal retail outlets in cities and towns. These volumes are normally shelved in the business department of the library.

7. The *Directory of American Scholars* provides brief biographical sketches of many professors, as does *Who's Who in Higher Education*.

8. A complete collection of your state's statutes is probably somewhere in the government documents department.

9. Check the subject index of the card catalog.

10. Mr. Huston's career is profiled in Halliwell's *Filmgoer's Companion* and the *Oxford Companion to Film*, among other sources in the reference department.

Well, how'd you do? If you didn't have a clue about any of these, don't worry—at least not yet. Just look at this as a wake-up call, and remind yourself to become better acquainted with your campus library.

What do you need to know? The information is probably in the library somewhere, and you can find it—if you just know where and how to look. The library is the heart of any campus, and most college libraries have the materials you need to see you through your undergraduate career, hidden though they sometimes may be.

Put it another way: You've paid for the privilege of using this literary country club. So get in those stacks and find the references you need!

During your first few days on campus, take some time to check out the library. Many schools offer group tours for new students. If yours doesn't, simply walk around to the various sections—Serials, Reference, Documents—and see what's in there. If you don't understand something, ask. Most librarians, despite their snippy image, are genuinely glad to help and look upon searches for answers as little mysteries to be solved. At a minimum, you should come away from your initial library orientation with an understanding of the card catalog (this may be on a computer), which is your key to the library's resources and databases, and you should be familiar with some specialized terms, including the following:

- Stacks—how they're organized; who can use them and when)
- Library of Congress numbering system
- Microfilm, microfiche, microcard—where they are, and how to use them
- Interlibrary loan
- Serials

The library may even have a brochure or orientation booklet explaining much of this; it also may offer some shortcuts.

CHEATING

In addition to plagiarism (see box, on page 139), some of the more common forms of cheating include the following:

- Stealing a copy of the exam ahead of time
- Copying from someone else's paper
- Sending or receiving signals during a test

- Turning in a paper that's been bought from a commercial research firm (also known as a "term paper mill")
- Using unauthorized notes or "cheat sheets" during a test
- Taking an exam for another student, or letting someone else take an exam for you

Sleazy practices all. So why do they occur? Why do people cheat? Pressure for good grades is the reason most frequently given. The dog-eat-dog competition for top grades has gotten out of hand at some "gunner" schools and in some academic disciplines, and it brings out the worst in people. Other contributing factors include stress, laziness, and, to a large extent, poor management by the institutions.

Teachers and universities need to emphasize personal integrity more. They also need to crack down on cheaters when they do catch them and establish a classroom environment that discourages cheating. (The kindly old professor who gives the same exam year after year, for example, needs to wise up.)

A number of schools, such as Vanderbilt, have honor codes, rigidly administered by students, to discourage cheaters. At other schools, such as the University of Maryland, faculty and administrators have dramatically reduced cheating by imposing tougher monitoring standards.

No matter what the atmosphere happens to be on your campus, no matter what other students are doing (as your mother might ask, "If they all jumped off the Empire State Building, would you do that, too?"), or what competitive pressures you feel, you don't really gain anything by cheating. If you're caught, you could be suspended or expelled and stuck with a blemish on your scholastic and personal record that will dog you for years to come (as more than one candidate for high national office has been embarrassed to discover). No grade is worth that, and your own sense of integrity should tell you so.

Even if you're not caught, you still pay a price in terms of guilt (and fear of being found out, if you did it with an accomplice who might brag to others about it) and the nagging feeling that you've shortchanged your fellow students and demeaned yourself. No grade is worth that, either.

ONE'S CALLED RESEARCH, THE OTHER'S CALLED PLAGIARISM: KNOW THE DIFFERENCE

Plagiarism means passing off somebody else's work as your own. It means using ideas without acknowledging that they're not yours or saying where you got them.

It's lame, and weak, and contemptible. And college professors don't like it one bit. In fact, it makes them mad. So if you're caught, you can, at a minimum, expect to get hit with a failing grade on the assignment. It's also entirely possible that you'll be given a failing grade for the entire course. If it's bad enough, and the professor is mad enough, proceedings could be instigated that could even get you kicked out of school, and/or kept out of graduate or professional school at that university.

The worst thing about plagiarism is that it's so easy to avoid. If you want to use somebody's ideas, fine—just say something like, "As Chaucer said . . ." and you're covered. So be very careful to cite the sources of the ideas and passages you include in your essays and research papers. Of course, you're going to consult and use the work of others—that's why there are libraries! Just make certain you don't pretend their work is your own.

Think about it. Your professor:

1. Reads widely in the field.

2. Has a long memory, especially where research is
   concerned (some professors even keep copies of
   students' papers for a certain period of time, such
   as five years).
3. Can be relentless in the
   pursuit of plagiarists.

It's late at night. You're
tired, punchy, and almost
beyond hope for a miracle
when you suddenly come
across ten beautiful pages in a
scholarly book that seem
made to order for your term
paper that's due tomorrow
morning. You're tempted. An
insidious little voice inside
your head insists, "Do it, do
it." (This cowardly, weaselly
voice—a fair-weather friend
indeed—is nowhere to be
found when you get caught
and you're looking to share
the blame.)
Don't give in.

All we're saying is that
you need to get your act
together, figure out what
you need to do, and when
you need to do it.

TIPS ON TIME MANAGEMENT

Point One: There are only 24 hours in the day, whether
you sleep or not, and therefore, it's possible to do only
so much.

Point Two: We're all different; what works for
somebody else may not necessarily work best for you.

When one of us was a freshman and then a
sophomore, he shared a room with "Dan," a guy whose
study habits were, well, appalling. Dan drank too much
and showed up for class only when he felt like it, which
wasn't every day. In some courses, he would skip the
readings entirely until the night before the final exam.
Then, he would crack the textbook—and a bottle of
Scotch—and cram all night, usually finishing the book
and the Scotch at about the same time. At dawn, he
would shave, shower, stride confidently across the
campus, and proceed to rack up an A on the final exam.
He was graduated cum laude. Of course, Dan has a
genius-level IQ and a memory like a sponge. He did all
the wrong things as a student, and yet he was
successful.

People like Dan (who now, by the way, is a highly
successful college administrator) ruin it for the rest of
us because they make it look too easy. Dan was a
marvel; we envied his style, but we would have fallen on
our faces—literally as well as academically—if we had
attempted to copy it.

What are your limitations? Maybe you're like Dan, and
you don't have any. Or maybe, like most of us, you have
to scramble and plan and work hard for what you get.

Now is as good a time as any to figure out what your
limitations are, deal with them, go on from there and try
to get a handle on those 24 hours, organizing them into
some kind of workable schedule that suits you. It may
not be the schedule your roommate or friend across the
hall follows. But how could it be? You're all different.

Kevin, for example, is simply biologically unable to
get to sleep before 2 a.m. Midnight is prime time to him;
his mind is sharpest then, and he does his best studying
late at night. Consequently, mornings are awful. Every
single morning of his life, for as long as he can
remember, he's awakened and thought, "Oh, God, do I
have to get up now?" Kevin doesn't think very clearly in
the mornings; he can barely function until he ingests

mass quantities of caffeine, and he's not really even fit to live with until at least 10 a.m.

Trevor, his roommate, is at the other extreme of the circadian rhythm clock. He is the definitive "morning person," who actually throws off the covers and bounds out of bed, unbelievably cheerful, bright-eyed, and not only ready but eager to face the day. He even sings in the shower. Knowing this about himself, Trevor has scheduled his classes from 8 a.m. to noon every day. This leaves his afternoons free for studying (and intramural basketball practice), and by about 10 p.m.—when Kevin, the night owl, is just getting revved up—he's drowsy and ready to nod off.

(By the way, in case you're wondering, it didn't take Kevin and Trevor long to figure out that their personal schedules were polar opposites. But they get along fine and are planning to room together next year. They worked out a system: Whoever's awake at odd hours makes an effort to be quiet and to keep as many lights out as possible; whoever's sleeping puts a pillow over his head. They also keep a portable fan set on "high," which provides the sleeper with some "white noise.")

No matter what your personal timetable is, you need to design a schedule that will enable you to do everything that must get done. And you need to do it now, or you could run into trouble.

This is what often happens: During the first few days of the semester, you make a fantastic discovery—college isn't like high school at all! Wow! The professor makes an assignment, but—get this—doesn't check at the next class to see if you've actually done it or if you've even begun to work on the major paper that's due in two weeks. What freedom!

One night, you actually do settle down to study, until a friend comes in and says, "Let's go see *Gone With the Wind* at the campus theater tonight." You put off reading that chapter in American history for yet another night. But, tomorrow comes and now you have two assignments to do. Then—oops! Your first exams are breathing down your neck, and you still haven't even read the material, much less organized and reviewed it. You panic so much that, even when you're frantically reading the material, you're thinking with every sentence and paragraph, "Oh, no, I'm going to flunk!"

No matter what your personal timetable is, you need to design a schedule that will enable you to do everything that must get done. And you need to do it now, or you could run into trouble.

Maybe for you the method used by Alcoholics Anonymous is the best way to go: One day at a time.

COLLEGE WORK-STUDY

If you qualify for College Work-Study (ask your financial aid office for information about this and other student work programs), you'll be offered a part-time job as part of your financial aid package. The number of hours you can put in will depend on the limits set by the admissions office. The average is about 10 hours a week.

A fringe benefit: There is now some interesting evidence to suggest that students on College Work-Study actually improve their grades, if only slightly, as a result of their jobs.

The reason seems to be that Work-Study jobs, which typically involve clerking, filing, and photocopying (entry-level, part-time office work) around an academic department, seem to engage the student more closely with college faculty, staff, and (never to be underestimated) gossip.

The student becomes more plugged into (and interested in) the place, develops a little savvy about dealing with it, and grades improve accordingly.

Many students don't consider the College Work-Study program; they prefer jobs that are more career-related and that will make a nice addition to their old resume.

But qualified students who do choose Work-Study may pick up that nice academic fringe benefit (and, incidentally, may get to know some professors who might provide good references later) in addition to a regular paycheck.

The message? Don't be like Scarlett O'Hara and say, "I'll think about that tomorrow." Because tomorrow may be too late.

No, we're not daring to suggest that you're supposed to be a total grind and spend the next four years having absolutely no fun and no adventures. All we're saying is that you need to get your act together, figure out what you need to do, and when you need to do it.

BASIC APPROACHES TO TIME MANAGEMENT AND HAPPINESS

Happiness can mean feeling that you're controlling time—rather than the other way around. There are lots of time management techniques; here are three that we recommend.

Method one: The big picture

- Go out and get a large desk calendar, the kind with a generous square of space for every day
- Take every class syllabus, and write down the dates of labs, exams, paper deadlines, and special activities
- Fill in all your fixed commitments—the weekends you plan to go home, holidays, your job schedule, other noteworthy events

Now look at what you've done, and you'll be able to get a pretty good idea about the crunch times and slack times ahead.

As school gets under way, you'll discover that some classes need systematic attention. In math, accounting, and foreign languages, for example, the material is presented to you in steady doses. You learn one or two new things each day and build on them, which means you need to study these subjects on a regular basis.

But in other classes, such as literature and history, the effort may be required in big chunks—reading an entire novel or play, for example—that must be planned for well in advance. Looking at your calendar, you can find some big blocks of free time and plan your work on these courses in advance.

Method two: The not-so-big picture

Even though it's nice to know at a glance what's in store for you down the road, you may prefer to plan your time week by week. For this you'll need a weekly calendar. You can buy one or make your own. Schedule in class time, work time, study and research time, and even the times you'll need open for reviewing lecture notes and preparing for specific classes (see our example).

This is a very effective approach. In fact, many business and professional types use the weekly calendar to keep track of meetings and appointments, so if you get started now, you'll be an old pro at this kind of schedule keeping when you're out in the working world.

Method three: The relatively small picture

But some students are overwhelmed by having their month, or even their week, laid out for them. They think, "I can't possibly do all that!" or worse, "I just sentenced myself to prison!"

So, if you're one of those who feels more pressured than organized by looking at the big picture, then think smaller. Maybe for you, the method used by Alcoholics Anonymous is the best way to go: One day at a time. It's very simple. Make a list of the things you need to do each day, and don't go to bed until you've done them. A sample list might be:

- Study for French test tomorrow.
- Go to library. Work on bibliography for English paper.
- Borrow notes for Wednesday's biology class (which you missed when you had the flu).
- Work this afternoon 1–3:30.
- Go to International Students meeting, 6:30, Shriver Hall.
- Read American history chapter for tomorrow.
- Send birthday card to Aunt Winton.
- Call about ride home for next weekend.

A final word. As a general rule—even though it's important to know what's lurking out there in your immediate future—it's best not to think too much about your total load. If you dwell on how much you have to do and how far you have to go, you could psych yourself

Even though it's important to know what's lurking out there in your immediate future, try not to think too much about your total load. If you dwell on how much you have to do, you could psych yourself right into inactivity.

right into inactivity; you could decide that the weight of your burden is simply unbearable.

- Think of yourself as a rock climber, scaling a sheer, vertical cliff, hanging only by a thin rope attached to pitons that you've driven into the solid rock. It's ironic that the farther you climb, and the closer you get to reaching your goal at the top—the farther you would fall if your rope didn't hold.
- The message? Don't look down at how far you've come; there's no point. And don't look up at how far you have to go; it could make you dizzy. Look straight ahead and stay focused. Concentrate on short-term objectives—building blocks—that will eventually get you where you're going.
- By just plugging away steadily and using your spare time wisely, you'll find that, somehow, it will all get done. Or—worst case—if it doesn't get done, there's still hope. Before long, there will be a new semester, and you can start all over again with a clean slate. (See sample time chart on page 146.)

WORK AND SCHOOL

You may not have much choice about this one. If you're entirely self-supporting, you may need to put in at least a 40-hour week on the job just to make ends meet. When you're trying to pass tough courses at the same time, that kind of load can be brutal. Sure, we know you can do it—a lot of students do, every year—but do you have any other options? Yes, very probably, you do.

Talk to the financial aid office at your school and explain your situation. You may be able to cut back on your work hours—and your stress level—by taking out a student loan, which you won't have to pay back until after you've graduated.

Work is fine. Work is good. But you've got another job, too—educating yourself—and if you don't give it your best effort, you may miss out on some great career and educational opportunities down the line. We believe—and this is supported by financial aid officers—that any full-time (15 hours a week) student whose part-time job consumes more than 20 hours a week is stretched pretty thin and is quite possibly headed for emotional or academic stress.

Work is fine. Work is good. But you've got another job, too—educating yourself—and if you don't give it your best effort, you may miss out on some great career and educational opportunities down the line.

Other part-time jobs

Check with the dean of students or, on larger campuses, the student employment office for other work opportunities. The local newspaper and school newspaper (some universities also have a newspaper for faculty and staff) will list still other job openings. If you want part-time work, you'll almost certainly find it; college communities are geared to handle a lot of part-timers. The pay may run less than for comparable work elsewhere—it's a college town, there's a big labor pool, and local employers can get away with it—but you should be able to earn enough to pay a fair-sized chunk of your expenses without shattering your grades in the process.

Note: Because it is highly unlikely that you will be the sole applicant for part-time work at your school, start looking ASAP. Expect some competition for the cushiest jobs and do your best to be the early bird that gets the worm. In other words, if you know now that you'll be needing a part-time job during the semester, make finding employment one of your first priorities when you arrive on campus. Or better yet, make a few calls around campus (to the offices listed above and any place else you can think of), and see if the school issues a weekly or monthly list of available jobs that could be mailed to you at home or faxed (at your expense, if need be) someplace nearby.

If you know now that you need the extra income of a part-time job but wait until the middle of the semester to start looking, the pickin's may be slim. (And so may your wallet.)

GETTING COURSE CREDIT

Even if you haven't taken a college course, you can still get credit for it. Here are some avenues you may want to explore.

"Testing out" of a subject

Consider the case of Hailey, a history major, who is also an amateur photographer. She has shot pictures under all types of conditions, processed the film herself, even had some of her photos published. The fine arts

CREDIT FOR LIFE EXPERIENCE

It's also possible to use knowledge acquired elsewhere to bypass prerequisites and move immediately into an advanced subject. Suppose, for example, you spent last year as an intern in your city's Department of Human Resources, where you developed a real interest in social work. You want to study the subject, but you find out that all the upper-level courses in your school's social work department carry a prerequisite called "Introduction to Social Services." If you can convince the professor that you're already familiar with the content of the introductory course, you may be allowed to skip that one and enroll in the advanced class.

Sample Time Chart

	Monday	Tuesday	Wednesday	Thursday	Friday	Saturday	Sunday
7:45	English 101		English 101		English 101		
8:50	Biology 101	Theater Arts	Biology 101	Theater Arts	Biology 101		
9:55	reread + organize notes		reread + organize lecture notes		same		
11:00	prepare for French 101		prepare for French 101		same		church
12:05	lunch	lunch	lunch	lunch	lunch		
1:10	French 101	work	French 101	work	French 101	soccer game at McPherson Field	
2:15	study for chem		study for chem		study for chem		
3:20	Chem 101		Chem 101		Chem 101		
4:25	relax, write letters		relax, do errands		same		
5:30	dinner	dinner	dinner	dinner	dinner		dinner
6:00	socialize, play ping-pong						study
7:00	study	study	study	study			
8:00		library research			dance in Adams Hall	Joe's Tavern for pizza	
9:00							
10:00							
11:00	bedtime		SLEEP				

146   THE ULTIMATE COLLEGE SURVIVAL GUIDE

department of her college offers a course in photography that covers subject material and techniques she mastered a long time ago.

Because Hailey needs to pick up some more credits to avoid having to go to summer school, she decides to ask the fine arts department for a special examination in this course. To show that she's serious (and that she's not just some joker who "likes to take pretty pictures"), she backs up her request with a portfolio of her best photographic work.

Now it's up to the chairman of the fine arts department: If he believes that Hailey is, indeed, reasonably prepared, he will arrange a special exam for her. (In this case, the test would probably include a photo assignment as well as a written quiz covering terms and procedures.) If Hailey passes, credit for the course will be added on her transcript.

If you think you already know the material in a certain course (perhaps a prerequisite for a more advanced course you would like to take), you might be able to "test out" of it—and get credit for the course without having to sit through it. (This is also called "challenge by special examination," or "challenge credit.")

Courses on many campuses are available for challenge credit, no matter how you came by this knowledge—whether you've studied the material independently, are currently enrolled, or have acquired the skills through experience. These special exams, which are comparable to the final exams in the actual classes, are developed and administered by the academic departments concerned. There's usually no charge for these exams, so you have nothing to lose by trying. If you feel legitimately prepared to take (and pass) such a test, go for it!

"Testing out" of a subject can help qualified students get their degree more quickly, escape superfluous basic requirements, or simply buy more time.

Placement exams

The idea here is for you to enroll at the level of study that's right for you. In certain subjects (especially math and languages), students can qualify for advanced placement and/or credit by scoring above a certain minimum on departmental exams given during freshman orientation.

CLEP CREDIT

The College-Level Examination Program (CLEP) is a nationally recognized means of acquiring college or university credit for what you may have learned elsewhere, including through on-the-job experience, extensive reading, correspondence study, or television courses.

The CLEP examinations, usually 90-minute multiple-choice tests, are offered in both general and subject areas. These tests are designed to measure knowledge and achievement; if you can prove through one or more of these tests that your knowledge compares with that of the typical college student who has had the specific course work, you can receive the credit without having to take the class.

The CLEP general examinations are available in English, history, the humanities, mathematics, natural sciences, and social sciences. CLEP subject exams are offered in a variety of specific areas. In business, for example, there are tests in computers and data processing, introduction to management, introductory accounting, introductory business law, and introductory marketing. Other subject areas include composition and literature, foreign languages, science, and mathematics.

Say you've taken two years of Spanish. You take a placement test, and your score qualifies you for a second-year course. You don't have to accept your advanced standing—maybe you feel the need to review some of the material taught in first-year classes—but the option to move ahead can be useful for those who want to take advantage of it.

Advanced Placement. Most colleges and universities participate in the College Board Advanced Placement Program and will award credit for those tough AP courses you took in high school—and release you from having to take some basic required courses. A high enough score (check with your college for specific score requirements) could earn you at least six semester hours of credit, spring you loose from a portion of your general studies requirements, and provide you with immediate entry into more challenging, upper-level classes.

Policies vary somewhat from one campus to another, and even among departments in one university (some departments, for example, may require an essay in addition). Also, better be safe than sorry: Make sure your tests results have been forwarded to your college registrar's office.

CHAPTER 9

This Is a Test

College students take tests:

- Every time class meets
- Once a week
- Once a month
- Once a semester
- Twice a semester
- All of the above
- None of the above

The answer to the question is all of the above. Although a few professors give only one big, all-or-nothing (talk about pressure!) test at the end of the semester, most give at least two. Thus, at the very minimum, you can probably expect to take a midterm exam (usually given in a regular class meeting) and a final, which is scheduled during a special exam period at the end of the term. A final exam normally lasts two or three hours; you may finish in less time, or you may still be scribbling as someone pries your blue exam book out of your cramped hands.

It's likely, however, that more than two tests (and other factors, such as papers and discussion) will contribute to your final grade. In some classes, especially science-oriented ones in which you're continually being bombarded with new terms and concepts, you may be tested once a week or more.

Which really isn't such a bad thing. In a way, getting lots of tests is better than having only one or two. For one thing, these tests tend to be "little": Each one doesn't count for a major chunk of your grade, so if you bomb one, it won't kill your overall average in the class. The sum total of these tests, however, may count for a lot—a third of your entire grade, perhaps. So if you do well on these little tests—and have a healthy grade going into the final or midterm—you might be in pretty good shape and feel much less pressured as you prepare for the big ones. Also, being tested regularly forces you to study and keep up with the material, which also is good; this way, you aren't trying to re-learn in December what you digested (and promptly forgot) way back in September.

WHAT TYPES OF TESTS TO EXPECT

In huge lecture courses, you'll probably get "objective" tests, which deal with hard information more than ideas. In smaller discussion classes, you're much more likely to get essay exams, in which you'll be expected to organize concepts and write thoughtful responses to questions.

Preparing for an objective test

Objective tests typically deal with true-or-false questions, matching, multiple choice, identifications, and completions. As you've probably figured out, these tests are more convenient to grade and are often handled by machines or teaching assistants. For some students, however, these can be worse than essay tests. Particularly nightmarish are questions without an obvious answer but rather a confusing array of answer options, such as:

A
B
C
D
A, B, and D
B and C
A and C
All of the above
None of the above

A, B, and D? What kind of mind, you may wonder, dreams up such a test? We don't know.

But we do know that this kind of test—which might cause you to have acid flashbacks to the SATs, Advanced Placement, or any other "achievement" tests you may have endured on your journey to college—throws a lot of people.

No test is a perfect instrument for measuring a student's progress; each semester, some of the most capable students—people who think clearly, write and talk well, and work hard—fail to come through exams with the good grades they genuinely deserve. Maybe they suffer from what educational psychologists call "test anxiety"—believed to affect about 25 percent of all students, some much more than others. The numbers are thought to be even higher for minority students. For whatever reason, some good students just don't "test well."

If you do well on the little tests—and have a healthy grade going into the final or midterm—you might be in pretty good shape, and feel much less pressured, as you prepare for the big ones.

Professors often goof up on their own exams— unintentionally dropping hints for those students clever enough to take advantage of them. Hey, a break for you!

Others, however, seem to outdo themselves, to perform above their capabilities during exams. These students may not be brilliant, but they're shrewd enough to squeeze the full mileage out of the knowledge they do possess. Also, they take everything they're given—and sometimes professors give away quite a bit. Most professors have never taken Tests and Measurements, Educational Psychology, or other courses in teaching methods and techniques. Partly as a result, they often goof up on their own exams—unintentionally dropping hints for those students clever enough to take advantage of them. Hey, a break for you!

This question, for instance, might show up on an American History exam:

At the onset of World War II, the President of the United States was:
A. Harry S Truman
B. Dwight D. Eisenhower
C. Franklin D. Roosevelt
D. Herbert C. Hoover

Okay. Assume you're stumped by that one. Later in the same test, however, you find:

During the early days of World War II, President Roosevelt's Secretary of State was:
A. Henry Wallace
B. Cordell Hull
C. George C. Marshall
D. Douglas MacArthur

Well, you may not know who the Secretary of State was (Mr. Hull), but you would have to be pretty unobservant not to have noticed that the second question provides a big clue—the answer, in fact—to the first.

"I've left myself open to just this kind of thing many times," admits one professor, "and I'm amazed at how few students have grabbed the freebies that have been available to them."

The take-home message here: Grab the freebies. If you really study the test, you can pick up clues that add points to your score. It may not be much, but every little bit helps. Here are some other tips:

- **Don't leave anything blank.** You have a shot at points if you make a stab at an answer. You get diddley squat if you leave it blank. On true-or-false questions, you have a fifty-fifty chance of getting it right; on a multiple-choice question, your odds are usually no worse than one in four. On short-answer questions, a professor may give you a mercy point or two for at least making the effort—any effort—even if your answer is almost entirely wrong. *(Warning: Some professors penalize their students for guessing. Be sure to find out what your instructor's policy is before you take the test!)*

- **Be ruthless with your time.** Suppose you're asked to identify the term "rationalism." Each identification is worth, say, five points and should be answered briefly. But wait! It just so happens that you studied the heck out of rationalism; therefore, you're tempted to write three full pages on the subject to show off your hard-earned knowledge. Don't. It's not worth it. Let it go. You're only going to get five points, tops, no matter how much you write. So answer the question swiftly and move on.

Don't tell everything you know on this question; nobody cares. The shrewdest test-takers respect the Point of Diminishing Returns and are ruthless in allocating their time. They demolish the easy stuff quickly and efficiently, saving up those precious extra minutes for the really tough questions that carry big point values.

Preparing for an essay test

The essay exam, some professors assert, calls for a higher order of mental processes. Instead of merely recognizing material, as in objective tests, you must also be prepared to organize it, evaluate it, argue with it, generalize and particularize from it, and relate it to other situations. If an objective test calls for knowledge, then an essay exam calls for knowledge, judgment, and skill. Your judgment will be demonstrated by how well you organize your thoughts (what you use and what you leave out), and your skill by how well you present what you know.

The essay exam, states Jared, a Brigham Young University student, "is when you spew your guts out."

Whatever.

Here's an example. Suppose that your professor for Introduction to Sociology concludes a unit on the subject of advertising with this essay question:

You have a shot at points if you make a stab at an answer. You get diddley squat if you leave it blank.

The outline is crucial. It will be the key to your essay test success.

In essay exams, as a general rule, the more specific your points, the more credible your case.

Support or refute this statement: "Advertising causes people to buy things they don't need with money they don't have to impress neighbors they don't know."

Your approach? First, consider the teacher's objective, which is probably to find out how familiar you are with the effects of advertising on society. Then, take a few minutes to make an outline. The outline is crucial. It will be the key to your essay test success. Here's one way you could do it:

I. Advertising critics make these points:
   A. Advertising is wasteful and expensive.
   B. Much advertising is in poor taste.
   C. Advertising can foster materialism and a false set of values, especially among children.
   D. Some advertising is misleading in that it seems to promise instant cures for all problems, both personal and social.

II. On the other hand, supporters of advertising claim the following:
   A. By stimulating demand, advertising speeds up the marketing process and can actually result in the lowering of some prices.
   B. Advertising supports the media of mass communications; without advertising, newspapers, radio, and television might have to be financed—and therefore controlled—by the government.
   C. Advertising fulfills a massive educational function, teaching us about new products and services, helping us spend our money wisely.

III. But if advertising is out of control, who should regulate it?
   A. The government. (But could this lead to censorship and thought control?)
   B. The industry itself. (But how effective is industry self-regulation?)
   C. The public, through education. (But this is slow and uncertain.)
   D. Possibly a combination of all of the above.

IV. Conclusion.

It probably won't matter much which you do, praise advertising or bury it, because there's no simple solution. Your professor will be more interested in seeing how well you understand all sides of the issue, and how skillfully and persuasively you present your case.

In preparing for an essay exam, then, you'll need to search through the material and your notes for major themes you can pull together into convincing arguments. Just because a topic is broad, however, doesn't mean your approach can be vague. There's a difference. In essay exams, as a general rule, the more specific your points, the more credible your case.

CRAMMING ALL NIGHT

The All-Nighter is out there, somewhere, in your future. At some point during your college career, you will have to study into the wee hours of the morning, or, at least, with your mind clouded by fear and fatigue, you'll think you have to.

Is cramming all night for you? Despite what other students may tell you, there's really no magic formula that's guaranteed to keep you awake and productive while you're pulling an all-nighter. Tiny catnaps, for example, may refresh you; they work for some people. But they also could zonk you out for the rest of the night, depending on your individual constitution. Caffeine pills work well for some students. They make other students climb the walls.

"Once, I got so wired on [an over-the-counter 'wake-up' pill]," says Jon, a student at Centre College in Danville, Kentucky, "that I couldn't do anything. I couldn't be still for more than a few minutes at a time. I kept moving around my room, just picking up things like tape cassettes and examining them, and then putting them back down again. I couldn't concentrate at all; I had the attention span of a flea."

Not only did Jon waste the whole night—he couldn't make himself study—but the next morning, he "crashed" and felt so worn out and drained that he could barely function, much less take the test. How'd he do? "To say I got an F would pretty much cover it."

So, what are you going to do if you're in that bad situation the night before a test or a paper's due date, when you need to cover a lot of ground and it's going to take you half, or all of, the night to do it? Again, that sage, Nike, comes to mind: Just do it. Your best bet—and

At some point during your college career, you will have to study into the wee hours of the morning, or, at least, with your mind clouded by fear and fatigue, you'll think you have to.

KNOW THE PROFESSOR'S OBJECTIVES FOR EACH TEST

If you can get your professor to say, for example, "I'm primarily interested in checking on how well you understand basic terminology at this point," you can prepare accordingly.

The best cure for test anxiety is just to study the material thoroughly, all semester long. Then, when exam time comes, you'll probably get lucky and be asked about things you know and understand. As one highly successful football coach is fond of saying, "The harder I work, the luckier I get."

yes, it's easier said than done—is to just convince yourself that what you've got to do is necessary and important and then get in there and do it.

A surgeon, called to the hospital at midnight, knowing he'll work until dawn sewing up victims of an accident and then see patients in his office all the next day, simply grits his teeth and does his job. Because he has to.

Tips for all-nighters

Still, we can offer a few tips that may make this gritty job easier:

- **Plan ahead.** For example: If you're going to need a blue book for the test you're about to cram for, get it today. (A blue book is an inexpensive writing tablet professors often require you to use when taking an essay exam.) On top of everything else, you don't want this hanging over your head. You don't want the distraction of having to rush over to the bookstore on the way to the exam.

  Also, allow some time at the end of your marathon session to compose yourself, to do a quick review, and to stroll unhurriedly to the exam. You want your brain to be as clear as it possibly can be, so you can focus on the task ahead.

- **Take frequent breaks.** At least once an hour or so. Your attention span isn't going to be that great anyway. Get up, stretch, take a walk, hang your head out the window like a dog and get some fresh air, turn on the TV for five or ten minutes. Take a cold shower. Splash cold water on your face.

- **Exercise.** Again, don't do too much—you need your energy for studying—but do enough to get your heart rate and energy level up. Do some calisthenics or some aerobic steps. Jump up and down. If you're not the athletic type, at least take a walk around the dorm, jog down six flights of stairs (come on, you can do it!), or run in place for a few minutes. It really does help.

- **Cover all the material, even if you just skim it.** If your choice is to know half of the material thoroughly or all of it superficially, pick option number two. Even a fleeting familiarity with some chapters of a textbook may be enough to allow you to wing it through part of an essay exam. Study the table of contents to see how the material is organized and presented (as in, is there a helpful summary at the end of each chapter? Is there an outline at the beginning of each chapter?). Then, methodically divide the material into blocks and decide how much time you can afford to spend on each unit. Be ruthless.

- **Avoid speed and other controlled substances at all costs.** What's the point of being wired if you can't think? You need all the brain cells you can get. You need to be able to focus your thoughts. These stimulants may get you through the night, but if you're so hung over the next day that you can't think straight, or you're actually incoherent during the test, what's the benefit? As the long-distance company commercial says, "Where's my big savings?"

- **Take a nap early in the day.** You know what you're going to be doing tonight. Even if you can't sleep but just rest for an hour or so, it will help you psychologically, so that you might not feel as tired going into the all-nighter.

- **Study at your desk, or in the student union, or at a local all-night diner.** Why? Think about it: If you're studying on your nice, soft bed, with your pillows fixed just the way you like them, and your roommate snoring blissfully just a few feet away, you're sending your body the same sensory cues it gets every night when you're actually trying to go to sleep. How do you think your body's going to respond? Is this going to make you more alert?

- **Plan to reward yourself.** This is the carrot-and-stick theory. You've already got the stick—your fear of flunking the test you'll be taking in, let's see, six hours now. So why not give yourself even more incentive (the carrot) to make this last push? Tell yourself, "In nine hours, I will be in my bed. I will turn off the lights and pull down the shade. I will turn on the fan, and I will sleep. I can do this now because I know I'll be asleep soon."

You can get through anything if you know it's only temporary. And this is. Plan on getting some extra sleep tomorrow. If need be, and you can swing it, plan to cut your next class after the test,

FEED YOUR BRAIN

We're not talking the basic food groups here. The best brain food for an all-nighter, many students believe, is caffeine—cola, coffee, chocolate, tea—but don't overdo it. Too much of a good thing can be counterproductive.

Next best, if caffeine is not an option for you, is orange or other fruit juice. (Now is not the time for the turkey sandwich and glass of milk—these foods, which release a chemical called serotonin in your brain, make you sleepy. That's why they're such great late-night snacks.)

Eat snacks throughout the night—an apple, cheese and crackers, a bowl of ramen soup, a slice of pizza, microwave popcorn. Keep something in your system, so your blood sugar won't drop (which could also make you sleepy).

so you can get this sleep you've promised yourself. (You'll worry about that class later.) Or, if sleep is not the best reward you can think of, then find something else you can use to psych yourself up, and reward yourself with it.

CHAPTER 10

AFTER HOURS

Guess how much of your time, every week, you'll be spending outside the classroom? Nearly all of it—about 90 percent.

Yes, that's right—this isn't high school, and the overwhelming majority of your time in college is not spent shuffling through halls, propped up at an uncomfortable desk or chair, listening to lectures, participating in labs or group discussions.

There are 168 hours in a week. Assuming you have a normal class load, your in-class time will average only about 16 hours—rarely more than 20—a week (as opposed to the average, 35-hour week you spent in class when you were in high school). Figure in the time you can reasonably expect to spend eating, sleeping, commuting, studying, perhaps even holding down a part-time job, and you're still left with a whole lot of time on your hands to manage, or mismanage, or even totally screw up—it's your choice.

Ideally, you'll dedicate some of this time to keeping yourself in shape, working toward that goal of *mens sana in corpore sano*—a sound mind in a sound body. But there are other dimensions to a sound mind that are just as important; they involve personality.

Your ability to function in social situations isn't the kind of thing that's taught in the classroom. Or if it is (students at Bob Jones University in South Carolina, for example, actually do learn to master some social niceties, including the art of dinner-party conversation), it's usually not taught very extensively. It's up to you to learn this on your own. Now, while you're in college, is a great time to do it—by getting to know lots of people from different backgrounds and by opening up your mind to new and different viewpoints and ways of thinking from any you've heard before.

MEETING PEOPLE

We've hammered home this point because it's important: Now is your big chance to become a more well-rounded person. Never again in your life will you be surrounded by so many different kinds of people—most of them your age, most of them actually eager to meet new people, too. So get out there and encounter them! Learn to do things you've always wanted to do but never had the opportunity to learn. Master a new skill—learn to play the guitar, swim, ride a horse, paint, sculpt, speak Italian, or hit a tennis ball. Improve your mind. Broaden your horizons. Grow.

Didn't we do the "clique thing" in high school? Didn't you cling, like a herd animal, to a pack of some kind, all of you dressed about the same, adopting pretty similar variations of the same basic persona? Well, maybe your entire clique isn't together now. If so, be grateful, this means you have a shot at freedom—a chance to make some new friends, to open yourself up to new ideas. Take it!

Look: You've got the rest of your life to hang out in a safe group, with people just like you, as you all grow old together in a limited, confined, safe, boring, shrinking world. Yawn. Shh! What's that? Creak! It's the sound of your mind closing. Save yourself!

Or, conversely, maybe you were the consummate loner in high school. Maybe you never quite fit in. Maybe the cliques were rigidly formed long before you got there, and you could never find a way to break into the group you wanted. Maybe you pretended like it didn't matter, or that it didn't hurt, but it did.

Or maybe you just don't want to be the person you were in high school. Maybe you're not too proud of the group you hung out with or the things you did, and you don't want college to be a continuation of the past—you'd like to make a break with the old and explore something new.

Well, this is your fresh start, too.

The best way to make new friends is to get involved in something. Strike up a conversation. Show up for club meetings. (In college, unlike high school, many clubs are much more open-ended and glad to welcome new blood, and it's rarely too late to join.) Make the effort.

GETTING INVOLVED

Don't just stand in line. Get busy. Join the Chinese Students Association, or Students for the Ethical Treatment of Animals, or the College Republicans, or the

DON'T BE A STRANGER

Because the atmosphere on a college campus is usually open and friendly—except during exam week, when people you think you know can change before your eyes (usually, it's only temporary!) into total, panic-ridden strangers who might bite your head off if you even dare to ask them the time of day—introducing yourself should become an easy, natural thing to do.

Start at the beginning of the semester, when college is an endless line, and you spend hours just standing around, waiting with other students to pay your fees, get your health card, have your I.D. mug shot taken, write a check for your textbooks, register for classes. Get good at standing in lines because you'll be doing a lot of it throughout your college career—two or three times a day in the cafeteria, whenever you want to check out books at the library or get tickets to ball games and concerts. Learn to make the most of them.

Get the point we're trying to make here? These lines offer a natural opportunity for you to start talking to the person behind or in front of you, even if he or she isn't your "type," whatever that means. You never know. If you're normally shy, force yourself to become friendlier. What do you have to lose? Maybe the person you speak to is just as shy and just as interesting but hasn't read this book and, therefore, has been waiting for somebody else (you) to go first.

If the person you're talking to turns out to be a jerk and is either rude or ignores you, big deal. You haven't lost anything, and it's not like high school; the social dynamics are different. In other words, the jerk is not going to rush away and tell everyone else what a goofball you are and encourage them to shun and ridicule you! Aren't you glad you're not in that brutal arena anymore?

Go your own way when you reach the end of the line and get on with your life. (Psst: Chances are, if you think he or she is a jerk who's got some growing up to do, others probably will, too. Sadly, nobody here is going to care if she was the prom queen or he was the star quarterback. That was then, this is now. In college, it's who you're becoming, not who you used to be, that counts most.)

Marine Science Undergraduate Society, or the Geology Club—name your special interest, there's probably a group for you to join. Try out for the marching band, student symphony, or jazz band. Audition for a part in a dramatic production or sign up to work behind the scenes. Volunteer for work in student government. Join the newspaper or yearbook staff. Involve yourself with people whose interests are similar to (or different from) your own. Ask to borrow someone's notes from biology class. When you return them, offer to buy coffee or lunch to show your gratitude.

Other good places to meet people include sorority or fraternity houses, the campus health club, gym or running track, or plays or concerts.

Of course, there are also houses of worship. Many provide free or very inexpensive suppers for college students. Local congregations or on-campus religious groups also arrange picnics, dances, hold social events, and form intramural sports teams. There are lots of possibilities here, as endless—or as limited—as your imagination and effort.

Student government

Wherever you go to school, you'll find the student body organized (if that's the word for it) into an official-sounding agency that, technically, has some legislative authority in certain areas affecting student life and that represents the students to the real policymakers of the institution—the president and (even more powerful, because they control the purse strings) the Board of Trustees.

Not to burst your bubble or anything, but your Student Senate probably won't have much real clout. Therefore, the guy who runs on a "Make All Classes Pass-Fail" and "A Keg in Every Dorm" campaign—though he might win the election—has no hope of actually seeing his dream come to pass in this lifetime. Cynical students, in fact, have referred to their power (or lack thereof) as a "Tinkertoy democracy."

But even though you probably won't be able to effect major changes in "the system," participating in student government is a good way to get to know people and to find out just how your campus community operates. Any number of successful careers in politics have been launched by campaigns for student government positions. Who knows? The next governor of your state could be one of the people you work with (you could be telling people, years from now, "Yeah, I remember her before she sold out"), or it could even be you (in which case, please disregard the cheap, cynical political shot we just made; we love politicians—honest).

Actually, if you play your cards right, you might even get paid for being a student leader: At California State University in Chico, the Associated Students president—who oversees a $16 million budget and 1,000 employees—gets around $700 a month. According to a survey of 150 schools done by *Student Leader* magazine, 70 percent of colleges offer their student leaders some financial incentive—either a monthly payment, or a break in tuition and/or board.

Campus elections are usually held in the spring. There may be a special election in the fall to choose officers for the new freshman class. If you want to stake out your claim as an up-and-coming student leader, these freshman elections are a good place to start.

If you're not interested in running for office but still want to get involved, you can work on student government committees. There are usually a boatload of these—for recreation, student life, entertainment, cultural attractions, publicity—and they offer fun and challenging opportunities for service and leadership. These committees have much to say about how student activity fees are spent, which means you could find yourself in on some big decisions about special events, convocation speakers, bringing top-name entertainment to campus, and managing the student union. Members of these committees are usually appointed by the elected student leaders, so if you'd like to serve, just drop by the student government office and volunteer.

Intramural sports

Intramural sports are played with enthusiasm, if not ferocity, on just about every college campus. You may hear most about flag football, a game that offers enough action to satisfy even the most aggressive student athlete, but the intramural program goes far beyond the gridiron. Individual, dual, and team activities are arranged to suit a vast spectrum of sports. The competition is as spirited, or as genteel, as you care to make it.

At Vanderbilt University, a school that has one of the more extensive intramural programs, the schedule

You don't have to try out for intramurals. You just sign up.

A WORD ABOUT CLUBS

College students are great joiners. So get ready—from the moment you set foot on campus, people are going to attempt to recruit you for clubs and causes that cover the waterfront of professional, political, religious, and social concerns.

To be honest, a lot of these clubs don't amount to much. They meet early in the fall to elect officers, then schedule an "urgent meeting" later on to have their picture taken for the yearbook, and that's about it. Other student groups do meet regularly, and at great length, and involve their members in projects that can only be described as "busy work."

includes soccer, volleyball, basketball, flag football, golf, table tennis, tennis, handball, racquetball, cross-country, billiards, punt-pass-and-kick, free-throw shooting, wrestling, swimming, diving, track and field, softball, and bowling.

Intramurals provide excellent opportunities to meet people. They're also great for clearing out the cobwebs after a long afternoon in the library or the physics lab.

Perhaps best of all—anybody can play. And thousands do—more than 50 percent of the students on many campuses. You don't have to try out; you just sign up. For team sports, you'll probably participate with your living group (dorm floor, sorority, town club). For individual and dual sports, you can register through the intramural office.

If you're really gung-ho, you might go out for a club sport, such as rugby or water polo, or even skydiving. Or maybe you'll want to sign up for a recreational sport as part of your academic schedule; these usually include swimming, tennis, racquetball, scuba diving, ballroom dancing, and aerobics. There may be an additional fee for some of these (such as karate, equestrian sports, or sailing), but the charge will be only a tiny portion of what you would pay at a private club.

Minority student groups

Racial prejudice is intrinsic to every race—after all, ignorance knows no skin color—and to deny its existence is to lie to yourself. So, while most of us would like to dream of racial harmony, the reality is that we're not there yet.

Which is why minority student groups are important.

They offer role models (older students, faculty, and members of the community); they're support groups. And, they do fun and important things. At the Johns Hopkins School of Medicine, a faculty member describes a minority program this way: "It's outreach programs within the community, faculty helping students, students helping faculty, and students helping each other, especially minority students. The way this occurs is informal . . . (we have) a tight community of students, faculty, and staff working together to create the educational opportunities and programs they know to be meaningful."

Here's what some other Johns Hopkins minority students had to say about some of the things they've accomplished together:

- "A group of us wanted more inner-city outreach programs. We worked with city officials, organized a training session for medical students, and put together a complete program for adolescents on human sexuality. We're in our second year now, and it's going great."
- "Every year, we get together and organize a weekend program for incoming minority students. It includes lectures, tours, and social events, but mostly it's a time to get to know other minority students and faculty. I loved it."
- "Our annual Black Student Organization symposium focuses on major health issues affecting minorities. It's a great opportunity to make an impact."

Volunteer work

Donating time and talent to worthy causes is a fine tradition among college students. Each year, tens of thousands of student volunteers work on their campuses, in their communities, with religious and government programs that take them across the world.

One Southern Methodist University student we know contributed her communication and fund-raising skills to a successful campaign to help a local chapter of the Urban League put a black-oriented radio station on the air. A George Washington University student cooks breakfast and washes dishes four mornings a week at a Washington, D.C., soup kitchen. Another friend of ours at Stanford University puts in a dozen evenings a month as a nurses' aide and volunteer counselor at a community-run spouse-abuse center in Palo Alto, California. A Johns Hopkins student in Baltimore takes her dogs, Jake and Penny, to visit a nursing home a few hours a week. An Indiana University graduate student we know, who works too many hours a week putting himself through school, still finds time to be a Big Brother to a child from a broken home and is, literally, just about the only sane and stable force in that child's life.

Other student volunteers read to the blind, work with emotionally disturbed children, become teachers' aides

That's the negative side of Club College. On the positive side, campus activities can plunge you right into the social life of the school, develop new talents, skills, and interests you never knew you had, foster friendships, and get would-be grinds out of the library once in a while.

A lot of student organizations do some good. Campus environmental groups on one southern campus helped mobilize enough public opinion to block a plan to strip-mine beautiful forest land that had been donated to the university. Black student groups have successfully diminished racism at some schools. Student clubs opposing alcohol abuse have done much to raise the level of awareness to this urgent problem (and probably also saved a few lives). And often, the most interesting speakers on the campus are not the ones on the official lecture schedule, but those controversial figures like Rush Limbaugh or Louis Farrakhan invited by a campus club. Love 'em or hate 'em, they could never be called dull.

One last bit of advice from a professor we know: "Pick your clubs carefully. Join only those in which you have a legitimate interest or in which you think you can make a contribution." In other words: Don't join just because you think "it'll look good on my resume." That's a waste of time—yours and the members who really believe in the club.

CAMPUS RELIGIOUS GROUPS

Most major religious faiths have established a presence on or near the campus. Larger church units, such as the Methodist Wesley Foundation, may maintain their own quarters, complete with chapel, recreational facilities, kitchen, and seminar rooms. But even religious groups with only a handful of students can usually arrange to schedule regular worship services somewhere—perhaps in a meeting room in the student union building, for example.

One of the most extensive campus ministries is the Roman Catholic Newman Center, which, near one large midwestern state university, operates a self-contained parish church. The staff includes three priests, two nuns, and two highly trained students who act as peer ministers. The Newman Center conducts Mass each day and sponsors a wide range of other activities, such as parties, classes, discussion groups, and an inexpensive spaghetti supper on weekends.

In another large campus organization, the Baptist Student Union, the emphasis is on weekday fellowship, the idea being that the BSU should serve as a link to the "regular" churches downtown or back home. The campus BSU does schedule a number of worship meetings and Bible study sessions, a midweek prayer service, seminars, and retreats. But it's also a social organization, engaged in intramural sports, service

at inner-city schools, repair rundown houses in poverty areas on their spring breaks, and conduct recreation programs in nursing homes and centers for battered children.

Somewhere on your campus is an office that coordinates volunteer efforts. The program may be run by the student government, the placement center, or the dean of students. You can quickly find out which agencies need volunteer help. Experience is helpful, but it's usually not necessary. All you really need are the interest, the dedication, and the time to share.

Religious fellowship

Some parents and grandparents out there fear the worst about college campuses. They darkly suspect that it must be easier to push a camel through the eye of a needle than it is to lure a college student into the pews on the Sabbath.

Well, we're not about to say that campuses are islands of unrelieved virtue. But they're not Sodom and Gomorrah, either. Actually, at most schools there are great opportunities for religious—Christian, Jewish, Hindu, Muslim, and others—fellowship, and increasing numbers of students are taking advantage of them.

"Student involvement with us is on the upswing, and students are more serious about their religion," says one Protestant minister. "They may not spend as much time with us as they'd like to—more students have jobs now, and they don't have as much free time—but the quality of their interest is stronger now than it's been in some years."

This may be partly because our politicians have been talking a lot about "traditional values." But also, college is a time when many people start figuring out their own personal values. As one campus leader of Hillel, an organization of Jewish students, explains, "It's an attempt to find personal meaning in a highly competitive society."

The youth ministers we've met are bright, well educated, unflappable, capable of sustaining enthusiasm through long and irregular hours and, best of all, sensitive to the particular concerns and uncertainties of college students. Campus youth ministers mostly listen. Sometimes they talk. They hardly ever lecture.

"Often, we're dealing with impatient young people who see things in stark terms of black and white," says one priest. "They point out that the Church itself doesn't have its own act together—and sometimes it doesn't. Their longing for quick and simple solutions can at times make them vulnerable to groups that promise easy, permanent, black-and-white answers. I try to get them to be patient, to appreciate the wait, and to have the courage to take steps into the world of shades of gray."

BROADEN YOUR HORIZONS

People from other countries are fun—just look at Mujibar and Sirajul, who became quasi-cult figures because of their running acquaintance with David Letterman.

Well, actually, people from other countries can be as fun, or as boring, as sweet or nasty as anybody else.

But they might, however, be a little more lonely than most of us.

Not too long ago, the authors of this book invited several international students home for Thanksgiving Dinner. We found that two of them, one from Hong Kong and one from Taiwan, had been off the campus only twice in three months. One had been downtown only once—and downtown was just five blocks from the campus.

American teachers and students haven't always been very good hosts to international students, which is a shame, because they enrich a campus in so many ways. Getting to know them helps you widen your own horizons. They're bright students; in fact, some of them will eventually hold positions of great importance when they return home. Who knows? That shy, possibly lonely international student you meet today may become some nation's prime minister in a few years.

Getting to know international students is easy. Many larger schools have an International Students Office; smaller colleges may have an international student adviser. Find out from the adviser or office about the upcoming events sponsored by the International Students Association. Most colleges have an organization of this kind, even if there are only a few international students, and involvement by Americans is generally welcomed. Many international student associations put on some memorable social events. At a recent international student dinner at the University of Kentucky, for

projects, community activities, suppers, and parties. The BSU minister's records show that about 8,000 Baptist students are enrolled on one particular campus; on a given Sunday, about 1,000 of these attend local Baptist churches, and an estimated 500 more students go home for the weekend and attend church services in their local communities.

Many Americans, for better or worse, are conditioned to respect privacy—and if you are shy, or if you have a hard time breaking through the language barrier, some students might believe, mistakenly, that you want to be left alone. Or, sadly, they might not make the extra effort to get past cultural differences and get to know you.

example, the menu included Thai shish kebab and spicy peanut butter noodles, Japanese miso soup and sushi, Vietnamese lemongrass-fish soup, Palestinian stuffed squash, marinated olives and roasted peppers from Provence, yogurt-filled ravioli from Afghanistan, and curried vegetables from India. The entertainment included Irish singers, dancing groups from Indonesia and Romania, and classical Spanish guitar music. What a party!

Advice for international students

It's a big dilemma: You're from another country. Where should you live? American students are notoriously myopic—many of them so self-involved that they may not take the time to get to know someone from another culture, particularly someone whose English may not be so great. Maybe you should live with other international students. If so, you've got two big choices: On campus, or off? The big advantage to living on campus is that you're minutes away from everything; class, the library, computer labs, your professors, and campus dining halls. This is probably the best option for you if housing close to campus (within a mile or so) is hard to get and much more expensive, if you don't have a car or bicycle, or if public transportation from other parts of town to college is inadequate.

However, if you have your own car or good source of transportation, you may want to consider living a little further off-campus, particularly if you can find one or more roommates. (Check with Off-Campus Student Services, or Student Affairs, for information on finding places to live off-campus.) For one thing, it's usually cheaper to live a little further away from school. There are "real" grocery stores out in the suburbs, for example, where you can make a little money go much further than it does in the convenience stores near campus.

Our advice, no matter which option you choose: GET INVOLVED. Regrettably, the first move may well be up to you. Many Americans, for better or worse, are conditioned to respect privacy—and if you are shy, or if you have a hard time breaking through the language barrier, some students might believe, mistakenly, that you want to be left alone. Or, sadly, they might not make the extra effort to get past cultural differences and get to know you, so try to get to know them. Join clubs. Talk to everybody. Smile like crazy. And don't put all your eggs in one basket, as the old saying goes: Make friends off-campus, too. Find a church in the community, for instance. Or join a local theater group, or volunteer at the hospital. Go to free lectures at the local library. Check out the local park, zoo, and hometown sports teams. Get yourself out there, and try. If you're having a hard time, talk to somebody—your adviser, your RA, if you have one, a professor. If your adviser's a dud, try someone in the dean of student's office, or a secretary— find a friendly ear. You may decide to stay here, and this may be your future hometown—in which case, you'll need to start putting down roots. Or, if you plan on returning to your own country, don't go back home with regrets. Don't say, "I didn't make any friends. I didn't meet anybody I liked. The people just weren't friendly." Trust us. They are—but you may have to find them first. The main thing is to keep trying.

THE GREEK THING

It begins with Rush Week, a limited, high-pressure period when people in Greek letter fraternities and sororities recruit, or "rush," new students in hopes of nabbing a good crop of pledges to keep their organizations alive and kicking for another four years.

It's not a great system, mainly because it's hard to get to know anybody in a week, much less potential "sisters" or "brothers." Rush at many institutions is characterized by intense pressure—on Greek organizations to "produce," or fill up their houses, and on new students, or "rushees" to "get in," or be accepted by the "right house."

The key to Rush is that it's a mutual selection process—in other words, it works both ways. Rushees are shoppers, too, looking for the best Greek organization for them. Each fraternity and sorority is limited by Rush rules to issuing a certain number of invitations to join (these are called bids); each rushee can accept only one bid, so the mutual selection process sometimes misfires if it's not a perfect match (if, say, a rushee ranks houses A, B, and C and gets accepted to house C but rejected by A and B).

Rush can get pretty brutal. Many students choose to skip it, and either participate in the more informal

A GREEK GLOSSARY

Active—a member of a sorority or fraternity who has been fully initiated into the group. (As opposed to a pledge, a not-yet-full-fledged member.)

Bid—an invitation to join a sorority or fraternity.

Chapter—the individual franchise of a national Greek-letter organization on a campus.

Depledge—to bow out of a sorority or fraternity before initiation, if you find it's not right for you.

Fraternity—A group of men united in brotherhood, ideally for life.

Hazing—A moronic practice of subjecting potential members of a group to various tests of endurance or humiliation. Thank goodness, it's becoming obsolete on many campuses.

Invitational parties—these are longer and somewhat more elaborate than the open-house parties. The objective here is to provide smaller groups of rushees with a more intimate impression of the personalities of the individual sororities.

Legacies—close relatives of current and former sorority or fraternity members, whom that member's chapter is basically obliged to accept.

Open-house parties—short receptions of about 30 minutes each, designed to bring every rushee into every sorority house on the campus. From these brief encounters, the rushees are supposed to begin narrowing their choices a bit for the next round of parties, the invitationals.

Open Rush—a series of relaxed, informal parties after the main rush is over. The advantage here is that rushees have much more time, and much less pressure, to make a decision.

Panhellenic Council—the group that regulates Rush (and all sorority) procedures.

Pledge (verb)—to join a sorority or fraternity. A pledge is a new, but not yet permanent, member.

Preferential, or pref parties—the final rounds of formal rush.

Rushee—someone going through Rush, who's considering joining a sorority or fraternity.

Rush Week—A limited, high-pressure period when people in Greek letter fraternities and sororities recruit, or rush, new students in hopes of nabbing a good crop of pledges to keep their organizations alive and kicking for another four years.

Sorority—A group of women united in sisterhood, ideally for life.

Suicide—this is an all-or-nothing decision where some desperate person says, "If I can't get into Sorority A, then I'm not interested in anything else."

"Open Rush" or bag Greek life altogether. But many others, conversely, find Rush Week exhilarating, an addictive whirlwind of parties filled with new faces and new friends.

It's different on every campus, and, generally, fraternity rush is far less tightly structured (can you say, "keg?"—just kidding; the National Interfraternity Council has established a policy of alcohol-free rushing, which most fraternities are abiding by) than sorority rush. But the ultimate goal remains the same: Matching the rushee's top choice with the fraternity or sorority's top choice.

Sorority rush at one midwestern campus

On a Sunday late in August, a week or so before classes begin, all the rushees assemble on the campus for an orientation meeting with representatives of the Panhellenic Council, the group that regulates Rush (and all sorority) procedures. The rushees then move into dormitory rooms, where they'll sleep, or try to sleep, between the strenuous rounds of parties that follow during the next days and nights. Some kind of general entertainment or informal social program may be scheduled for all the rushees later that evening.

The next two days are devoted to open-house parties, short receptions of about 30 minutes each, designed to bring every rushee into every sorority house on the campus. From these brief encounters, the rushees are supposed to begin narrowing their choices a bit for the next round of parties, the invitationals. (Note: Some houses have so many "legacies"—relatives of former sorority members, whom they're basically obliged to accept—that these open houses are, in effect, already closed. They have to cut somebody, so they cut the people without any connections no matter how wonderful they may be. As we said, not a great system.)

The invitational parties are longer and somewhat more elaborate, and the objective here is to provide smaller groups of rushees with a more intimate impression of the personalities of the individual sororities. (Be prepared; they always trot out the house achievers: "Have you met Erin? She's our Rhodes Scholar, who also just won an intense piano competition in Moscow.")

Each rushee can sign up for as many as ten invitationals. The sororities, meanwhile, have done some narrowing down of their own. *(Secret information: Many of them rank rushees based on personality and—yes, really—appearance. Not that they're superficial or anything.)* By choice (or not, if few people opt to go back to their house), they may extend a smaller number of invitations, so they can concentrate on the rushees they consider especially promising.

After the invitationals come the final parties, the preferentials, or return parties. By this time, each rushee is supposed to have narrowed her choices down to three. The sororities, too, knowing they have only a limited number of bids available, usually invite back only those rushees they regard as top prospects. These pref parties are usually more serious affairs; most of the screening has been done by now, and it's hard-sell time (be prepared for tender squeezes of the hand and tearful, meaningful songs). It's like an emotional, hourlong, no-holds-barred infomercial.

When the preferential parties are over, the rushees retreat to their rooms to draw up a list of their sorority choices in order of preference. The sororities, usually after an all-night meeting, decide to whom they want to extend bids. Both the rushee preferences and the sorority bids are secret. A computer discreetly and dispassionately matches up the two. If a rushee listed Sorority A first and Sorority B second, but only received a bid from Sorority B, she will then receive a bid from Sorority B, and only she—not the sorority—will know that she didn't receive her top choice.

A few tips on surviving Rush and staying sane

- **Don't "suicide."** A "suicide" is an all-or-nothing decision, where some desperate person says, "If I can't get into Sorority A, then I'm not interested in anything else." Some people suicide from the beginning of rush—they've got their heart set on one sorority and view parties at other houses as a waste of time.

  This is a mistake. Give every group a good chance to get to know you, and keep an open mind. *Note: No house is always going to be the best on campus. It's just not possible.* Houses change every year, as seniors go and new freshmen come on board. Therefore, the house that was last

The key to Rush is that it's a mutual selection process—in other words, it works both ways. Rushees are shoppers, too, looking for the best Greek organization for them.

Every fraternity and sorority has its legacies, and some of them are colossal misfits. In other words: Maybe Dad was a cool Greek, but Junior's a total geek.

year's rage might be well on its way to mediocrity this year. So don't just buy into a group's reputation—judge it for yourself. Be smart. Make your own opinions.

- **Don't take Rush Week too seriously.** Don't torment yourself, and don't buy anybody else's vision of you—popular, unpopular, pretty, not pretty, whatever. Your sense of self can't be determined by anybody but you. *Remember: No matter how it comes out, this is just the first week of your college career. Who you are and what you will become matters a lot more than anything that happens during Rush.*
- **Ask about "Open Rush" and Spring Rush.** Many sororities participate in "Open Rush," a series of informal parties after the main rush is over. Note: The sororities participating might be those that didn't make their bids; in other words, they've got some vacancies. There might be a good reason for this—a well-known drug problem in the sorority, for example—or no reason whatsoever; maybe they just didn't have a good rush. It can happen to anybody. Spring Rush is just what it sounds like—more informal rush parties in the spring, more opportunities to meet sorority members and much more time to make your decision.
- **One option: Go through Rush, meet everybody, and drop out.** Don't commit to anything. See how you like it. If it's something you want to pursue, go back next year—Rush isn't limited to freshmen—after you've had a chance to get to know the campus and after you've made some friends in various sororities. This way, you'll be more well rounded and confident; you may have more to offer the sorority of your choice, and you won't feel so pressured.
- **Rent the video *Animal House*.** Get yourself in a healthy mind-set before you go into Rush, and do your very best to hang on to your sense of humor—you'll need it!

Pros and cons of Greek life

On the good side. The Greek system really does promote fellowship. Beginning with Rush Week, you and your fraternity brothers or sorority sisters will go through a lot together—everything from house cleanup to beer blasts to silly costume parties to fancy-dress formals. This is the stuff of which friendships and memories are made; bonding is inevitable. Some of the memories may be painful and a few of the friendships may be more trouble than they're worth, but you'll have them anyway, and most likely, you'll get misty-eyed as you think back on them years from now.

Overall, for many people, the Greek experience is a positive and happy one.

Living with your friends (which, presumably, your new brothers and sisters will become) is good, especially on a big, impersonal campus. At least within the fraternity or sorority house (ideally) you feel that you belong, not just floating along in limbo as one of thousands of faceless, numbered students who are processed and computerized into oblivion by the university. You're not just another bug on the windshield of life; you're part of a group.

Despite the *Animal House* image, fraternities and sororities can teach you something about social graces. This is more important than it sounds. The ability to meet and talk with people comfortably and to show polish and consideration in your dealings with other people are invaluable skills to have; they'll serve you well, in social as well as business settings, all your life.

On the downside. Greek life can take its toll, and the price may be more than you care to pay. The relentless social whirl brings on what some students feel is a pressure to perform—to show up with a stunning date for every occasion, to think and act and dress in ways that will suitably impress everyone. You may not feel this pressure—and you shouldn't—but a lot of students do, and a lot of them don't handle it well. The obligatory participation in everything—intramurals, service projects, parties, and dances—can easily drain away time and energy from your studies.

Hazing

Whack! "Please, sir, may I have another?" Whack!

Smacking anybody's backside with those decorative wood paddles is illegal. So is making somebody chug vodka until he passes out, vomits, or both. So are sleep deprivation and other "endurance tests" designed to make you prove how "tough" you are (and therefore, how worthy you are to join this wonderful group).

Don't buy anybody else's vision of you—popular, unpopular, pretty, not pretty, whatever. Your sense of self can't be determined by anybody but you.

Remember: No matter how it comes out, this is just the first week of your college career. Who you are, and what you will become, matters a lot more than anything that happens during Rush.

It doesn't matter why you did it, or even that nobody got hurt. Hazing is wrong, it's stupid, and it's evil. Don't let yourself get swept up in it. Walk away.

Once tolerated or even encouraged (the same way people smirk and say patronizingly, "Boys will be boys"), hazing in any form—no matter how subtle—is actively discouraged today. On many campuses, we're happy to report, it's almost obsolete. Colleges and universities, as well as national Greek organizations, have cracked down on it. Students who participate in it are severely punished, and their organizations may be banned from campus forever. Some people have gone to jail for crimes committed in the name of hazing. Worst of all, a few people have died because of colossally stupid actions, all done in the name of fun and fellowship. In the last 20 years, at least 75 college students have died from hazing incidents, most of them involving extreme amounts of alcohol (see "Binge Drinking," below), but some involving other forms of punishment. Here are some recent, shameful examples:

- At Southeast Missouri State University in Cape Girardeau, a journalism student died of internal bleeding caused by pledging activities at Kappa Alpha Psi fraternity; the activities involved punching.
- Six members of the Omega Psi Phi chapter at the University of Maryland were seriously injured due to hazing; 23 members of the fraternity agreed to a plea bargain after being charged with beating pledges.
- The State University of New York-Cortland permanently abolished the Beta Phi Epsilon fraternity after some members used a lethal mixture to paint the fraternity's letters on the backs of 13 pledges. Two students were hospitalized with kidney failure; 20 students were suspended, put on probation, or otherwise punished for hazing violations.
- At the University of Iowa, the Lambda Chi Alpha fraternity was ordered to close its house after a student died as a result of pledging activities.

What is hazing? This is the definition at one large southeastern university: "Any activity undertaken by a group . . . or member of that group . . . in which members or prospective members are subjected to activities which harass, intimidate, physically exhaust, impart pain, cause undue mental fatigue or mental distress, or which cause mutilation or alteration of the body or parts of the body. Such activities include . . . tests of endurance, submission of members or prospective members to potentially dangerous or hazardous circumstances, activities which have a foreseeable potential for resulting in personal injury, or any activity which by its nature is so profound that it would have a potential to cause severe mental anxiety, mental distress, panic, human degradation, or public embarrassment."

No excuse for it is acceptable: "It shall not constitute a defense to the charge of hazing that the participants took part voluntarily, that they voluntarily assumed the risks or hardship of the activity, or that no injury in fact was suffered."

It doesn't matter why you did it or even that nobody got hurt. Hazing is wrong, it's stupid, and it's evil. Don't let yourself get swept up in it. Walk away. No organization—especially one that tolerates such garbage—is worth the price.

Ask Eileen Stevens. In 1978, her son died in a fraternity hazing incident involving alcohol. Ask Rita Saucier. Her son, Chad, called her one evening and left a message, "Hi, Mom. I'm dressed like an elf and going to the frat Christmas party. I'll be home early tomorrow." At that party, he had to drink a lot of alcohol, given to him by his "big brother," Saucier says. A few hours later, Chad had passed out; he was carried to a room and left there. He soon began to turn blue, and at 1:20 a.m. was pronounced dead. His blood alcohol level was .353. In efforts to stop sick hazing incidents like these from killing any more mothers' sons, Stevens and Saucier each have formed organizations that can help. Saucier's is the Committee Against Hazing, P.O. Box 850955, Mobile, Ala., 36685. Stevens' group is the Committee to Halt Useless College Killings (C.H.U.C.K.), at P.O. Box 188, Sayville, New York, 11782.

Many universities are fighting back: For example, in an ambitious overhaul of its Greek system, the University of Maryland has set standards that its fraternities and sororities must meet, including: At least a 2.30 grade-point average with a minimum of 12 college credits, community service projects, cutbacks on new member activities or pledge periods, and restrictions on alcohol use.

BINGE DRINKING

Colleges are steeped in the moronic tradition of binge drinking—quaffing four or five drinks in a row. At least. As John Belushi tells new pledge "Flounder" at a critical moment in the movie "Animal House": "My advice to you is to start drinking heavily."

Look in your campus newspaper. How many ads are there for local bars touting such stellar features as "Ladies Night," "Bladder-Busters" (in which bar drinks are cheaper until somebody has to go to the bathroom), "All You Can Drink" specials, and "Dollar Pitchers?" Look up and down the hall of your dorm. Chances are, your neighbors spend more money on alcohol than they do on soft drinks and textbooks combined. A recent study of America's undergraduates found that they're drinking 4 BILLION cans of beer—on average, 55 six-packs each—a year. They do it with fake I.D.s, with the help of older friends who buy it for them, with corrupt bars that deliberately (wink, wink, nudge, nudge) do a pathetic job of enforcing the legal drinking age of 21. They make a game out of it, by playing quarters, or counting the number of times people say, "Hi, Bob," on "The Bob Newhart Show," or whatever. If they can't drink fast enough, they use "beer bongs" or "funnels," airless rubber hoses that shoot an entire can of beer through somebody's mouth and into the stomach in about six seconds.

In 1997, just after the fall semester began at Louisiana State University, a 20-year-old student named Benjamin got his pledge pin from Sigma Alpha Epsilon. His celebration with his new "brothers" began with a keg party that featured "funneling," escalated to stronger stuff—151-proof rum, whiskey, and liqueur—and ended with the upperclassmen wheeling their incapacitated new pledges home in shopping carts because they couldn't walk any more. Hours later Benjamin was dead of alcohol poisoning; three of his fraternity brothers were hospitalized. The autopsy found that he had consumed about 24 drinks, and his blood-alcohol level was six times the state's legal intoxication limit.

Also killed that year, among others, were Leslie, 21, a senior at the University of Virginia, who fell headfirst down a flight of apartment stairs after a night of drinking; her blood alcohol level was .27—more than three times the state's limit. And there was Melinda of

Virginia Tech, an 18-year-old freshman who was "sleeping off" a night of heavy drinking. She rolled off her bed, out her dorm window, and fell eight stories to her death.

A binge drinking spree can hit the brain like a nuclear holocaust, causing permanent memory loss or even death, if the brain becomes so poisoned by alcohol that it can't tell your lungs to keep breathing, or your heart to keep pumping.

Very important note: If someone you know passes out from drinking too much, DON'T LEAVE HIM OR HER ALONE! Tell your RA, and make sure somebody stays until your friend is no longer unconscious.

Who are these binge drinkers? Well, many of them are affiliated with Greek houses—fraternities and sororities. A recent study by the Harvard School of Public Health, of 14,700 students at 115 colleges, found that 86 percent of fraternity residents and 80 percent of sorority residents are binge drinkers. Maybe not every day, but at least once within the two weeks prior to the study, these students had a binge episode—they downed five or more drinks in one sitting. Binge drinking was also high among Greeks who didn't live in their fraternity or sorority house—71 percent of men and 58 percent of women. The numbers for students not affiliated with Greek houses were significantly lower—45 percent of men and 36 percent of women admitted binge drinking.

One recent study found that binge drinkers are seven to 10 times more likely to have unprotected sex or spontaneous (not planned, and therefore probably not protected) sexual activity, get into trouble with campus police, damage property or injure themselves. An estimated 90 percent of all campus rapes, and 95 percent of all acts of violence on college campuses are committed when alcohol has been consumed. The U.S. Department of Health and Human Services calls binge drinking by college students "the most dangerous and most ignored element on college campuses today." Worse yet—among regular student binge-drinkers, half of women and 60 percent of men report driving while drunk.

But it's fun, right? Recently, the *Herald-Journal* newspaper in Spartanburg, S.C., interviewed some particularly stupid enrollees of the University of South Carolina-Spartanburg. One of them was Chris, who said he drinks at least a six-pack a night and as many as 20

A recent study by the Harvard School of Public Health, of 14,700 students at 115 colleges, found that 86 percent of fraternity residents and 80 percent of sorority residents are binge drinkers.

drinks when he's at a party. "I'm a fifth-year junior, so it's held me back a little bit." DUH. "It's pretty much eight days a week."

Also interviewed in the story was Scott, a senior at Clemson, who was on his twenty-first beer of the night—a brew to celebrate every year of his life. He had two beers to go. "I'm legal. What are they going to do, tell me I can't drink beer? Scott said. "This is college; we're all about getting trashed."

Right. The families and friends of Benjamin, Leslie, Melinda and the string of students who, like them, died senseless deaths, would give anything for him to be wrong.

Sundresses and Backstabbers: One Sister's Story

Ask Martha, a recent college graduate, about her sorority and suddenly she's off on a series of bittersweet flashbacks: She's a brand new freshman at the University of Kentucky in Lexington, meeting the thirty other girls in her pledge class for the first time, resplendent in the mandatory sundress and pearls and cute sling-backs that matched her little summer purse.

"I just knew, when I graduated from high school, that I wanted to join a 'good' sorority," says Martha, a "townie" from Lexington. (Because she would be living at home, not a dorm, her first semester, she viewed sorority rush as a way to become part of a group.) "It was my number one priority."

"I just knew, when I graduated from high school, that I wanted to join a 'good' sorority," says Martha, "It was my number one priority."

And so, scared and excited, Martha signed up for rush in the fall. As she made the rounds from house to house, Martha smiled gamely and tried ("probably too hard") to impress, made conversation, pretended to like people she had detested in high school when she met them again, and faded under the blazing hot sun and grueling days of eight-hour parties. She suppressed her distaste at the gooey sweetness of "Preference Night," (where rushees and sororities make their final choices), and convinced herself, tearfully ("since everybody else seemed to be crying, too"), that this was the true sisterhood she'd been waiting for all her life. The candles and the plaintive, quivering, sugary songs, the tearful smiles and tender squeezes of hands worked their intended magic, and Martha wanted desperately to be part of it.

By Bid Day, Martha—and the five hundred other girls left out of an original group of more than a thousand—was exhausted, mentally and physically. Some girls had "suicided" (put all their Rush eggs in one basket and picked only one house) and lost; they would be prey later, during Open Rush, for the sororities they had rejected earlier. Others had dropped out. Still others, sadly, were "No-Bids," also fair game for Open Rush.

Martha was astounded to learn how some sororities cut applicants: "At one house, a friend later told me, I was cut because, when they asked me if I wanted seconds—every house served snacks—I said yes. Who knew it's not considered 'ladylike' to take seconds? It was hot and I was hungry, and I thought they meant it when they made the offer; I didn't know it was just an easy way to rule out someone."

Once "in," the hysterical euphoria faded somewhat as she trudged through one mandatory exercise (amid the ever-present song and ritual of sisterhood) after another. But Martha did well in the sorority—the "Actives" were impressed with her enthusiasm (she had dutifully attended every single event), her intelligence (her academic grades were good) and her leadership potential (she worked on the campus newspaper). She became liked, depended upon, and trusted. She made some good friends, most of whom she's kept ever since.

But after a while, Martha decided she didn't want to "do the sorority thing" anymore. "You know, they even taught us how to clap? When it was our turn to hold rush parties, and we'd stand on the steps of the house and sing, we had to do this 'perky clap.' It was gross."

The character of her sorority had begun to change: "When I pledged, there were thirty-seven seniors; I didn't make much of this at the time. But the next year they were all gone, and we had a comparatively small house—which made us all even more tense for Rush next year; we felt this big pressure to make up those numbers. We didn't do very well at all in the next Rush, and our chapter, which had been pretty good, started to feel a little like a sinking ship; I noticed a defensive quality in myself and some of the girls, especially when we met with other sororities. What's amazing to me is how, when you have a vulnerability—real or perceived—people can smell it. It was an awful feeling. A lot of us

The candles and the plaintive, quivering, sugary songs, the tearful smiles and tender squeezes of hands worked their intended magic, and Martha wanted desperately to be part of it.

"When it was our turn to hold rush parties, and we'd stand on the steps of the house and sing, we had to do this 'perky clap.' It was gross."

thought, ' What have I gotten myself into?' After that bad Rush, a lot of the girls felt rejected, like, 'What's wrong with us?' "

Eventually, Martha began to feel trapped by the whole thing. She stuck it out for two years, then transferred to Emory University. ("One of the big reasons I went there was because they didn't have a chapter of my sorority.")

Now, looking back, Martha wonders "why they ever made sororities anything but a social club," she says. "The original founders of our sorority were just a bunch of girls who wanted a club." But they veiled it in mysticism, candlelight, robes and ceremony; they proclaimed scholarship and, worse yet, philanthropy. That a hundred girls would voluntarily unite, draped in their expensive clothes, to fight heart disease and cancer, didn't make much sense to Martha—"especially when we got slapped with a big fine if we tried to skip" a philanthropic activity. In my experience, nobody ever joined a sorority because she wanted to do some good for the world. That's bull. At least 99.9 percent of girls join sororities for the social aspects."

"Also, it was hypocritical," Martha continues. "These girls promise to be your sisters forever. But I guess it's like any group—some good, some bad. A lot of them were really catty. You never knew who they'd turn on next—other sororities, fraternities, or our own sisters. I found myself constantly doing P.R., just to make sure I was still in good standing with these people who were supposed to love me!"

Also disturbing to Martha were some activities she considered degrading. "We had this one Spirit Contest, sponsored by one of the supposedly best fraternities, where we basically had to go and scream spirit chants—you know, 'WE'VE GOT SPIRIT, YES WE DO, WE'VE GOT SPIRIT, HOW 'BOUT YOU?'—until we were hoarse, and put on a talent contest to show how much 'spirit' we had. We worked so hard, and we all pulled together. That part was good. But we came to find out later that it wasn't a real contest, which was devastating. They had already picked the sorority house that was going to win, and it wasn't ours.

"A few weeks later, we had a Greek Spirit Sing contest, where we had the big privilege of serenading a fraternity whose reputation was that they were a group of Southern gentlemen. Not! Most of the guys were so drunk when they got to the quad (where our house was) that some of them urinated against the side of our building, and they were shouting comments and laughing while we were standing there, trying to sing this routine we'd rehearsed for a week. Some girls cried afterwards. I felt like a prostitute."

Greek life also costs money. Dues, special assessments, pledge and initiation fees, gifts, party favors, photographs, and other miscellaneous items can run several hundred dollars a year, on average.

The potentially most damaging aspect of all is the danger Greek societies pose of perpetuating a questionable set of values. Too often, Greek life seems to place a premium on superficial qualities like conformity and gloss, which starts with Rush Week and, for some, never ends. Not every Greek organization is like this, but many are.

So, should you pledge? Only you can answer that question. Note: Beware of anyone—your parents, friends—who wants to make this decision for you. There's a certain snobbishness among some Greeks, sure. But there's also a reverse snob appeal, an anti-Greek sentiment that can be equally vicious and unfair.

The bottom line. If you feel comfortable with a particular group of people and think you would enjoy their activities and fellowship, then join. If you feel uneasy about all or even part of it, then don't. Wait a while. Neither decision is permanent—you can always consider pledging, or "depledging" (getting out of a sorority or fraternity) later.

A few tips:

- **Don't pledge blind.** Don't join a fraternity or sorority (or anything, for that matter) until you feel you really know something about the group. This means doing some homework. If possible, before you go through Rush, ask friends or older classmates from your high school who've gone to the same college for their opinions on various Greek organizations.

  At every campus, each fraternity and sorority has a general reputation—they're "the jock house" or a bunch of party animals, druggies, achievers, nerds. *(Note: As always, beware of these and any generalizations and make your own judgments about each group—but do keep them in mind.* It's far better to know exactly what you're getting into

"Most of the guys were so drunk that some of them urinated against the side of our building, and they were shouting comments and laughing while we were standing there, trying to sing this routine we'd rehearsed for a week. Some girls cried afterwards. I felt like a prostitute."

than to say one day with dismay to your fellow pledges, "What? This is the druggie house?") This may even require a delay in your going through Rush until you've lived on campus a while and seen all the Greeks in action. Rush Week, with all its emotional intensity and excitement, can be a terrible time to attempt to make a rational decision.

- **Don't pledge a certain sorority or fraternity just because your mom or dad once belonged and you feel pressured to continue the family tradition.** Greek organizations are uneven from chapter to chapter. The Kappa Sigmas at one campus, for example, may rule; at another campus, they could be the pits. Greek houses undergo massive personality changes from one year to the next. There's no way your dad's old lodge you heard so much about can be the same today as it was a generation ago.

- **One bad Rush can set a depressing chain of events in motion; one good Rush can change a chapter's fortunes.** Also, every fraternity and sorority has its legacies, and some of them are colossal misfits. Maybe Dad was a cool Greek, but Junior's a total geek. Therefore, look over all the houses carefully. Then, if you do pledge the family fraternity or sorority, you'll be sure you did it for the right reason—because you really wanted to.

- **Beware of rushing alumni.** Sometimes, if a chapter is having a particularly hard time, it might bring in some ringers—alumni or active members from other campuses—to help out during Rush. They're supposed to have some helpful designation on name tags, but they may not. One easy way to tell is to look at the big composite picture—the big framed "yearbook," with individual mug shots of all the members. If you're being rushed by a house of thirty, and there's only twelve people on the composite, get suspicious.

CHAPTER 11

DATING AND OTHER GAMES

First of all, lighten up.

Here is as good a place as any to add this bit of advice: *Don't look at every member of the opposite sex as a potential girlfriend or boyfriend, and don't think of every person you date as your future mate for life.*

Lydia, for example, a University of Maryland student, doesn't get asked out much. Also, since she never does the asking (it wouldn't be "ladylike," she believes) it's always up to some guy to make this first move. But on those rare occasions when she does get asked out, it's not unusual for her either not to accept or to find something wrong with the guy right away.

"Once, I had some doubts about a guy I had dated for a few months, so I had my mother come down from New York to meet him." Naturally, Mother didn't think this guy was good enough for her little girl and quickly made Lydia see this—and, like the dutiful daughter she is, Lydia promptly cut herself off from this poor guy, whose only crime had been to see something promising in Lydia that made him want to know her better. Lydia actually has a list of criteria for the perfect man. If the guy is not a potential marriage candidate, Lydia isn't even interested; it wouldn't be a good use of her time.

Therefore, because her time is so precious, Lydia spends a lot of Saturday nights eating popcorn and watching TV in her dorm room. She misses out on a lot of fun because she's such a snob. And fewer "eligible" men are showing an interest in her. Why should they? If she doesn't watch out, she's going to be alone for the rest of her life because Mr. Perfect never came along. But there were lots of Mr. Pretty Goods and even a few Mr. Greats—and one of them could have turned out to be Mr. Right.

This is what we would like to say to Lydia: Wise up, honey! You don't have to marry the person or become joined at the hip. Just enjoy your contact with that individual for what it is. One date doesn't have to lead anywhere or even enrich your life. You can be friends without becoming romantically involved. You can even be good friends. Or, you can just be acquaintances. (If you're not destined to become buddies or fall in love, it doesn't follow that you have to dislike each other or become enemies. Your conversation, or date, or chance encounter doesn't have to be a peak or valley on the Richter scale that is your life—it could just be a "blip" on your personal radar screen. Blip, he's gone. That was mediocre. Now move on.)

It's a sad thing that so many people won't even try to get to know, much less go on a date with, another student who is not a jock, or preppy, or Deadhead, or some other trite stereotype that can be summed up in one word—whatever he or she is looking for in a spouse. It's entirely possible (and definitely a lot more relaxing) to have a cup of coffee or play Putt-Putt golf or go see a movie with someone without worrying about your "future" life together.

Lighten up! You're a freshman, for crying out loud! You don't want to get bogged down too soon in a romance—it can be devastating this early in your college career, particularly if you become "lovebirds" and isolate yourselves from everyone else. Have a little foresight: If it's meant to be, you'll be together forever. But if it's not, and you break up, you're going to be alone in many respects, primarily because your self-imposed isolation will have kept you from making any other friends. What will you do if you put all your eggs in one basket and suddenly that basket's gone? You'll have to start over again from scratch.

Go out in groups. Groups are good. For one thing, going out in a group lets you see how he or she acts around other people. If she's a total clod, for instance, or a psycho, this might be more obvious when you're sitting around a table with six other people having pizza than when you're making out in somebody's dorm room. (And, you can extricate yourself from the relationship nice and early.) Or if you're not sure about him (see "Date Rape Really Happens," page 197), going out in a group is safer and wiser; things tend not to get out of hand, because you're not alone. *Our advice: If you're going to become serious, do it slowly. Get to know each other in safe, casual settings.*

Find cheap ways to have fun. Because so many students share the same condition—they don't have a lot of money—you should feel absolutely no embarrassment about being unable to entertain your date in the grand manner. So you can't afford escargots at the Chateau. So what?

DATES ON $5 OR LESS

At Gordon College in Wenham, Massachusetts, resourceful students, in the hallowed tradition of impoverished scholars everywhere, compiled a list of 50 suggestions for dates that cost less than $5 each. Here are some of their ideas:

- Cheer on the basketball team
- Attend a free concert or recital
- Make a late-night coffee date or a breakfast date to start the morning
- Take a scenic drive
- Support your local campus artists by attending a showing
- Share a pizza
- Get tickets for a campus play, movie, or variety show
- Invite someone over for Monopoly and popcorn
- See a movie in the afternoon before the prices go up
- Spend 19 quarters on video games
- Browse around a local shopping center or mall
- Play Ping-Pong in the dormitory
- Take a study break at a nearby snack shop
- Play tennis
- Fly a kite in the park
- Have a picnic at a quiet spot
- Play miniature golf
- Skate on the ice rink
- Hike through a nearby forest
- Stage a snowball fight
- Try canoeing or rock-climbing
- Spend a day at the beach of a nearby state park

Don't get stuck on the idea of dazzling or impressing your dates; charming them is less important than just communicating with them. With a little imagination, you can have fun on even the most severely limited budget. (In fact, if you look at it as a challenge, not a handicap, you may wind up doing much more interesting things than the boring old "dinner and a movie" or "night on the town." Make it an adventure: "Hey, I've got a coupon for a free dessert at Cappucino Cafe. Want to go?")

Going Dutch is a treat. That is, unless one or both of you would feel your principles—in other words, your ideas about the roles men and women are supposed to play in dating—were being compromised. (In which case we say: "Oink! Wake up, pal! It's the nineties! It's okay if she pays! It's okay if he doesn't pay every time! It's okay if you always split the check right down the middle!")

Going Dutch almost certainly beats spending a lonely Saturday night in your cold dorm room with only your pride for company, while she's doing the same in hers. There's no shame in pooling your resources. In fact, it makes a lot of sense. Another possibility: take turns paying. You cover all the expenses for one date, and let her pay next time. (*Hint: Try to work out the details in advance, so you can avoid a mood-dampening discussion over who picks up the check!*)

You're probably going to find that college is a pretty informal and unpretentious place, despite the fancy image many outsiders have of it. Most college students are broke at some point or another; for some, poverty is a more or less continuous condition.

Let's face it: If all dating waited until students had ample funds and could entertain in what they considered to be first-class style, very few people would ever go anywhere.

Ladies, one nice bonus about going Dutch: Pay your way and have your say. Of course, you should always have your own say anyway. We know that. You probably know that. But a lot of women—encouraged by a lot of jerks—are made to feel they owe the man some reward, and we think you know what we mean here, for being taken out on an expensive date. As if money correlates with other favors.

A college junior we know—we'll call her Sandra—was out on a double date recently. Her date was Ben; her friend, Carla, went along with her boyfriend, Jeff. One evening, at the end of a very nice dinner and show at a nightclub in Cincinnati, Jeff actually pulled Sandra aside and said, "You know, Ben is really disappointed that he didn't get more from you—after all, the guy spent more than 100 bucks on dinner tonight!" Hey. So, to recap: Not only did Ben think he didn't get enough for his money, he proceeded to discuss the situation with his friend, Jeff. What a pig. (To make it worse, Carla, who was already sleeping with Jeff—and who, perhaps, was threatened by the fact that Sandra wasn't having sex with Ben—agreed that her friend should express her gratitude in a more generous way!)

Sandra felt hurt and angry at all of them. She whipped out her checkbook, wrote Ben a check for $60 (a sum, by the way, she couldn't really afford; it was about half of her bank balance)—"That should cover the tip, too," she said—and added, "Sleep with this!" (Or words to that effect.)

You're high school sweethearts going to the same college: Should you get married now?

No, absolutely not. Forget it.

Oh yeah, we forgot—both of the writers of this book got married when they were students. (Ron was in graduate school, and he was slightly older than most students—he'd worked for five years after college before going back to school. Janet, however, got married to a medical student right before starting her senior year in college.) In both cases, the difficulties—being poor, trying to make good grades, and make the marriages work—actually made the relationships stronger. But other student couples, friends of ours, haven't been so lucky; their marriages haven't lasted. Maybe they wouldn't have anyway—maybe the college environment wasn't a factor in their breakups; then again, maybe it was. It's probably safe to say that being in college didn't help their marriages too much.

Everybody's different. Some people are as mature, centered, and emotionally healthy at age 18 as people several times their age. Others, on a good day, have about as much maturity, personal depth, and sensitivity as Beavis and/or Butt-head.

No matter how wise and mature you feel now—and we say this gently and with the utmost respect for your dignity and personal maturity—you're still pretty young. You haven't seen that much of the world yet. Now, the dawn of your freshman year, is one of the most exciting times of your life. You know—or at least, having read

HAS YOUR FUTURE SPOUSE CUT THE CORD TO HIS OR HER PARENTS YET?

Does he or she relate to them as an adult, or is it still "Daddy's little girl," or "Mamma's boy"?

Danger!

Will your future in-laws (or your own parents—be honest) have something to say about every decision you make in the marriage (and will your future spouse be overly swayed by their opinions)? Will they get a detailed account of every aspect of your married life? Will they try to interfere financially or have a say in such intensely personal decisions as when you should start a family, what jobs you should take when you graduate, or even where you should go on your vacations?

Look long and hard at those relationships, too. Be prepared to stand up for yourself—and fight for your marriage—by nipping such meddling in the bud.

Are you secure enough, in yourself and your future spouse, to do this—to establish your own independence as a couple? If not, your marriage may be in big trouble. Do the words "living hell" or "end of life as you know it" have any meaning for you at all?

"Mamma says you're not feeding me balanced meals."

"Daddy says you're not ambitious enough—you should work harder."

"Mamma says if you loved me, you'd give up this crazy

idea of a Ph.D. and go to work for Uncle Jimmy at the company. He's got a job all lined up for you."

"Daddy says he read this article in *USA TODAY* on couples who couldn't get pregnant, and you should start wearing boxer shorts. What do you mean, how does he know you don't wear them?"

Give college a chance to do what it's supposed to do. Wait and get married next year, or better yet, the year after that, or the year after that.

this far, you should have a big clue—that you're probably going to change this year. You're probably going to be a different person at the end of this year than you were at the beginning. You won't be able to help it—when people get exposed to new ideas and experiences, they tend to grow. This is good. It's what's supposed to happen. It's what college is all about.

Give yourself the opportunity to experience all this. Give college a chance to do what it's supposed to do. Get married next year, or better yet, the year after that, or the year after that. If it's truly meant to be, your true love isn't going anywhere. And give him or her the chance to grow and change, too—doesn't your future spouse deserve that chance? By the time you're both seniors, you'll have a much clearer idea of what you want to do with your life (besides just "being together forever").

Say, for example, you both want to go to graduate school. Will you both be able to get into the same school? What if he wants to go to journalism school at the University of Missouri, while you want to go to medical school at Johns Hopkins? Who wins? Who sacrifices? If you both get what you want, can the marriage survive the next several years apart? Take some time to consider the big plan for both your lives and tread carefully—this is a big life choice you're making here.

"I frankly tell students that the odds are against a successful marriage in this situation," says one college counselor. "The problems with any marriage—problems with money, sex, in-laws—seem to be intensified in a college marriage. There's also the matter of getting used to each other, insisting that one spouse behave the way the other spouse wants him or her to. The behavior patterns of college students are obviously different in many ways from those of high school students."

Married college students, he continues, "work all day, then come home at night—with hours of studying they know they ought to do—and they are exhausted. Some men thought they were impotent, but, after a vacation, they found they were not. They had just been working too hard. The old story of getting your degree and your divorce at the same time is too often true here."

Another counselor at a different college put it this way: "The first years of our lives are spent in what might be called the 'dependent' stage. Next comes the 'independent' period, a time for spreading wings, for exploring, for thinking and acting on one's own. Marriage represents still another stage, that of 'interdependence.' Until now, any young person has probably thought of the world in terms of 'me.' But after marriage, it's supposed to become 'we.' 'We' is the operational unit for planning, for socializing, for earning and spending money, for everything. Many students aren't ready to begin thinking as 'we' just yet, which suggests they may not be mature enough to sustain a marriage relationship."

So, in addition to everything else you need to be thinking about, it's probably pretty important for you to know where you and your spouse-to-be are on this dependent/independent/interdependent scale before you contemplate a college marriage—or a marriage of any kind.

DON'T BE STUPID: A FEW WORDS ON HAVING SEX

This decision—to have a sex life or not—is about as personal as it gets, and it's a choice only you can make. But, like any important decision, it should be an informed one. There's a lot to think about here—and, in these days of AIDS, it can concern not just your health and well-being but your life.

We hope you know by now that sex isn't an event that just happens all by itself. Pardon us for borrowing from song lyrics, but for every "Some Enchanted Evening" . . . "There's Got to Be a Morning After." There are consequences, even if you use condoms or various other methods of birth control (a detailed discussion that we're not going to get into in this book!).

Pregnancy

It could happen, no matter how careful you are. Ladies, are you prepared to deal with an unexpected pregnancy? How would you take care of a baby? Would you give it up? Would your family support your decision? Could you deal with the emotional, moral, and spiritual ramifications of having an abortion? What would all this do to your education, your career, your life?

How would you take care of a baby? Would you give it up? Would your family support your decision?

MORE INFO ON HIV

To learn more about HIV and where to get the test in your town, call your local health department, or 1-800-342-AIDS (English language) or 1-800-342-SIDA (Spanish language). Also, you can call AmFAR (the American Foundation for AIDS Research), a nonprofit group whose work includes getting information to, and protecting the rights of, people with HIV and AIDS at 1-800-39-AMFAR.

TRIALS AND TREATMENT OPTIONS

To find out more about participating in a clinical trial, ask your doctor or clinic or call 1-800-TRIALS-A.

Also, a toll-free telephone reference service called ATIS is available for people with HIV who want to know more about treatment options. That number is: 1-800-HIV-0440 (TDD/Deaf Access: 1-800-243-7012).

Gentlemen, are you ready to be a father? Or to let somebody else raise your kid if it's given up for adoption? Could you handle it emotionally if your girlfriend had an abortion?

AIDS

Briefly, here's what you need to know: AIDS stands for Acquired Immune Deficiency Syndrome, a disease caused by HIV (human immunodeficiency virus), a virus that knocks out the body's ability to fight infections, ultimately leaving someone powerless when attacked by illnesses that otherwise would be thrown off easily. Everything—a stranger's cough, a baby's runny nose—becomes a potential health risk.

Your perspective changes. Ultimately, your central focus inevitably shifts from, say, spending the next 30 to 40 years of your life as a lawyer, or accountant, or social worker, having a family, making something of yourself, accomplishing great things, to simply beating the clock to just staying alive and keeping healthy.

Note: This doesn't mean that life is over for someone who tests positive for AIDS. Far from it. People who are infected with the AIDS virus can live for 10 to even 20 years; with new and better forms of treatment—most exciting are new drugs called protease inhibitors—it's reasonable to expect an even brighter prognosis in the future. But your perspective changes—it has to—from that of someone who may never have valued good health to that of someone with a chronic illness. Many college students, if they think about the long haul at all, tend to think, "I've got the rest of my life to do whatever I want." Whereas many people with the AIDS virus may think, "I've got maybe 20 more years. I want to make them all count."

Who gets AIDS? Well, technically, nobody's immune to the disease; anybody who has sex or uses IV (intravenous) drugs could get it. HIV is spread through sexual contact when infected body fluids (notably semen and blood) are introduced into the body of another person. In this country, AIDS is passed along most commonly by gay or bisexual men (mainly through anal sex) and among IV drug users who share dirty needles. Increasingly, as an AIDS expert from the National Institutes of Health points out, it is affecting the women who have sex with these men. Don't think, "I'm a woman, I can't get it," or "I'm a heterosexual man, I can't get it." Sure you can.

In the past, a tiny number of people with AIDS got it when they received transfusions of infected blood. Now, with vastly better techniques of testing and treating transfused blood, your risk of getting AIDS through a blood transfusion is practically nonexistent. AIDS can also be transmitted during sexual intercourse (in the seminal and vaginal fluids). In Africa and many other parts of the world, this is very much a heterosexual disease, with about equal numbers of men and women infected with AIDS.

Some groups of people, by the nature of their activities, are at much higher risk of getting AIDS than others. They include the following:

- Homosexual males (not involved in monogamous relationships) and bisexual males
- IV drug users
- Prostitutes, male and female
- Any man or woman who has, or has had, many sex partners
- Any man or woman who has contracted other sexually transmitted diseases

Is there such a thing as safe sex?

In his book *Safe Sex in a Dangerous World*, Dr. Art Ulene says that " 'truly safe sex' is an all-or-nothing thing. Sex is either 100 percent safe or it's not, even when it's 'almost safe.' If you can't find a safe partner (one who has never been infected with the AIDS virus), don't kid yourself into believing that there is a perfectly safe alternative—other than abstinence."

Condoms, as Dr. Ulene and others have pointed out, are not perfect. They may be put on incorrectly, they can slip off, they can tear or break or leak. A number of women—perhaps as high as 10 percent—who use condoms as their sole means of birth control find this out every year, when they get pregnant. It makes sense that people who use condoms for AIDS prevention are similarly at risk.

Tip: Until you know for sure, just assume your sexual partner has it and take precautions. Sometimes, people lie about things—like who and how many people they've slept with. Sometimes, people don't know things, like

THE NUMBERS ARE SCARY

The World Health Organization estimates that by the year 2000, more than 40 million people worldwide will be HIV-positive; an estimated 1.5 *million* people in the United States are infected with HIV. Unfortunately, the vast majority of those people probably don't realize they're carrying—and passing on—a time bomb. A 1994 article in the *Journal of NIH Research* described AIDS as a "13-year-old epidemic that continues to reinvent itself in creatively malevolent ways. From the meanest street to the most impregnable ivory tower, no one is sure how bad it really is or is going to get."

So, what does this mean to you, Joe or Jane college student? "If I'm careful and practice safe sex and use protective devices," you may be telling yourself, "I won't get AIDS." Yeah, probably.

However, it may also oversimplify the situation. Many people (including a lot of health officials) have bought into the notion that devices like condoms and spermicides are to AIDS what strings of garlic and the cross are to Dracula; they offer total, complete, absolute protection. That's why condom dispensers are showing up everywhere—in restaurants, on college campuses, in malls.

OTHER SEXUALLY TRANSMITTED DISEASES (STDs)

Gonorrhea and syphilis haven't gone anywhere; they've just been bumped out of the limelight by AIDS. They're still around, they're still serious, and you can still catch them. According to the Alan Guttmacher Institute, an estimated 12 million new STDs occur every year, and two-thirds of them are among women and men under age 25. At current rates, the institute predicts, at least one person in four will contract an STD at some point in life.

Other STDs out there include:

- Human papilloma virus (HPV), which may manifest itself in genital warts, and which, in women, may be deadly—it could lead to cervical cancer
- Chlamydia, which, if not treated, can damage a woman's reproductive organs and result in sterility
- Genital herpes (like HPV, this can be "the gift that keeps on giving")
- Trichomoniasis, which, in men, can lead to painful infections in the prostate and urethra
- Hepatitis B, which can cause major liver problems and may even be fatal; there is a vaccine available, and doctors strongly recommend it for anyone who plans to be sexually active. For more on this, see Chapter Twelve.

the fact that their last sexual partner occasionally used IV drugs. Sometimes, people have weird ideas—like one guy we talked to who thinks "if I have sex with men, but I also have sex with women, I must not be gay, therefore I can't be at risk for AIDS."

Get the point? You can't be sure, so be safe. Don't do IV drugs. If you're going to have sex, have the safest sex you can. Wear a latex condom (animal skin is more porous and therefore easier for the virus to get through). Use it correctly. And, advises an AIDS expert from the National Institutes of Health, "use a different one for each act—don't reuse them." In addition, experts advise that you use a spermicide with an ingredient called nonoxynol-9, which may also protect against other sexually transmitted diseases (STDs) like chlamydia and gonorrhea.

Also, avoid anal sex (the tissues in the rectum are thinner and crack open or tear more easily). Although it's become kind of a cliché, remember that you're not just having sex with your partner; you're sleeping with all the other people your partner has ever slept with. (Which is kind of gross, if you really think about it.) You take on their histories, reflecting their previous decisions, some of which may have been really stupid and careless.

You could pay dearly—with your health and/or your life—for somebody else's stupidity.

Promiscuity is bad for a lot of reasons. It also raises your odds of getting AIDS or another STD. If abstinence is not an acceptable choice for you, then it's absolutely essential that you take the steps mentioned above to keep your AIDS risk to a minimum. Until there's a cure (which doesn't look to be anytime soon; the AIDS virus continues to stump the brightest minds in the world medical community) then using latex condoms and avoiding IV drugs are good defenses, and abstinence is the best defense of all.

Note: Birth control doesn't mean "disease prevention." While the pill, diaphragm, IUD, and spermicides might be good (or fair) contraceptives, they don't do much to prevent the transmission of disease. Only latex condoms have been proven to block the spread of disease from one partner to another—and even then, only if they're used correctly.

Who should get tested for AIDS?

According to the National Institute of Allergy and Infectious Diseases, the branch of the National Institutes of Health (NIH) that handles AIDS, you should think about having the AIDS test if you answer "yes" to any of the following questions: Have you ever:

- Had sex without knowing for sure if the person you had sex with does not have HIV?
- Had sex with someone you know has HIV or AIDS?
- Had a disease passed on by sex, like genital herpes or syphilis? (Having these diseases makes it easier to get HIV.)
- Had sex with many men or women or had sex with someone who has had sex with many men or women?
- Had sex with someone who has used needles to take drugs?
- Shared needles to take drugs?

Information about the HIV test

An expert at the NIH has this advice for anyone thinking of getting the test: "First, find an anonymous test site, where no one knows your name and your results won't get on any records—school, medical insurance, etc. You should be offered pretest and posttest counseling. If your testing site won't do these things, go someplace else."

HIV is diagnosed very carefully. If the first blood test, called ELISA, is positive (in other words, if it shows signs of HIV), your blood will be tested again. If the second test is positive, another kind of test, called a Western blot, will be done to confirm the result. Nobody should make a definitive diagnosis of HIV in your blood based on a lone test.

If the test is positive. This simply means that your blood has signs of HIV. It does not mean that you have AIDS. Many people who test positive for HIV don't get symptoms of AIDS for eight to ten years, or even longer, after the virus infects them.

What a positive test does mean, however, according to experts at the NIH, is that you need to do two things: Avoid giving the virus to anybody else and take good care of your own health. (Note: Having safe sex and not sharing drug needles is just as important now as ever. After you're diagnosed with HIV, such activities can

GUYS WHO ACT LIKE IDIOTS

A recent study by the University of Minnesota Hospital and Clinics found something surprising: Many teenage and college-age guys know the facts about AIDS but don't take precautions. In other words, there are a bunch of idiots out there playing Russian roulette with their sex lives.

Even though they knew what to do to protect themselves against the disease, more than 60 percent of the 239 young men surveyed went ahead and participated in dangerous sexual behavior and were considered at "extreme risk" for exposure to HIV, the AIDS virus.

This strikes us as particularly stupid because AIDS is completely preventable!

And yet, the study's leader said, "Some teens have a fatalistic view about AIDS. They believe they will get AIDS, regardless, because they are gay." And therefore, they feel it's useless to fight it.

That's like saying, "There are cars on the road, I'm going to get hit by one; therefore, because it's inevitable and there's nothing I can do to change my destiny, I won't look both ways when I cross the street."

Also, many of the young men said they were hesitant to ask their partners to use condoms because they are shy or don't want to "spoil the mood."

Okay, let's get out the old scale: What weighs more—"spoiling the mood" or dying a horrible death from a wasting-away disease for which there is no cure? Figure it out for yourself. Take charge of your life and your health; don't leave it up to somebody else, and don't worry about something so very inconsequential in the grand scheme as "spoiling the mood."

MORE INFO ON STDs

You can write: National Institute of Allergy and Infectious Diseases, National Institutes of Health, Building 31, Room 7A50, 9000 Rockville Pike, Bethesda, MD 20892-0031, or call (301) 496-5717 or check online at www.nih.gov.

make your situation worse by exposing you to diseases that could threaten your health.)

Find out about clinical trials. In a relatively short time—a decade—scientists have made incredible progress in the fight against AIDS, and many new medicines are being developed to help people with HIV. You may be able to take part in a research study, called a clinical trial, to test one of these new treatments.

SMART THINKING ABOUT RAPE

Think it can't happen to you? Wake up; it can. The numbers are scary: One out of every four American women, according to FBI projections, will be the victim of rape or sexual assault in her lifetime.

Rape is the fastest-growing crime of violence in the country. Between 1977 and 1986, the number of rapes increased by 42 percent.

Given the statistics, you'd think colleges and universities would be able to do a lot better job of preventing rape than most of them do. Unfortunately, the typical campus police force is at minimal strength, especially in these austere budgetary times. And the typical "Barney Fife" campus cop is much better at writing parking citations (and, of course, eating doughnuts) than preventing crimes. Campuses are not well lighted. Those beautifully secluded spots, landscaped in a more innocent era, are made-to-order for a would-be attacker; they provide excellent cover and opportunity.

In many cities, students who rent apartments near the campus find themselves living in neighborhoods populated by transients, where strangers aren't noticed as they would be in more settled parts of town; where nobody cares who belongs to an apartment building and who doesn't.

So, ladies—be alert, be careful, don't take stupid chances, don't be naive. To quote every football coach we've ever heard, "The best defense is a good offense." (See "Steps you can take," below.)

And don't count on other people to take care of you in social situations—especially if you and others are drinking or taking drugs.

Steps you can take to minimize your chances of rape

When you walk:

- Be sociable. Take a friend along whenever possible.
- Don't gamble. If you're not sure an area's safe, take the long way around—not the shortcut through the trees.
- Walk with a purpose. Look confident, even if you aren't.
- Take help if you can get it. Many schools have security guards or student volunteers who will walk women home late at night.
- Don't hitchhike. Ever.

In your car:

- Do basic maintenance. Keep your car in good working order and always, always, have at least five bucks' worth of gas in the car (at least a quarter-tank).
- Lock your doors. When you're driving or parked.
- Have your keys ready. Don't spend five minutes turning your purse inside out as you stand unprotected beside your car.
- Park in well-lighted areas.
- Check the back seat before you get in.
- Don't open your window for anyone, particularly panhandlers, at traffic stops.
- If someone pulls alongside you, warning frantically about some problem like "flames shooting from the back of your car," assume they're lying. DO NOT STOP. Drive to the nearest exit and find a service station. A still-unsolved string of rape-murders of young women in central Virginia centers around a "Good Samaritan" from hell who pretends concern for some faked auto emergency, offers the women—all of them, alone in their car, all of them on the petite side—a lift for help. Sometimes he even uses a flashing blue light, and pretends to be a cop.
- If a plain-clothes policeman stops you, leave your door locked and ask to see his ID. If it's in the middle of a deserted area and you feel extremely uncomfortable stopping, put your flashers on to

COULD DATE RAPE HAPPEN TO YOU? FOUR DANGER SIGNALS

(From the National Organization for Victim Assistance)

- Watch out when your relationship seems to be operating along classic stereotypes—of dominant male and submissive female. The "Me Tarzan, you Jane" scenario just doesn't cut it in the real world. Some men, particularly in adolescence, are very domineering—they need to make women feel small or inadequate just to assert themselves and make themselves feel more important. Does this sound familiar? Your boyfriend orders for you in a restaurant, plans every date activity, and always gets his way. If this is the case, it may be that he will do the same thing in an intimate setting.
- Watch out when your date tries to control your behavior in any way—for example, trying to restrict the people you meet or forcing you to do something (as silly as ordering a particular entree when you go out to eat, or deciding what video you're both going to watch for the evening) you don't want to do.

  Be especially careful when a man pressures you—and when he's betting that you'll be too embarrassed to tell mutual friends about it, or that you wouldn't be believed. Every time a little incident like this happens, it takes a little chink out of your wall of independence and makes you just a little more vulnerable.

- Make sure your signals are clear. Don't send ambiguous messages. For example, if you're making out, don't say you don't want to go any further—and then start making out again. What are you really saying here? If you've made a decision not to have sex, then be clear about it up front; this may keep things from getting difficult (and your signals from being misunderstood) later.
- On a first date, try to go with a group.

Most rapes aren't committed by psychos in ski masks who stalk women on dark streets.

signal that you intend to obey, drive SLOWLY (so there's no mistaking this for a high-speed chase), and stop where there are people around. Because of some police impostors (like the one discussed above), most savvy state troopers understand why women are afraid to stop.

When you jog:

- Run with a partner, if you can. If you can't, see if you can borrow a friend's dog. The exercise will do you both good.
- Vary your route.
- Jog in populated areas. Okay, it may not be as scenic as the rural route, but somebody's more likely to hear you if you scream.
- Get to know people in your neighborhood in case of an emergency.

In social situations:

- Don't be mysterious. Let your roommate, friends, or even your parents know where you're going—and with whom—and when you expect to be home.
- Develop a support system. If you see a friend—or anyone, for that matter—being pushed or talked into something she doesn't want, help her. (Offer a ride home, for instance.)
- Don't be stupid. Think about it: If you're drinking or taking drugs, it's going to be harder to use good judgment, particularly in unfamiliar situations. If your date is drinking excessively or the situation's getting out of hand, get out of the situation as soon as possible and find another way home. If you're scared, disappear; no apologies, no explanations—and no opportunity for argument or arm-twisting. Do something you wouldn't ordinarily do in more polite company: Excuse yourself to go to the bathroom (be sure to take your purse), call a cab or friend to pick you up, then find the bartender or bouncer (preferably, a guy built like a tank), and see if you can wait in the kitchen or office for your ride to come. (Note: No matter how nice they seem, don't let the bartender or bouncer give you a ride home; you might just be exchanging one trouble

for another. As a general rule, it's safer not to let too many people know exactly where you live.)

If you're being stalked: If there's the slightest possibility that someone is taking an unhealthy interest in you and may be stalking you, play it safe: Tell EVERYBODY. (Remember, as Hillary Clinton says, it takes a village. Let your own village—your dorm neighbors and friends—help keep an eye on you.) Start with your roommate, your RA, the campus police, and even the local police. Tell your parents, who can put pressure on your school to take steps to help protect you. There is a lot you can do, including getting a restraining order against the stalker, if necessary. The main thing is to put your friends on alert. The net effect of this is to make the stalker, in a sense, radioactive—so he or she can't get anywhere near you without a dozen people's radar screens being activated. Get a buddy or campus escort to walk with you in secluded areas or at night. Do the common-sense things: Keep yourself out of vulnerable situations (see "Steps You Can Take"); don't lower your guard with drugs or alcohol. Keep the door to your room locked at all times—even when you're in it, unless there are a lot of people nearby and you want to socialize. Be completely unavailable. Screen your calls, either by letting your roommate, voice mail, or an answering machine answer the phone. In class, sit with friends, or—if you don't know anybody there—park yourself right up front, under the professor's nose. Your best protection is never to give him or her a chance to get at you. Maybe the stalker will get over it; or maybe he or she will transfer the unwanted attention to someone who's a lot more accessible.

Date rape really happens

Beware of strangers. That's a given. And follow the steps listed under "Steps you can take to minimize your chances of rape," on page 195.

Most rapes aren't committed by psychos in ski masks who stalk women on dark streets. Instead, they're committed by respectable-looking guys you might know well enough to go out with socially. Date rape is a big problem on college campuses, and the numbers are growing. Increasing numbers of college women have been forced by acquaintances and dates to have sexual relations against their will.

SECOND CHANCE

"Looking back," says Jayne, a student at the University of Kentucky, "it terrifies me to think about how close I came to being raped. It wasn't the middle of the night, either—it was broad daylight. I was so drunk, I didn't know what I was doing.

"I can't believe I was so stupid," Jayne continues. "I was at a football game with my friends and a guy I particularly wanted to impress. We had all been drinking, and I fell down some steps and ripped my tights. So I decided to zip back to my sorority house and put on a new pair.

"I didn't tell anybody where I was going. I left the stadium and stepped out in the street, in front of the first car that came by, and hitched a ride. There were two scuzzy guys in the car. I thought I was so cute—I sat on one guy's lap, and gave him directions on how to get to the sorority house.

"It was Homecoming, and everybody—I mean everybody—was at the game. The campus was deserted. It didn't dawn on me that I might be in any danger until we reached the sorority house and they came inside with me. The house was completely empty. Even in my drunken state, I was dimly aware that something wasn't right as we got up to my room.

"I opened the door and saw the most beautiful sight in the world—the six-foot, five-inch tall boyfriend of my roommate! My roommate is one of those people who is always late, and even the Homecoming game was no exception. She was still getting ready, and John, her massive boyfriend, was sitting there waiting on her. Thank God! He took one look at me and at those guys and told them to get lost. But the really scary part is that they followed us all the way back to the stadium.

"I'll never be that out-of-control again."

The bottom line is that a lot of men—deliberately or otherwise—have trouble reading a woman's signals.

Drinking lowers your shield. It diminishes your ability to look out for yourself. It makes you vulnerable. Combine a drug—any drug—with that, and you may not be able to stop something bad from happening.

A recent study of 6,500 students, funded by the National Institute on Mental Health and conducted by Professor Mary Koss of Kent State University, found that more than 10 percent of coeds questioned—about 1 out of 8—had been forced to have sex without their consent. In this study, 9 out of every 10 students who had been raped knew the men who did it. Nearly half of these sexual assaults, 47 percent, were committed by first dates or romantic acquaintances.

Another disturbing revelation. While a number of the men interviewed admitted having forcible sex with unwilling partners, none was willing to identify himself as a rapist.

The bottom line is that a lot of men—deliberately or otherwise—have trouble reading a woman's signals. They think "no" means she's being coy, playing hard to get. "Some men have the capacity to fool themselves into thinking date rape is normal behavior," one clinical psychologist at Ohio State said in an interview in *The New York Times*. "They believe the myth that when a woman says no, she really means yes." And that they're just "man enough" to change her mind. Yuck.

This and other mistaken notions are being dealt with in conferences on campuses around the country. In one such seminar, held at the University of Wisconsin and sponsored by a group called Men Stopping Rape, women and men acted out anxieties and frustrations they typically experienced on dates.

Guess what emerged as a major triggering cause of date rape? A communication breakdown. Ironically, during these discussions, a number of women felt that they were to blame, for overlooking some character flaw in their dates or using poor judgment. They wondered what they had said or done to provoke the assault.

This clearly misplaced sense of guilt may be one reason that the overwhelming majority of date rape victims compound their problem by not talking about it—to friends and counselors who could offer support. Nine out of 10 cases of date rape are never reported to the police.

The "Date Rape" Pill

It's called Rohypnol, but the street name for this sedative is "roofies." It's a sedative, banned in the United States but available on the street, particularly in Florida, Texas and California—get this—TEN TIMES more powerful than Valium. (The drug was originally intended as a treatment for insomnia, and as a sedative to be taken before surgery). It dissolves easily in the drink of an unsuspecting person, who wakes up with no memory of what happened a few hours before—not even if it was rape. Recently, cases of "roofie rape" have made the news, and the stories sound like nightmares: An evil jerk slips the drug into a girl's drink. She gets dizzy and disoriented, and has trouble moving her arms and legs. Finally, she passes out, unable to stop what happens next.

Hoffman-LaRoche, the maker of the drug, has launched a campaign to fight its abuse, producing radio, TV and print public service ads in English and Spanish, and offering free urine testing kits for law enforcement. In one ad, a man slips drugs in a woman's drink when she becomes distracted by approaching friends. When he slides the drink toward the woman, one of her friends pushes it back to him, saying, "Here, you drink it." Their message, and ours: Drinking lowers your shield. It diminishes your ability to look out for yourself. It makes you vulnerable. Combine a drug—any drug—with that, and you may not be able to stop something bad from happening.

"Rohypnol has been called a party drug of today," said U.S. Customs Service commissioner George Weise, when Customs officials announced that they would immediately begin seizing all imports of the drug. "Well, the party is over."

WHAT TO DO IF YOU'RE SEXUALLY ASSAULTED

The first thing is to tell someone—ideally, the police. Call 911, not the local police number, whether it's been a few minutes or even a few hours since the attack. This is definitely an emergency. Says a Baltimore police officer: "If you call the number for the precinct, you're going to waste a lot of time. If you call 911, you'll get the dispatcher right away—that's how we're set up—we can reach an officer who's already out cruising in your immediate vicinity, and help can be there within a few minutes."

Talking about it, especially to police officers, may be exactly what you don't want to do, but it's extremely important that you notify the police right away, for many

WOMEN WHO'D LIKE TO TURN BACK THE SEXUAL CLOCK

Now that so many people seem to be having sex, a quiet new sexual revolution is taking place: An increasing number of teenagers and young adults are opting to hold out for a while. You've probably seen them on the news—groups of teens, all over the country, signing "no-sex" contracts and promising to remain celibate until marriage.

Their lives will probably be a lot less complicated because of this decision. And, if recent polls like a survey of 500 women for *Redbook* magazine indicate, more people are wishing they'd done the same.

Two out of three women would want to be a virgin if they were getting married today, and half believe neither men nor women should have sexual experience before marriage, according to the survey. EDK Associates, the firm that did the research, reported that 64 percent of the women said they'd want to be a virgin; 31 percent said they'd rather not.

If a woman does not get married, those surveyed said, on average a woman should experience sex by age 23; 27 percent said a woman should stay a virgin all her life.

Some 53 percent said they believe having sex with the person you are going to marry is the same thing as being a virgin; 42 percent disagreed.

Of the women surveyed, 42 percent said they were virgins when they got married; 41 percent were not.

ONE SCHOOL'S PROTOCOL

At the University of South Carolina, this is part of the official protocol of immediate care and treatment for an assault on or off campus (your school will probably have a similar set-up, with a designated Rape Crisis Network number to call):

The sooner a sexual assault is reported, the easier it is to collect valuable evidence. To facilitate evidence collection, the victim:

- Should not bathe or douche
- Should not urinate
- Should not drink any liquids
- If oral contact has occurred, the victim should not smoke, eat, or brush teeth
- If clothes are changed, soiled clothes should be placed in a paper bag (plastic destroys crucial evidence)

University Police may transport the victim to an area hospital for medical attention and a rape protocol exam. If the victim does not want to contact the police, a friend or relative may transport the student to the hospital. When the victim arrives at the emergency room, the hospital will call Rape Crisis Network to arrange for a volunteer advocate to accompany the victim throughout the exam. The hospital staff may also contact the University Police and/or the police where the incident occurred. If the victim chooses, the University Police Victim/Witness Coordinator typically assists the victim throughout the criminal pro-

reasons. One is that the sooner the police have a description of your assailant, the sooner they may be able to catch him. Also, most city police departments have counselors specially trained to help women who have been sexually assaulted—and, like it or not, you're going to need to talk about it to someone. Another important reason is that the police will help you get medical attention. (In many cities, there is a certain designated hospital, which is particularly well-suited to handle the physical and mental needs of women who have been raped, as well as to look for any physical evidence—semen, body hairs, blood—that could be used in identifying and convicting the rapist.)

You need medical attention to make sure you're not injured internally. You may also have been exposed to AIDS or venereal disease.

There is also the possibility of pregnancy; thus, you'll probably be offered the "morning after" pill, which will prevent you from becoming pregnant. (Don't worry—its effects are not long-lasting, and it won't prevent you from becoming pregnant in the future.)

Among hundreds of other emotions, women who have been raped tend to feel unclean, numb, shattered and terrified. They have been violated, and the first—completely natural and understandable—reaction for many is the intense desire to take a shower, to scrub away all physical traces of the man who assaulted them. *Don't do it.* Don't immediately bathe or shower—don't even wash your hands—and don't take off or destroy the clothes you were wearing at the time. Valuable evidence could be lost.

As soon as you're able to, write down a complete description of the assailant, and as many details of the crime as you can remember.

It's good to write about it. It's good to talk about it. Get it out—don't keep what you're feeling inside, don't lock it up, and most of all, don't be ashamed. Nobody asks for rape. Nobody "deserves" it. Such talk is a load of garbage, and anyone who tries to make you believe it is an idiot. Nothing you said or did made this an acceptable action for someone. There is no justification for this awful crime. Nobody had a right to do this to you.

Which brings us to the next point, which is also hard for many women to accept: Whoever did this should be punished for it. Reporting a rape and pressing charges are far easier said by us than done by you. We know that. We know that most rape victims want more than anything to forget what happened to them, to make it go away—not compound it with the added stress of police, publicity and the courts. There have been horror stories about police skepticism, about the social and emotional pressure placed on the victim, about the difficulty prosecutors have in obtaining a conviction in rape cases. But attitudes and sensitivities have been changing. Police and prosecutors are far more sympathetic, and they definitely take rape far more seriously than they did even a few years ago. Much of this heightened consciousness is due to the courageous women who did recognize sexual violence for the profoundly serious crime it is—and were willing to fight back.

Note: You don't have to deal with this alone. Enlist the support of your family, friends, dorm buddies, a campus counselor, minister or rabbi, a professor you're close to—anyone who can make this at all easier for you, and who can be your advocate. Many schools have detailed sexual assault policies, extensive follow-up and recovery services, and volunteer or paid advocates whose job is to help you get through this. At the University of South Carolina, for example, there is even a 14-point "Victim's Bill of Rights."

You are not alone. Many women have survived this, and with a lot of counseling and over time, they've actually gotten their life back. You can do it, too. Believe it.

Call 911. "If you call the number for the precinct, you're going to waste a lot of time. If you call 911, you'll get the dispatcher right away—that's how we're set up—we can reach an officer who's already out cruising in your immediate vicinity, and help can be there within a few minutes."

Nobody asks for rape. Nobody "deserves" it. Such talk is a load of garbage, and anyone who tries to make you believe it is an idiot.

Nothing you said or did made this an acceptable action for someone. There is no justification for this awful crime. Nobody had a right to do this to you.

PRANK PHONE CALLS

When they were kids, one or more of your grandparents, nearly doubled over with suppressed laughter, probably

cess and informs the victim of services specifically available to him or her.

Medical attention is crucial to assess possible internal injuries or sexually transmitted diseases, as well as to collect medical evidence should the victim/survivor choose to pursue prosecution. The police will be contacted by the hospital to take possession of evidence collected while the victim/survivor makes a decision about whether to pursue charges.

Many obscene calls are random—numbers dialed arbitrarily. If you take part in the game, you might make this random event personal, and it could escalate into something really ugly.

used to call the local drugstore, asking, "Do you have Prince Albert (tobacco) In a can?" Hee, hee. If the pharmacist was dumb enough to fall for this one, and answered in the affirmative, your grandparents would then scream, "Well let him out! He's suffocating!" Another favorite would have been "Is your refrigerator running? Better go catch it!"

When It's Not So Funny: What To Do If You Get an Obscene Phone Call.

Sometimes, it's not so funny. Sometimes it's annoying, and sometimes, in fact, it's scary.

Here are some tips from the division of Law Enforcement and Safety at one large southern school:

- Hang up as soon as you hear an obscenity, an improper question, or no response to your hello. Then IMMEDIATELY dial *69 (which tells you the number) or *57 (which puts a tracer on the call for the phone company—see below. Note: Depending on your school's location and campus phone technology, these services may not be available).
- Don't play detective. Don't prolong the call by trying to figure out who's calling.
- Remain calm. Or, if you do get upset or angry or frightened, don't let the caller know it.
- Don't attempt to be clever. A witty response might be taken as a sign of encouragement.
- Don't attempt counseling. The obscene caller obviously does need professional help, but will only be encouraged by your concern and may continue the calls.
- Don't tell everyone you know about your calls. Many calls of this type are actually made by "friends."
- Report obscene or annoying calls to your campus police department.

High-tech help: Check with your local phone company. In many parts of the country, for instance, available services include:

- Call Trace, a short code such as *57. This lets you trace the number of the last call you received, and have it automatically reported to the phone company. (There is a small charge for each successful trace.) Note: This only traces the very last call you received; if you get another call, or your call waiting kicks in, you're out of luck. "You should use it only in the case of life-threatening, obscene or harassing calls," advises C & P Telephone of Maryland, which is owned by Bell Atlantic.

- Call Block. This lets you block calls from up to six phone numbers. "When someone calls you from one of these numbers, your phone will not ring," the phone company says.
- Caller ID. This lets you (within specifically equipped areas) actually see the phone number of the caller before you pick up the phone. (Note: To get this service, you need to buy a separate display unit.)
- Return Call, another code such as *69. This lets you call back the last number that called you, whether you answered the phone or not. If the number is busy or doesn't answer, Return Call will keep dialing for up to 30 minutes. Note: We strongly recommend that you NOT use this to "get back at" an obscene phone caller. Say you get an obscene call from someone we'll call Psycho Ed. You hang up, but then call him back, and say something witty like, "How does this make you feel, Psycho?" This is probably not the smartest move you've ever made in your life. Many obscene calls are random—numbers dialed arbitrarily. If you take part in the game, you might make this random event personal, and it could escalate into something really ugly. And think about it: If you call Psycho Ed back, now he's got your number— he may not have remembered what he dialed before—and he can do the same thing to you.

Other options:

Screen your calls. Buy an answering machine. This solution is so simple, it's brilliant, if we do say so ourselves: Just wait for whoever's calling to start to leave a message, then decide to pick up—or not pick up, or call back later—at your own discretion. One bonus: If it's Psycho Ed, you'll have a nice little tape recording of his voice to hand over to the police.

Call in the troops. If this is a continuing problem, do not hesitate to seek help—from the phone company and maybe even the police, if the caller is really creepy and

Is the ultimate purpose of this some bizarre matchmaking rite? Does any guy actually follow up on these phone numbers, and does any girl actually go out with the creep who caught her undies?

IF YOUR ROOMMATE IS A DRUGGIE

If you want no part of it, agree to disagree. Let him or her go one way, you go yours. Make new friends who will be your "support group" and draw strength from them. If it's a real problem and you feel pressured, your options include trying to get a new roommate (see Chapter Two) or never being there except to sleep. Spend most of your time elsewhere—somebody else's room, or the student union, the library, a sorority or fraternity house. Remember: You have choices. You're not helpless.

says things that reveal some knowledge of your daily activities. Among other solutions, the phone company may be able to place an electronic "trap," or surveillance device, on your phone, which could help them catch the caller.

PANTY RAIDS AND OTHER KNEE-SLAPPERS

We can't believe people actually still do such things, but lo and behold, they do. Adolescent freshmen boys still engage in such games of hilarity as panty raids with freshmen girls. Unbelievable. And desperate or misguided girls actually write their names and phone numbers on suggestive-looking pieces of lingerie (ideally, on lingerie that has never been used), and throw them out their dorm windows and down to the outstretched arms of these still-stuck-in-puberty, overgrown, drooling, moronic junior high schoolers.

Let's just think about this. Is the ultimate purpose of this some bizarre matchmaking rite? Does any guy actually follow up on these phone numbers, and does any girl actually go out with the creep who caught her undies? What kind of winner—of either sex—do you think you're going to find participating in this? The future father or mother of your children? Someone to make your parents proud? Picture them saying, as they wipe a grateful tear from their eyes, "Thank God I sent you to this university—because here's where you met Goober, the son-in-law we always dreamed we'd have. Now, our life is complete." What unsavory tone is this going to set for your first special date? ("I called you because I really like Maidenform.") Do us, yourselves, and your parents a favor. Grow up. Don't participate. Get a life.

DRUGS AND ALCOHOL

Have some sense and set some limits. When we urge you to broaden your horizons, we're definitely not saying you should open yourself up to every new experience—particularly those involving illegal drugs (don't forget, alcohol is a drug, too). Even in their purest forms, drugs violate the sound mind/sound body rule. When drugs are tainted (mixed with cheaper chemicals by a cost-cutting dealer, for example), they can be hazardous to your health. In addition, when drugs are administered with dirty needles, they can be deadly. When you inject a drug, you're opening the door to the unsavory outside world, inviting plague illnesses such as hepatitis and AIDS into your disease-free body.

So ask yourself: Is it worth it? In the words of one teenager recovering from a cocaine problem: "Does my life suck so much that I need to risk dying to escape from it?" If it does, you've got a problem that drugs aren't going to fix, and they could make it a lot worse.

Many drugs, including alcohol, aren't stimulants; they're depressants. They activate chemical pathways in the brain that can make you depressed, which might make you want to take another drink.

The drug scene

The main drug of choice seems to vary from town to town. Emergency room physicians at Johns Hopkins Hospital in Baltimore, for example, report that a high percentage of their patients—many of them from the inner-city—who do drugs inject heroin. "This is a shooter town," as one Johns Hopkins internist puts it. But 30 miles away, in Washington, D.C., doctors at hospitals such as Georgetown see a much higher incidence of crack cocaine (which is smoked), and relatively few needles.

Crack, by the way, is a highly toxic, addictive, and fairly cheap way to ruin your brain and your life. It's also the drug that sends the grim and very sad message, "I don't care about myself or anything else; I see no beauty in the world; I'm willing to become a prostitute and steal to support my drug habit; I want to die soon."

At colleges and universities, many experts in the field—counselors, physicians, residence hall directors, and people on the staff of the dean of students at several institutions—have reported a considerable decline in the use of some "hard" drugs on their campuses. Some of the pills (amphetamines, barbiturates) are tougher to get now, and more students seem to have wised up to the scary consequences of hard-core drugs such as heroin and the toxic angel dust. But other drugs, such as cocaine and marijuana, remain readily available for students who are looking for them.

Heroin, for incomprehensible reasons, is making a small comeback among losers in elite circles who

BE PREPARED WHEN TALKING WITH A FRIEND

If you're trying to talk to a friend whom you think may have a real problem with alcohol, don't let yourself get sidetracked. Go into the discussion prepared—with other friends, if you think it's appropriate—and bring a list of the points you hope to make and the conclusion you hope to reach. This may help keep the conversation focused. Addicts are often sly, gifted manipulators who can turn the tables on you and cloud the issue so well that nothing gets solved.

Don't, for example, buy a defensive line of reasoning like "Caffeine (or cigarettes, or whatever) is a drug, too." Therefore, it's "the pot calling the kettle black"—*you're* an addict because you can't get through the day without a cup of coffee or six Diet Cokes. So what? That doesn't mean your friend doesn't have a problem.

Anyway, it's not the same: Caffeine is a drug, sure, and a lot of us are indeed addicted to it. (It's also true that cigarettes, though much slower-acting drugs, are highly addictive; they may ruin your health—or, if you smoke enough of them, they'll kill you. But, like caffeine, they don't impair your ability to function or think; they don't alter your personality, and they aren't ways to escape from reality.)

But, last time we checked, they didn't have anonymous groups where people who are hanging on to self-control by their fingernails, one day at a time, meet to discuss how caffeine has ruined their lives. Nobody ever wakes up in a pool of his own vomit from drinking one too many Espressos and then passing out.

Nobody ever gets so crazy on cappucino that, in a fit of uncontrollable, blind rage, she hits her kids and then breaks down sobbing about the disgusting mess she's made of her life. They don't make Breathalyzer tests to check for traces of Pepsi. Nicotine doesn't make people forget what they did the night before. Nobody hides little "emergency" bottles of Coke in potted plants and under the car seat where they won't be found by the family members and friends he or she's been lying to for months, insisting "I don't have a problem."

consider themselves hip; speed labs continue to crop up, like zits on the face of the earth, throughout the country. Marijuana remains readily available for students who are looking for it. (Pot has actually surged slightly in popularity in the retro-hippie, Woodstock, "I may have been too young to experience the seventies, but I can dress in tie-dyed garments and bell bottoms, pierce my body parts, smoke pot, flash the peace sign like I really care about world peace and love, and pretend I'm there now" generation.)

Basically, if you want it, and you're willing to look for it, you'll be able to find it.

Some housing officials, with rose-colored remembrances of their own college days, have mixed feelings about marijuana and will look the other way. Others will not. If you're caught with a marijuana joint, you probably won't be expelled—not for a first offense, anyway—but repeated violations could get you kicked out of your dorm (for breaching the housing contract you signed), and you may find the sudden change of address awkward to explain to Mom and Dad. Drug dealing, on the other hand, is a far more serious offense—one that's almost certain to get you expelled from school and prosecuted by the police.

In general terms, you'll probably find that the college drug scene is no worse—in some cases, it's actually less serious—than the one you faced in high school. With the additional maturity you've presumably acquired by now, you should be able to handle the peer pressure more confidently.

But actually, there may not be as much peer pressure. If there is, you've most likely got a bigger population base now than you had in high school. Find the kind of people you want to be around, and hang out with them.

Alcohol on campus

Actually, most students seem far less vulnerable to the temptations of drugs than they are to alcohol abuse. "Eighty percent of the student problems I deal with," grumbled one experienced housing director, "are connected directly to booze. I'm talking about disorderly conduct, damage in the residence halls, arrest reports, personal troubles, flunk-outs—these are primarily alcohol-related. The biggest offenders are freshman men—kids who try to knock off three fifths of bourbon in a weekend. It's a macho thing with them, I guess, though many became seasoned drinkers before they ever left high school."

An associate dean of students at the University of Kentucky—a state, by the way, where much of the country's hard liquor (bourbon) is made—has this to say: "I'm amazed at the number of students who begin drinking even before noon. Instead of a cup of coffee, they get a beer. Many seem unable to function, much less have fun, without alcohol. The party revolves around the bar or the keg. For too many, alcohol is the crutch."

Ways to avoid being around alcohol. In all likelihood, no one is going to force an alcoholic drink on you or make a big deal out of it if you say, "No, thanks." Actually, they'll probably respect you.

However, in all honesty, we do have to say that a few insecure people might feel threatened by your strength, self-control, and values in refusing a drink; some boorish clods may even feel the need to put you down for saying no. But you can deal with them; vote with your feet—by moving them. If someone's giving you a hard time, you don't have to stay and convert them to your side, or even get into an argument at all. If it's a party, find the people who aren't drinking—there are almost always some—and hang out with them. (Alternatively, find the people who are least drunk.) If it's in a dorm room (or, worst case, your dorm room) and you don't feel comfortable staying, take a walk down the hall. If it's late at night and you're sleepy, just put in your ear plugs and go to sleep.

You don't have to prove anything to anybody, and if you don't make an issue of it, chances are, they won't, either. You're not the enemy, and (unless they're driving as well as drinking) they're not the enemy; you just have different ideas of what constitutes a good time. That's fine—the world is made up of people who don't agree; but most of them manage to get along. Actually, you may be pleasantly surprised to find out that there's less peer pressure in college than there was in high school. If you just tell the truth and say you'd rather not drink, it's probably not going to matter to most people.

If you're uncomfortable but don't want to leave or cause a scene, do what a lot of us do—nurse one drink all evening. Just because there's a drink in your hand doesn't mean you have to chug it or even drink it.

Actually, you may be pleasantly surprised to find out that there's less peer pressure in college than there was in high school. If you just tell the truth and say you'd rather not drink, it's probably not going to matter to most people.

IF YOU'RE REALLY WORRIED

There are other alternatives, including the following:

- Stay away from parties where the main objective is to get wasted. Do you really want to be friends with these people? You're not going to have a good time, and they won't either—to them, you'll be a stick-in-the-mud. Let them tell you all about the "good time" you missed.
- Join a support group. There are a lot of them on college campuses now— organizations such as Bacchus or SADD (Students Against Drunk Driving). It shouldn't be too hard to find other students with similar concerns about alcohol abuse.
- Some larger campuses have dorms or houses that are, by the choice of the students who live in them, reserved for nondrinkers. Check into this possibility at your school.
- You might be more comfortable at a church-related college or another university where drinking is an official no-no. At these institutions, abstinence is easy; since you'd be risking suspension to drink, you have a perfect excuse to stay sober.

Master the art of the "fake sip." Or bring your own—take an alcohol-free beer, for instance, to a keg party. Who's going to test your beer for alcohol content?

If they're drinking gin and tonics, without making a lengthy, self-righteous, party-stopping statement about what you're doing and your many good reasons for doing it, simply fix yourself a tonic and lime, with no gin. Who's going to know?

Or, lie: "I just took an antihistamine," is a good one. (An even better one, although it might spark a whole other discussion is, "I may be pregnant." On second thought, better not use that one!)

There's really no need to rearrange your life just to dodge the problem of alcohol. Whatever else college life is, it's manifestly a place that cherishes the principle of laissez-faire; in other words, what you do—or don't do—is largely your own business, unless it gets out of control.

IF ALCOHOL IS A PROBLEM FOR YOU OR A FRIEND

Which brings us to alcohol abuse. Anybody—children, old people, men, women, rich, poor, people with advanced degrees and high-school drop-outs—can have a problem with alcohol. College students are definitely not immune. (See also "Binge Drinking," in Chapter Ten: After Hours.)

If you (or a roommate or friend) are wondering if your drinking has passed the socializing stage, here's a brief quiz (adapted from the short version of the Michigan Alcoholism Screening Test).

Each time you answer "yes," make a check mark:

- Do you drink more than most other people?
- Does your roommate or friend ever worry or complain about your drinking?
- Do you ever feel guilty about your drinking?
- Do friends or relatives think you drink more than most people?
- Do you ever experience a loss of control? (That is, you fully meant to have only one or two drinks, but you ended up having more?)
- Have you ever attended a meeting of Alcoholics Anonymous because of your drinking?

- Has drinking ever created problems between you and your roommate or between you and a parent or near relative?
- Have you ever gotten in trouble at work (or in class) because of your drinking?
- Have you ever neglected your obligations, your family, or your classes for two or more days in a row because you were drinking?
- Have you ever gone to anyone for help about your drinking?
- Have you ever been in a hospital because of drinking?
- Have you ever been arrested for drunken driving, driving while intoxicated, or driving under the influence of alcoholic beverages?
- Have you ever been arrested, even for a few hours, because of other drunken behavior?

If you have only one check mark on your paper, it's not likely that you have a problem. Two check marks mean you might have a problem. Three or more mean there's a good possibility you do have a problem and should seek counseling.

If you're still uncertain about your drinking, try one more test. Set a limit for yourself. One good suggestion is that you make sure you don't drink every day, and that you have no more than three drinks on the days when you do drink. (A drink here is defined as one twelve-ounce can or bottle of beer, a four-ounce glass of wine, or a mixed drink with one ounce of 86-proof distilled spirits.) If you discover that you're unable to keep to this limit, you may need help.

CHAPTER 12

When You Need Help

Bad news: It's inevitable because, as the bumper sticker says, STUFF HAPPENS. You will run into problems at college.

Good news: You're at the right place at the right time. Never before have colleges and universities been so aware of, and sensitive to, what their students are going through. They want to help, which means you won't have to deal with your problems—academic, physical, legal, social, economic, or emotional—all by yourself.

An example: The Counseling and Human Development Center at one southern university recently announced a line-up of workshops and support groups for the fall semester that included Couples Support/Therapy Group; Dissertation Writing Support Group; Drop-In Self-Hypnosis; "Fat Is a Feminist Issue"; Gay/Lesbian Students Support Group; Psychomotor Therapy/Counseling/ Support Groups; Understanding Your Personality; Appreciating Oneself; Assertiveness Training; Burnout Prevention/Coping with Stress; Healing the Wound: Recovering from Loss; Memory and Concentration Through Hypnosis; Self-Improvement Through Self-Hypnosis. The center also offers to arrange other support groups and to set up extra skill workshops.

Muhlenberg College in Allentown, Pennsylvania, also is emphasizing its supportive environment, aiming to be "the caring college" —combining small-sized classes with academic and career counseling. "What this means," says Marion, an alumna, now a vice president for corporate communications at a New York public relations firm, "is that from the president down there's a mandate to help students with schoolwork and personal issues, even at the peer level, to help educate and prepare them for the working world." However, buoyed by this nurturing environment, some envelope-pushers can't resist taking a good thing a little too far, Marion adds: "One mom actually called a prof to see if he could stop by her son's dorm to wake him up for his 8 a.m. class!" (The professor declined.)

Caring is the message, indeed, and it's being shouted by colleges nationwide: "Our sole purpose is to help YOU! Give us a problem, we'll try to help you fix it."

Your challenge: Learn when to ask for help, where to find it, and what to ask for when you get there.

HELP IF YOU GET SICK

First, some basic information: The health services you'll get for your tuition dollar vary from one college to another. So will the amount of your health service fee. Most colleges generally provide, at minimal cost, such benefits as unlimited visits to the campus infirmary for consultation and treatment by student health service doctors and nurses. (*Note: Many student health services are staffed mainly by nurses or nurse practitioners, who act as the first-tier, "screen-out" layer of care, with one or two doctors available to see more serious problems.*) Your student health service will probably serve mainly as a dispensary, offering a few basic services that may include the following:

- Prescribing commonly used medicines
- Performing routine diagnostic tests and X-rays
- Providing first-aid treatment of injuries not requiring surgery
- Offering psychological counseling for personal and emotional problems (unless your college has a separate counseling center, to which you'll be referred)

Your college will probably offer you a supplemental health insurance plan to cover hospital care and various other medical services not routinely provided for you on campus. You'll be urged to sign up for this additional service, unless you show that you're already covered by your parents' medical insurance plan.

Now, our advice: Don't expect too much from student health and you won't be disappointed. We hate to say it, but, in general, the country's finest physicians don't rush right out of medical training and sign up to work at college health services. (For one thing, the pay is probably not great. Also, as in most cost-controlled environments, neither is their autonomy—their ability to get the medications and order the diagnostic tests they feel their patients need.)

The health services you'll get for your tuition dollar vary from one college to another.

COLLEGE, PARENTS, AND YOUR RIGHT TO PRIVACY

Guess what? You've got rights as a college student—rights to privacy. Unless you're involved in a genuine medical emergency, your parents may never be contacted directly by your college or university (except to be invited to Parents' Day, or Graduation, or something equally innocuous). At one time, college officials would mail your grade reports directly to your family, along with other fun messages, like a notice that "Tremaine was placed on academic probation," or that "Gina has several books overdue at the library."

That doesn't happen much anymore. The main reason: fear of lawsuits. Alarmed about the new privacy statutes, the larger institutions (especially those that are state supported) have become extremely cautious about releasing information to anyone except the individual student concerned. ("Andrew, I'm a little confused—this report from the student health service says you were treated for syphilis. How can this be?")

At some schools, you may sign a release form authorizing the college to mail your grades and related messages home. Otherwise, your grade reports and other official communications will be dispatched directly to you. Whether you share this information with your parents, says the university, is your business.

It's a good idea, if you have a physician you like at home, to schedule your regular check-ups for vacations or other home visits. But in order to prepare in advance for any medical problems that may crop up in between those visits, find a local private physician or group practice before you need one. The big benefit of being already established as a patient in a local practice is that, if you get sick, you can always call the office and say, "I'm a patient of Dr. So and So's, and these are my symptoms. Should I come in?" You may be able to get away without needing (and therefore paying for) an office visit. You might even be able to get the prescription or advice you need over the telephone.

"At many student health services," says a Johns Hopkins physician, "when somebody gets sick, he or she ends up getting referred out (to an outside physician or hospital) anyway. It's a low-level primary care setting—they're able to treat things like common skin disorders, common infectious diseases, venereal diseases, and so on. But if you have anything more exotic—if you need a specialist or you need surgery—you're going to have to go somewhere and pay some physician in the community to see you. I guess student health is like most things—you get what you pay for."

Your ideal medical solution may be just around the corner, *if* your university has its own medical school and hospital. Why? Because academic teaching hospitals tend to offer the best medical care in the country.

When to see a doctor

This is the big question, and we can't answer it for you—only you know how you feel. But we can offer the following general guidelines, which were compiled with the help of a Johns Hopkins internist:

- If you have a fever higher than 101 degrees Fahrenheit that doesn't get better with aspirin or acetaminophen (the key ingredient in nonaspirin pain relievers such as Tylenol). "Especially a fever associated with a shaking chill."
- If you have severe pain that's unexplained. In other words, pain that's not caused by such things as a muscle injury, tension headache, menstrual cramps (or mid-cycle pain, which some women experience when they ovulate—usually about two weeks after their last menstrual period).

- If you're unable to keep down food or water for more than 24 hours.
- If you're unable to urinate, or you haven't had a bowel movement in several days.
- If you notice any unusual vaginal discharge, blood in your urine or bowel movements, or blood when you cough.
- If you experience burning when you urinate. "Especially in males, this could be urethritis (an irritation of the urethra) that's a symptom of a venereal disease," says the doctor. "This is important, because the symptom could go away, but you could still be spreading some form of venereal disease." (*Note: Women infected with a venereal disease, the doctor adds, often have no symptoms, or only minimal symptoms.*)
- If you're having upper respiratory problems. If you've been coughing for several days, cough syrups don't help and your chest is getting sore, or if you're short of breath and can't take a deep breath.
- If you have a sore throat that lasts longer than a couple of days.
- If you're feeling excessively fatigued for several days and can't "perk up."
- If you become depressed or begin to have suicidal thoughts.

An Ounce of Prevention

The very best way to handle being sick is not to get sick at all. And there's a lot you can do to make sure this doesn't happen. With help from an internist at the Johns Hopkins Medical Institutions, we've compiled a few sure-fire tips to boost your odds of staying well. They include:

- Wash your hands. Your mother was right. Do it before you eat, stick your finger in your mouth, or—this is really important—touch your eyes or nose. "Most common cold viruses are stable on hard surfaces," says the Johns Hopkins physician. "It's very common for people to get the common cold virus when they touch a doorknob, desk or other surface and then rub their eye—the virus travels down through the nasolacrimal duct." (Note: The doctor points out that there are "over

Note: At some private schools, however, especially at the smaller ones, efforts continue to make parents fully aware of the educational progress of their sons and daughters. This means if you make the dean's list—or get busted for possession—your folks may get a letter about it.

WATCH OUT FOR HEPATITIS B

This is a bad bug, and it's on the rise: Nearly 300,000 Americans contract hepatitis B every year. Like AIDS, it is spread in infected blood and other bodily fluids (semen, vaginal secretions, saliva, open sores, and breast milk). Note: It is NOT spread by casual contact; you can't get it from holding hands, having someone cough or sneeze on you, baby-sitting an infected child, "dry" kissing on the lips, or eating food prepared by someone who has the virus. Hepatitis B may also be present in tainted shellfish and contaminated beaches. As many as 10 percent of all people infected with hepatitis B develop chronic hepatitis. Fortunately, most people manage to fight off the infection successfully within a few months, developing an immunity that lasts a lifetime. So: If your body manages to clear itself of the virus, you're home free. You will never again develop hepatitis B (although you could still develop another form of hepatitis). Your immunity can be checked by a test called "anti-HBs," for "antibody to hepatitis B surface antigen" (the test registers the presence in the blood of a certain protein attached to the outside of the hepatitis B antibody). If you've ever had hepatitis B, or been vaccinated against it, antibodies to the virus will always be present in your blood, and—because there is a tiny risk that the anti-HBs test showed a false positive, and that you

100 serotypes of the common cold virus—so you can be infected again and again, each time with a different strain.")

- Take a multivitamin. You know it, we know it. Your diet probably isn't going to have representatives of each of the basic food groups you need every day—especially if your vegetable of the day is something like western fries. So do us and yourself a favor; take a vitamin. (It doesn't have to be expensive; get the generic brand at a discount store.) Put the bottle by your alarm clock, so you'll see it in the morning or at bedtime.

- An aspirin a day may keep cancer and heart disease away. Numerous studies have shown that aspirin is truly the "wonder drug." Taking just one aspirin—or even a baby aspirin—a day is proven to prevent the buildup of atherosclerosis ("hardening" of the arteries) that can lead to heart attack and stroke. Aspirin also is known to prevent or slow the growth of some precancerous lesions, including polyps in the colon (which may lead to colon cancer). Another bonus: Aspirin makes these intestinal polyps more likely to bleed, so they can be diagnosed sooner. Finally, there's also exciting evidence that aspirin may slow the progression of Alzheimer's disease, as well. Why should you care? Let's see. No reason to care now; do what you want. Unless you have a family history of heart disease, colon cancer, other forms of cancer, or Alzheimer's—which means that you, my friend, have been born with the deck stacked against you, genetically speaking. Pardon our frankness, but: Knowing that there's something you can do now—and not doing it—is just plain stupid.

- Get a flu shot. Check with the student health service; they may offer them cheap. Yes, the shot may make you feel bad for a day or two. But better a day or two of mild discomfort than two weeks of being out of commission with the flu, and then another month spent recovering from it.

- Make sure your immunizations are up-to-date. "Two things that have gone rampantly through college campuses are measles—because people got the old vaccine and no longer have immunity—and hepatitis B," says a Johns Hopkins gastroenterologist. "Hepatitis B is very infectious; it's a million times more infectious than AIDS. Like AIDS, you can get it through blood and body fluids. But you can also get it through more casual contact, like household exposure, and you can get it through kissing. The worst thing about it is that it's associated with what's called a 'chronic carrier state,' where people who harbor the virus may look and feel perfectly healthy, so they can spread it without even knowing they've got it." Plan ahead on this one; the vaccine is administered in three shots, given over a period of six months. Many HMOs and health plans offer this at minimal charge. Note: In order for the vaccine to be completely effective, you need all three shots. (For more, see "Watch Out for Hepatitis B.") We repeat—you can get it through kissing. Enough said! Another good vaccine to get, if you haven't already had it, is the chicken pox vaccine. This disease, bad enough when you're a kid, is really miserable when you're a grown-up.

- Don't do stupid things. "The big killers at the college age are accidents," states our friend the internist. "A lot of them are caused by drinking and driving and doing drugs." This is simple: If you're planning to drink, save some money for cab fare, or pick a designated driver (you and your buddies can take turns doing this). "But another, more subtle worry about doing anything that impairs your judgment is that it's a lot easier then to fall into other dangers—like getting exposed to the AIDS virus, or hepatitis B. People are more likely to do things they wouldn't do otherwise when they're in an altered state." In other words, if you're wasted and feeling on top of the world, you might think, "Who needs a condom? It's probably okay." Famous last words. (The classic "Saturday Night Live" skit, "Bad Idea Jeans" comes to mind.)

- Stock your own medicine chest. Like the commercial says, never underestimate the power of (chicken) soup, and of over-the-counter medications. They're no substitute for medical care if you're really sick (see general guidelines, above). But let's face it: If you have cold or allergy symptoms—including runny or stuffy nose, a

could still pass on the virus—you will not be allowed to donate blood or any other bodily organs or fluids.

An estimated one million Americans are lifelong carriers of hepatitis B. If you have had hepatitis B in your bloodstream for more than six months, then you're considered a carrier—even if you feel fine. This means that you can transmit the virus to others by having unprotected sex, sharing needles, deep kissing, sharing food or drinks, or engaging in any other risky behavior. Note: This also means that your liver is more vulnerable than normal to injury—particularly that caused by even small amounts of alcohol or drugs. If you're a carrier of hepatitis B and you get pregnant, you have an estimated 90 percent likelihood of passing on the virus to your unborn baby. (Fortunately, your baby can be vaccinated at birth to prevent the virus.) Inexplicably, in a tiny percentage of carriers, the hepatitis B virus spontaneously goes away on its own. Other people aren't so lucky: According to the American Liver Foundation, hepatitis B kills 5,000 Americans each year. However, most carriers lead normal lives, with no major health problems.

Getting enough fluids is more important than ever when you're sick, because you need all your strength to fight off whatever's ailing you.

cough, congestion, and itchy, watery eyes—a doctor can't help you. All a doctor can do, when confronted by the common cold, is suggest some medications and tell you to go out and buy them. Cold and headache remedies won't make the problem go away—only time will take care of that—but they can bring dramatic relief of the symptoms, so you can get on with your work and not fall behind in class. (See Mom's medicine cabinet, in Chapter One.)

- Force fluids, preferably juices. Getting enough fluids is more important than ever when you're sick, because you need all your strength to fight off whatever's ailing you.

"Montezuma's Revenge" and Other Forms of Intestinal Hell

It happens to everyone. For whatever reason, your gastrointestinal tract decides to call attention to itself. Violently. The symptoms are miserable, but they're almost always mercifully brief—sweeping in and out with the force of a hurricane. The main thing you need to know, if one of these maladies strikes, is this: Don't let yourself get dehydrated. Force fluids, even if you throw them up; at least something will get absorbed. Call your doctor if you have a high fever, if you can't stop vomiting or having diarrhea, if you have bloody diarrhea, or if you vomit blood.

Now, here's a brief run-down, no pun intended.

Traveler's Diarrhea. This is nicknamed "Montezuma's Revenge" for good reason: Of the 3 million tourists who travel to Mexico each year, an estimated 25 percent to 50 percent return with diarrhea. Traveler's diarrhea is almost always a bacterial infection, transmitted during unsanitary food preparation by the dreaded "fecal-oral" route. Basically, this means happens when food handlers don't adequately wash their hands after they use the bathroom. Yuck! The most common culprit (in an estimated 40 to 70 percent of cases) is *E. coli* bacteria; less common are parasitic infections, such as giardiasis (caused by a protozoan) or amebiasis (caused by amoebae). If you're planning an exotic trip for Spring Break, beware: Traveler's diarrhea also afflicts visitors to parts of Central and South America, Africa and Asia. But there's good news: In 80 percent of cases, symptoms last less than a week; in most people, three or four days.

More good news: IT'S COMPLETELY PREVENTABLE! Unfortunately, even for the very conscientious, one lapse is all it takes: For instance, you may do a great job of sticking to bottled water all day, but then slip up and brush your teeth with tap water at night. Or drink a bottled cola—good—with ice cubes made from tap water. Oops. If you're traveling in an area where this problem is common, your mantra should be: "Boil it, cook it, peel it, or forget it." Avoid ice, tap water, vegetables, salads, foods sold by street vendors, and fountain sodas. Drink bottled water, sodas, tea and coffee; brush your teeth with bottled water. If you wear contact lenses, use bottled water to rinse them. To be on the safe side, you might want to take your own supply of bottled water from home—estimate at least one quart-sized bottle per person per day. Limit your fruits to foods you can peel, such as oranges or bananas. Talk to your doctor about treating traveler's diarrhea before it strikes—with Pepto Bismol or prescription antibiotics, (which you'll need to take the whole time you're there)—or after the fact, with an over-the-counter drug such as Imodium AD (which slows the intestine down from warp drive).

Food Poisoning. Meet our good friend Ralph York (think about it). This fun illness usually manifests itself violently, with intense vomiting and diarrhea, cramps, abdominal pain, general weakness and malaise—but hardly ever a fever. (Note: If you have a fever, you may have a different problem, such as gastroenteritis.) Food poisoning is caused by extremely harsh toxins, made by bacteria such as *Staphylococcus* or *Salmonella*. Sometimes, the food is already contaminated, and the bomb-proof bacteria manage to survive inadequate cooking. Other times, food is contaminated by a food handler after the fact: When someone handling raw chicken, for instance, fails to wash her hands before touching other food. Food poisoning, although miserable and sometimes violent, usually lasts no longer than 24 to 36 hours. Some people may have vomiting or diarrhea only; others may be afflicted with both—sometimes simultaneously, which can be truly unfortunate. (The only possibly good aspect of this is that—believe us—you find out who your true friends are. Fast.) Other bacterial infections, such as shigella, cholera, are usually transmitted by the "fecal-oral" route described in the "traveler's diarrhea" section.

If you're traveling in an area where this problem is common, your mantra should be: "Boil it, cook it, peel it, or forget it.

Before eating in <u>any</u> restaurant, check for the restaurant's Health Department Grade, which, by law, is supposed to be hanging up somewhere public (in many restaurants, the certificate hangs on the wall near the rest rooms). If the grade is anything below an "A," leave. They don't deserve your business.

Like Montezuma's Revenge, food poisoning is often completely preventable. Cook your food thoroughly. Then, keep it either hot or cold, whichever it's supposed to be—particularly, egg salad, mayonnaise, rice pudding, cream, tartar sauce, and fried rice. Bacteria love lukewarm food. They start cranking out the toxins when food becomes a good "culture dish" - when it sits at room temperature for several hours (at a picnic, for example). Tip: Avoid like the plague those vats of mayonnaise or horseradish sauce at the cafeteria and fast food joints (although prepackaged containers are okay); choose mustard or catsup instead. Another tip: Before eating in *any* restaurant, check for the restaurant's Health Department Grade, which, by law, is supposed to be hanging up somewhere public (in many restaurants, the certificate hangs on the wall near the rest rooms). If the grade is anything below an "A," leave. They don't deserve your business.

Viral Gastroenteritis This lovely bug has many of the same dismal symptoms as the other two we've discussed—diarrhea, nausea, abdominal cramps, vomiting, muscle aches, loss of appetite, weakness, malaise—with two wrinkles: One is a low-grade fever; the other is that it hangs on, maybe for a week or longer. Like Montezuma's Revenge, viral gastroenteritis usually takes the disgusting "fecal-oral" route—mainly, this happens when food handlers, who apparently just fell off the truck, don't know they're supposed to wash their hands after they use the bathroom. Except here, the unwelcome intruder in your food is a virus, not bacteria. Viral gastroenteritis may also be present in shellfish that inhabit water contaminated by raw sewage.

If you don't have a high fever (in which case you should call your doctor, try an "anti-motility agent" (which slows the intestine down from warp drive) such as Imodium AD to treat the diarrhea. As always, call a doctor or student health if your symptoms persist or seem particularly severe. That's their job, to help you get better.

DENTAL CARE

Some universities include dental care as part of their student health service package. Most, however, don't; they expect you to solve your dental problems in your own way.

The best thing you can do to minimize dental problems is simply to take care of your teeth. You know what to do: Brush twice a day, floss daily, and get checkups twice a year. So do it! It's a good idea, also, to establish a relationship with a dentist in your college community. If you've already become known as a patient—say you've already been in for your six-month checkup and cleaning—you'll have a dentist to call in case of an emergency.

Ask around—local students, your dorm director, or faculty adviser (basically, anybody who lives in the town where you're going to school)—for a good dentist whose office is near the campus. Another option is to call your campus health service or the county dental society (if there is one) for names of good dentists. If you have a dental emergency, check the yellow pages for private dentists who are available to see patients on a round-the-clock basis.

You know what to do: Brush twice a day, floss daily, and get checkups twice a year. So do it!

HELP FOR EMOTIONAL PROBLEMS

First, know that emotional problems are extremely common. Everybody, at one time or another, has some trouble coping. Especially college students, who typically experience feelings of depression, insecurity, and anxiety at various points throughout their college careers. Maybe you're having trouble relating to your parents, handling your responsibilities, making new friends, or adjusting to your new environment. Maybe you're having trouble with your boyfriend or girlfriend. Maybe you've never felt so alone before in your whole life.

But you're not alone. And if you think there's no help, and nobody could ever understand, you're mistaken. Do you think your situation is so bad it would shock people? Forget it; there will always be somebody out there who has recovered from something just as bad or even worse, which means that if he or she can get better, you can, too.

First, try your college counseling center. On most campuses, psychologists and counselors are on hand—they're specially trained and employed for this purpose, they exist for it, it's their role, it's their mission in life—to help students solve personal, academic, and vocational problems.

Take an honest look at yourself and figure out why your grades are going down.

BEATING DEPRESSION: ONE SURVIVOR'S STORY

In 1992, Janet covered a press conference at the annual Mood Disorders Research and Education Symposium, held at the Johns Hopkins Medical Institutions. The star of the press conference was Dick Cavett—talk-show host and survivor of horrible bouts of depression—who held all of us spellbound as he described what it's like to feel barren inside, wanting to die, and being too despondent to pull the trigger.

"Depression turns everything sort of colorless," he said. "It's a permanent state of dismal, worthless, black despair, of not wanting to go out of the house. Your manhood becomes an instant casualty. You can't remember anything that ever gave you pleasure. You know it's permanent."

Cavett's first real bout of depression came when he was in college, during his freshman year at Yale University; the second struck several years later, when he was an out-of-work actor living in New York. He spent the time in his apartment, mostly sleeping, rousing himself only to watch the Jack Paar show, then going back to bed.

It was only after his most severe attack, in the early 1980s, that Cavett sought help, at his wife's urging.

Under the care of a New York doctor, Cavett found a medication that worked. When the drug "kicked in," he knew

Since the counseling offices are funded by your tuition money, there's usually no charge for the counseling. It's confidential, of course (you could sue the pants off the university if your confidentiality is violated!), and it's purely voluntary.

Depression

Should you seek help? Here are some warning signs:

- Changes in your eating habits—either having a poor appetite and losing weight when you're not on a diet or gaining a significant amount of weight.
- Changes in your sleep habits. Having insomnia or wanting to sleep all the time.
- Being too active or not active enough. Feeling noticeably restless or sluggish for prolonged periods.
- Loss of interest or pleasure in your usual activities, including a lack of interest in sexual activity.
- Having no energy, feeling tired all the time.
- Feeling that you're worthless or feeling inappropriately guilty. Blaming yourself for everything.
- Not feeling "normal"; feeling indecisive or unable to concentrate.
- Thinking a lot about being dead or about killing yourself.

Obviously, that last symptom is a big red flag. If you have any suicidal thoughts, talk to somebody immediately. Also seek help if several of these warning signs sound too familiar.

Almost everybody gets depressed sometime. With some people, depression happens because of a chemical imbalance in the brain—and this is a problem that can be fixed. We know it's hard to make yourself take that first step, but you have to do it. There are good treatments out there. The way you're feeling right now doesn't have to be permanent.

Anxiety

The same is true for bouts of anxiety, or "panic attacks." You wouldn't believe the physical symptoms that anxiety can cause. (The following list is adapted from the American Psychiatric Association's diagnostic criteria.)

- Chest pain or tightness
- Smothering sensations; feeling like you're choking
- Vertigo; feeling dizzy or unsteady
- "Unreal" feelings; feeling a sense of "weirdness"
- Tingling in the hands or feet
- Hot and cold flashes
- Sweating
- Feeling faint
- Trembling or shaking when you're not cold
- Fear of dying, going crazy, or doing something uncontrolled during one of these attacks

Some of those sound a lot like heart attack symptoms. Panic attacks can be terrifying. And, as with depression, there is help. Again, start with the counseling center. If you don't feel up to making the call or going to the counseling office, ask a friend to go with you.

Get your stress under control

Mental stress kills. Usually not instantaneously, but in increments; over time, its toll on the body is immense. Recent studies have shown that lowering the burden of stress on your body is better for you than exercise—and feeling hopeless is just as bad for you as smoking a pack of cigarettes a day.

Researchers at Duke University recently found that patients who learn to manage emotional and psychological stress factors lower their odds of having another heart attack or major heart problem by an astounding 74 percent. In another study, scientists at the Public Health Institute in Berkeley, California, found that men with high levels of hopelessness—defined as feeling like a failure, or having an uncertain future—had a 20-percent greater increase in "hardening of the arteries," or atherosclerosis (a condition that can lead to heart attack and stroke), than people with a more positive outlook. Hopelessness and worry can trigger your central nervous system to churn out "stress hormones," which besiege your poor heart, making it beat faster, and putting it in a constant state of "fight or flight." But get this: Laughing lowers your blood pressure, and makes your body produce "good" hormones like beta endorphins (which are chemically similar to morphine).

instantly—"The curtain rose. It was as if I woke up and there was color back in the world, and I could think of at least three reasons to live." He has stayed on medication ever since, he says, maintaining a base level of the drug in his system.

And he has "come out of the closet" to talk about his experiences, so others may be helped. One of his points is that depression can happen to anyone, at any time. "You can get it when you've been fired; you can also get it when you're happily married, everything's fine, and you've just been promoted. You can get it like the flu."

Among depression's most evil components, Cavett says, are the things it has made him believe about himself. "You think you're the exception, that one intractable case that will never be cured . . . that you will die wretched and unloved in an attic . . . that your talent was luck and you never were any good . . . that you deserve it." Seek help if several of the warning signs on page 220 sound too familiar. There are good treatments out there.

IF YOU NEED A TUTOR

Start by checking with the secretary at the appropriate department (for example, the Classics Department for a Latin problem). Chances are that the department has a list of students who are willing and able to tutor; it may even tell you their individual rates.

Then, make your own arrangements. *(Note: Get a copy of the list; if one tutor doesn't work out, don't give up—just move on to the next one.)* Prices are usually quite reasonable. Student tutoring fees begin as low as $5 an hour. Or, ask friends, your professor, and other classmates to recommend a tutor.

Another way to go is to seek off-campus professional tutoring offices, which are staffed by experienced teachers. Their services are usually advertised in student newspapers and on circulars posted on campus bulletin boards. These places almost always charge more; however, the results may be better than what you could get from a student tutor.

Many of the academic problems you're going to encounter in freshman French or college algebra, for example, can be solved with help from a student tutor in a few hours' time. *(Note: Whatever you decide to do, don't begrudge the money. Get this taken care of. If you need four sessions at five dollars an hour, that's about the cost of dinner at a decent restaurant and a movie.)*

These happy hormones produce a feeling of well-being. And what's good for the mind, researchers are realizing, is probably best for the body.

HELP FOR ACADEMIC PROBLEMS

If your grades head south . . . wring your hands. Hit a wall. Throw something. Panic. Get mad.

Then, when you've gotten all that out of your system, let's work to fix the problem. The first thing you need is clear: some no-nonsense self-analysis. Take an honest look at yourself and figure out why your grades are going down. The answer you get will suggest the most direct means of attacking the problem.

What's causing this? If, for example, your grades are in a tailspin because of an emotional problem—depression, perhaps, or anxiety or insecurity—then make a beeline to the counseling office, set up an appointment to see a counselor, and talk it out.

If the material in your courses is fairly standard stuff, but you just aren't getting it—math, foreign languages, and some sciences tend to set off this kind of confusion—your best solution may be simply to arrange for one or more private tutors to get you back on track. On the other hand, if your trouble comes in interpreting the material—if you're just not getting it (this often happens in humanities courses)—then try talking to your professor. *(Hint: You probably won't get a lot of help if you say something like, "You're just not explaining it well enough, Prof.")* Request an appointment and let your professor know you have a problem and—more important—that you're concerned about it. Some professors do their best teaching in individual conferences with their students.

Finally, if your self-analysis suggests you're headed for trouble because you can't or won't spend enough time studying (cheer up—this one is easy to fix!), then you might need to rethink your priorities and analyze the way you're currently spending your days and nights. If you're the high scorer on every video game at the student center, you might want to think about saving a few quarters and tapering off a little. Or you may need to take a leave of absence from the staff of the school newspaper, cut back your seven-dates-a-week social life, unload a time-consuming office in your fraternity or sorority, or even drop a hellish course if it's about to drag your other course grades (and you) down with it.

Don't just sit there and watch it happen—take action! The most important thing, though, is to do something now. Don't hold off until finals, when it's too late for the professor or your faculty adviser to do anything for you. Professors don't tend to be overly impressed with students who wait until the last day of classes to ask for help. ("I've been here every day, young man. Where have you been?" might be one question you could expect to get asked.)

Create your own feedback. So far, we've been talking about a situation in which it's easy to tell that your grades are slipping because you've got tangible proof—actual grades. But you may run into another problem, one more difficult to deal with, and that is when there are no grades until the final exam—and then it's all or nothing. A lot of courses are set up this way. You may think you're understanding the material as you go along, but you aren't sure. If that's the case, you need to create your own feedback.

So, every few days, ask yourself: "If the final exam in this course were held today, what questions would most likely be asked?" And, "How well would I answer them?" Once a week, review the material you've covered that week, and quiz yourself on it; then briefly go over what you've already learned. That way, you'll be building up a solid knowledge base—and you'll be in good shape long before the final exam.

Procrastinators anonymous

Let's talk about this subject later. No, really, we will get to it—we promise. WHAT! Come on, stop nagging, we said we'd do it. Can't you just give us a little more time? Why are you being so unreasonable? First thing tomorrow, we'll do it. Absolutely, that's the last word. Tomorrow. (Or, as Macbeth said, "Tomorrow, and tomorrow, and tomorrow . . .")

Okay, fine. Have it your own way. We'll talk about it now. Happy?

Procrastination is a big problem for a lot of people; in college, it probably accounts for more bad grades and, worse, more anxiety than just about any other single academic problem.

All of us prefer to put things off at times—mowing the lawn, cleaning the tub, writing that thank-you note,

GETTING A GRIP ON "MATH ANXIETY"

You are definitely not alone here. Millions of Americans suffer from some form of math anxiety. They're intimidated by the subject and avoid it whenever possible. Their eyes start to glaze over when they even look at a math problem, much less try to solve one.

But in this computer age, it's becoming increasingly more difficult to get through college without at least a low-level understanding of mathematics. Which means that, as a college student, you've got to get a grip on your math anxiety.

Many counseling centers offer some sort of help, using various tactics. One is to organize volunteer math-anxious students into informal support groups, where students can talk out their frustrations and begin to deal with them. Under the guidance of professional counselors, the students may then be given simple math problems to solve slowly and without pressure. Eventually, for many students, the math anxiety is either whipped outright or brought under sufficient control so they can get through their required math courses.

If your procrastination has become an entrenched life habit— and you can't shake it when you really need to get something done—then you need to see a counselor about ways to deal with it.

paying the bills, doing actual work. But in college, serious procrastinators can postpone themselves into scholarly oblivion.

We know what you're going through, and we have to admit that (at least for us) the urge to procrastinate doesn't go away after college. One of us has a lot of self-control, diligence, and discipline. He sets timetables and sticks to them. He describes himself as a "plodder," but day by day, he gets the job done.

The other one of us admires him. She is a major procrastinator who has to achieve a certain level of torment before she can make herself do anything. It has to be more uncomfortable for her *not* to do something than to just suck it up and do it. On a typical day, the farce begins as she fixes herself a big Coke, sits down at her home computer, and stares at the reproachful, blank screen. Then she notices something really important, like "There's a loose thread in this curtain." Or, "I bet the dogs would love a good, long walk." Sound familiar?

Procrastination is a big problem. In college, students with perfectionist tendencies seem especially vulnerable; they keep delaying work on a project until they finally find themselves overwhelmed by it.

Sometimes, procrastination reflects an actual emotional problem, such as resentment of authority (as symbolized by deadlines) or a longing to have more control over your own life. Sometimes it stems from a fear of failure or even a fear of success ("If I do well on this paper, I'll just put more pressure on myself to keep doing well on all the others. People will expect too much from me.")

If your procrastination has become an entrenched life habit—and you can't shake it when you really need to get something done—then you need to see a counselor about ways to deal with it.

Divide and conquer. For most people, procrastination is simply a time management problem. The procrastinator needs to learn how to analyze the tasks ahead and carve them up into workable, short-term objectives that can be attained one day at a time. Suppose, for example, you've got a test in freshman English next week on *King Lear*. You've leafed through the play, and what you skimmed over looks overwhelming. Don't panic. And don't procrastinate. Instead of muttering to yourself, a wild look in your glazed, bloodshot eyes, "I've got to read *King Lear* today," give yourself an easier, more manageable goal. Say instead, "Today, I'm going to read Act I of *King Lear*." Then do it. Pat yourself on the back for achieving a worthy objective, and go on with the rest of your life.

Your success with Act I will reinforce you for tomorrow, when you tackle Act II. By the end of the week, you'll have had the time and generated the momentum to read all five acts. *(Hint: Make little notes in the margin as you read, so you can find important passages later for review.)* Your next task might be to review the work, place the characters in context, go over your notes from your reading and class lectures, and anticipate any questions your professor might ask. You and the bard will be well acquainted by now, and you'll have won a series of impressive victories over your procrastination.

The same divide-and-conquer philosophy applies to papers you have to write. Don't—please!—hold off writing until you've thought up the perfect opening sentences. Just get something down on paper (or on computer, typewriter, or tape cassette—whatever works for you). Even if it's only a barely coherent smattering of phrases, sentence fragments and ideas you think are pertinent—even if it's really bad—at least it's *something*. And now you've got something to work with. Those first thoughts may not be elegantly expressed, but at least they'll give you a point of departure, something you can look at, coordinate, analyze, polish, and add to in later revisions.

Don't try to write the whole essay at once. Set a reasonable goal for today (three pages of a first draft, for example) and forge ahead. You'll get there. (Or, if you've already procrastinated, set a reasonable goal for this morning. Do it, then take a break. Set another goal for this afternoon, etc.)

Your college counseling office is used to answering questions and providing good answers about procrastination, so don't put off (no joke intended) seeking help if you need it. You may even want to sign up if they're offering any workshops on this subject. They're usually free, or available at a minimal cost, and in five or six study sessions, you can pick up useful insights into task and time management. You'll also find, in the process, that a lot of other students are coping with this same problem. Maybe you can help each other.

Your college counseling office is used to answering questions and providing good answers about procrastination, so don't put off (no joke intended) seeking help if you need it.

A RANGE OF SERVICES FOR STUDENTS WITH DISABILITIES

At one large southeastern university, the Office of Disabled Student Services offers a range of services for people with various disabilities. We're listing some of them here to give you some idea of the possibilities:

For deaf or hearing-impaired students: Interpreters for any academic required activity—lectures, advising, registration—for students who use sign language, and note-takers for those who do not. Also, it maintains a telecommunications device for the deaf (TDD), which is available for students making local calls.

For students with learning disabilities: Resources include course advisement, tutorial referral, personal and group counseling, help in obtaining course materials, in career planning and placement.

For mobility-impaired students: Modified housing in various residence halls and transportation to all academically related activities (except at night and weekends). The university also provides personal care attendants for students who need some extra help with personal hygiene and day-to-day living activities.

For visually impaired students: Resources include readers and note-takers, a special audio-book ordering service, with other assistance available on an as-needed basis.

HELP FOR STUDENTS WITH PHYSICAL DISABILITIES

It took a lot of years, with a lot of heartbreak during the wait, but there are now clear federal regulations aimed at ending the unjust and demeaning hassles affecting handicapped students. One of those is Section 504 of the Rehabilitation Act of 1973, which says that "no otherwise qualified handicapped individual in the United States . . . shall, solely by reason of his or her handicap, be excluded from the participation in, be denied the benefits of, or be subjected to discrimination under any program or activity receiving federal financial assistance."

Since your college or university almost certainly receives some federal aid, chances are excellent that massive efforts are being made on your campus to comply with this law. (It's funny how all you have to do is mention the possible loss of federal money to a college administration, and you immediately receive a top official's earnest and undivided attention.)

Section 504 does not require that every building or every part of a building be accessible to those with disabilities, just that the program as a whole be accessible. Some older classroom buildings may not yet have the ramps, elevators, and installations needed to accommodate students in wheelchairs. But if a student with a disability is assigned to a building that still has architectural barriers in it, then he or she must be reassigned to a comparable class in a building that is accessible, the entire class must be moved to an accessible location, or some other means must be employed, such as arranging to have the course material taught to the student at home. (This last alternative is clearly the least preferable; it's far better, educationally, to bring the student into the class, rather than bring the course content to the student.)

The Americans with Disabilities Act of 1990 (ADA) expands on the rights of the disabled by defining "an individual with a disability" as a person who has a mental or physical impairment that substantially limits a "major life activity," has a record of such impairment, or is regarded as having such an impairment. The ADA requires that public entities "must ensure that individuals with disabilities are not excluded from services, programs, and activities because buildings are inaccessible."

The University of South Carolina defines students with learning disabilities as having "a disorder in one or more of the basic psychological processes involved in understanding or in using language, spoken or written, which may manifest itself in an imperfect ability to listen, think, speak, read, write, spell, or do mathematical calculations. These disorders include such conditions as perceptual handicaps, brain injury, minimal brain dysfunction, dyslexia, and developmental aphasia." Should you be in college if you have a learning disability? You bet! "Students with learning disabilities are a part of every segment of the university," the statement continues. "They are undergraduate and graduate students. They are history majors and English majors. They are pre-med students and law students." Resources at your college may include academic, career and personal counseling; notetakers and readers, if you need them; textbooks and readings on tape; diagnostic assessment and referrals to specialists who can help you; tutors; computer-assisted learning; and study skills workshops. You may also be able to audit a course before you take it for credit, take alternative tests (this may mean an extended test time, or answering questions orally instead of on paper) and do alternative assignments (which will differ only in form, not substance), and take a reduced course load of nine hours or more, without losing your status as a full-time student.

While there is much work left to be done, most institutions have devoted a great deal of energy and money toward making their campuses accessible through ramps, curb cuts, and remodeled rest-room facilities. But that's just the tip of the iceberg, and it only deals with one form of impairment. Now, many schools also employ specially trained teachers to work with students who have speech or hearing disabilities, and many college libraries offer sophisticated magnifying equipment and a range of audiotapes to help students with severely impaired vision.

Note: Your college will probably have some procedure set up to handle complaints of discrimination based on a disability—and may even offer you assistance in composing and filing the complaint—but there may be a time limit (at one university, it's fifteen working days after an incident takes place). So if you want to file a complaint, make sure you don't miss this "window."

Our advice: Don't just show up at school determined to "mainstream" and let pride or independence keep you from getting some extra help if you need it.

A WORD ON HAVING SEX WITH A PROFESSOR

What are you, NUTS? This relationship may not be forbidden at your school, but it's probably not heartily endorsed. With good reason.

"A professional power differential exists in these situations, in terms of the influence and authority which the one can exercise over the other," says one university's sexual harassment policy. "If a charge of sexual harassment is lodged regarding a once-consenting relationship, the burden may be on the alleged offender to prove that the sexual harassment policy was not violated." Or more likely, the burden could be on you to prove that it was.

Think about it: No offense, but your professor must be pretty immature to be romantically interested in a college freshman. No matter how emotionally and intellectually sophisticated you may be now, ideally you will have matured even more in a few years—at which point you probably won't be dating 18-year-olds. So why is your professor?

Look: If it's meant to be, the attraction won't fade away. Give it some time, and definitely don't get involved while your grade depends on the professor's evaluation. (Just imagine how, if the romance sours, your life in that class could become a living hell.)

At larger schools, particularly state universities, there might be an office for students with disabilities (it may be called something like the Office of Equal Opportunity) to provide information and support. Each academic department should have a designated faculty or staff member to deal with specific concerns of such students—provisions for special exams, course scheduling, classroom changes, and similar matters. The names of these people may be announced during orientation; if not, get them from the office of the dean of students.

SEXUAL HARASSMENT AND DISCRIMINATION

Whether consciously motivated or not, sexual harassment does occur throughout society, and college professors, who should know better, can be as guilty as anyone else. Sex discrimination and harassment can take many forms. For example, your professor may not regard your career goals seriously, believing them to be unsuitable for members of your sex. You may be subjected to pressure by a professor to participate with him or her in social and/or sexual activities. Maybe you don't get a fair shot at financial aid, admission to a program, or some other academic benefit for sexist reasons. Or, you may find that the material in your course (lectures or textbook) demeans you because of your sex.

If you are discriminated against or harassed, you may feel helpless and alone. No need to. The law is on your side, and there are people on your campus, such as affirmative action officers, who can help.

Steps you can take

Here is a list of specific options if you're victimized by sex discrimination or harassment. These steps are adapted from a statement issued by the Utah State University Commission on the Status of Women and reported in that school's orientation book. They apply to campuses everywhere and, as warranted, they should be carried out in the order given.

Before you do anything, step back, scrutinize the situation calmly from all sides, and examine your own heart: Does your claim have substance? In other words, if you make a big stink because "he looked at me in a suggestive way," or "he gave me a C because I'm a woman," you're probably wasting your effort; you can't prove that. Did the incident really bother you? Did it truly hurt—badly enough that it's worth making an issue over? Was it absolutely offensive and unforgivable? Or could you let it roll off your back—this time—and save your fights for something more worthwhile? Like, if this happens again or becomes part of a continuing pattern of harassment. Can you *prove* that it happened, or will it be your word against the professor's? (Which doesn't mean you shouldn't pursue it, but you should think about what you're letting yourself in for.) Did you document anything? Did you write down what happened immediately after the incident, or has it been a few weeks? Examine your motives: Are you being self-righteous, or are you out to hurt the professor for some other reason—like a bad grade, or a put-down about a point you raised in class that had nothing to do with sexual harassment? Or, are you doing the only thing your conscience will allow? If so, and you want to pursue it, read on.

- **First, talk to the professor.** Explain why you consider a particular action or comment to be sexist. And give your professor the benefit of the doubt. The offense might have been committed through ignorance, not malice. A lot of times, people just don't realize how their remarks can hurt. (Ask the professor: Would you make fun of a person's skin color or religion? They why do so with sex?) In many cases, just "raising the consciousness" of the offender might be enough to prevent careless, perhaps unintentional, sexism in the future.
- **Contact relevant campus authorities.** Almost every college has an affirmative action officer (usually a faculty or staff member appointed for a given term). Your academic dean knows what the law says about sex discrimination and so does your dean of students. They will listen to you and provide help and advice.
- **Put your complaint in writing.** If you've talked to the professor and sex discrimination or harassment continues, write a letter to him or her outlining the specific incidents, and explain why they offended you. Send a copy of your letter to the professor's department chairman, to your dean, and to your campus affirmative action

If you are discriminated against or harassed, you may feel helpless and alone. No need to. The law is on your side, and there are people on your campus, such as affirmative action officers, who can help.

ANOTHER OPTION: TRY AN ADVOCACY GROUP

In Baltimore and many cities, the new trend in helpful local TV newsland is for stations to be your friend. One way they do this is by having a reporter serve as a consumer advocate. Some of their catchy slogans are "(Channel) Eleven On Your Side," or "Get Gelfman" (the name of the particular reporter)," or "Contact Two." Actually, these services seem to be pretty good.

Say you had a financial dispute with your landlord, who promised to remove the asbestos in your walls before you move in and now wants to do it while you try not to breathe as they dig out the insulation. Understandably, you want to move, but the greedy pig won't let you out of your contract. If a local TV advocacy service chose to take your case, what it would basically do is give the landlord a hard time and make him look bad until he released you from the contract.

Other groups might also be able to help: The Better Business Bureau, for example, takes complaints of unfair business practice and serves as a clearinghouse for consumer information about questionable companies or activities. The local or national chapter of the American Civil Liberties Union is especially vigilant in matters involving discrimination and freedom of speech, religion, and assembly. Your state or county Attorney General's office may operate a Consumer Protection Agency, to investigate questionable business practices.

officer. This should get some results. In addition, you can write out your complaints in your student evaluation of the course, if your school provides this option. These comments will be read by deans and department heads and taken into account in determining the professor's yearly performance rating.

- **File a formal grievance.** This is a very serious step—it's virtually a legal proceeding—and it shouldn't be undertaken without thought, discussion, and counsel.

Important note: The overwhelming majority of discrimination cases can be corrected without ever going beyond Step 1. Old prejudices are disappearing fast on most campuses, and the climate today is far healthier than it has ever been. But any sex discrimination is too much, and if it happens to you, know that you can fight back.

One school's policy

Almost every college has a detailed sexual harassment policy. Here's the setup at one large state university (we're quoting from the official policy statement):

"In order to maintain an environment in which the dignity and worth of all members of the institutional community are respected . . . sexual harassment of employees or students is prohibited. Such conduct is unacceptable and will not be tolerated. It is a form of behavior which seriously undermines the atmosphere of trust essential to the academic environment. . . It is also the policy of the University that willful false accusations of sexual harassment shall not be condoned."

(Note: We shouldn't even have to say this, but if your judgment is so bad that you're even considering making up a false statement to "get back" at a professor, forget it. You could be expelled and even sued for damages in a court of law. Remember, you're playing with two reputations here—yours as well as that of the person you accuse.)

"Sexual harassment offenders shall be subject to disciplinary action which may include, but is not limited to, oral or written warnings, demotion, transfer, suspension or dismissal for cause. . . .

"Sexual harassment may involve the behavior of a person of either sex against a person of the opposite or same sex . . . (it) is defined as unwelcome sexual advances, requests for sexual favors, verbal or other expressive behaviors, or physical conduct commonly understood to be of a sexual nature when:

- submission to such conduct is made either explicitly or implicitly a term or condition of an individual's employment or education;
- submission to or rejection of such conduct is used as a basis for academic or employment decisions or assessments affecting the individual's welfare as an employee or student;
- such conduct has the purpose or effect of unreasonably and substantially interfering with an individual's welfare, academic, or professional performance, or creates an intimidating, hostile, offensive, and demeaning work or educational environment.

"Prohibited acts of sexual harassment may take a variety of forms ranging from subtle pressure for sexual activity to physical assault. Examples . . . include:

- threats or intimidation of sexual relations or sexual contact which is not freely or mutually agreeable to both parties;
- continual or repeated verbal abuses of a sexual nature, including graphic commentaries about a person's body; sexually suggestive objects or pictures placed in the work or study area that may embarrass or offend the person; sexually degrading words to describe the person, or propositions of a sexual nature;
- threats or insinuations that the person's employment, grades, wages, promotional opportunities, classroom or work assignments, or other conditions of employment or academic life may be adversely affected by not submitting to sexual advances."

Sexual harassment may involve the behavior of a person of either sex against a person of the opposite or same sex.

IF YOU NEED LEGAL HELP

First, contact the office of the dean of students: Many universities retain an attorney who visits the campus several hours a week to answer students' legal questions.

If you're living away from your parents and you don't have a lot of money, check out the Legal Services office in your area. If you qualify financially, this federally funded, free service can provide you with civil (but not criminal) legal assistance.

If you want to hire a lawyer and don't know how to find one, consult the telephone directory for the number of your local or state bar association. Someone there can help by matching your particular need with the type of law practiced by one or more attorneys nearby.

Try working within the system. If you need help with an academically related problem—if you've been verbally abused by a teacher, for example, or wrongfully accused of cheating—then find out what your options are. At many institutions, committees (made up of students, faculty, and staff members) are set up to handle academic and other grievances.

At the University of South Carolina, a "nonacademic" grievance committee handles "dissatisfaction occurring when a student thinks that any condition affecting him/her is unjust, inequable, or creates unnecessary hardship," which may include "mistreatment by any University employee, wrongful assessment and processing of fees, records and registration errors, racial discrimination, sex discrimination, (and) handicapped discrimination."

Such committees are there to handle fairly serious injustices (so don't come to them with your campus parking tickets, no matter how heinous and unfair they may truly be—they won't want to hear it), and there's usually a time limit in which the grievance must be filed.

Another good option: See if your college has an ombudsman. On many larger campuses, the ombudsman conducts impartial investigations into student complaints, and the findings—as professors and administrators can tell you—are listened to with great respect. The ombudsman is usually a senior, tenured member of the faculty who has been asked to serve a year or two in that delicate position. (The term ombudsman, for you "Jeopardy" hopefuls, is Swedish and was originally used to describe an official who investigates complaints against public officials.)

Working independently of the college administration and all other groups on campus, the ombudsman, like Superman, seeks to combat injustice and resolve conflicts. Students can communicate with their ombuds-

The ombudsman, like Superman, seeks to combat injustice and resolve conflicts.

man in confidence. Though most ombudsmen don't have the power to reverse decisions or to punish people, they do have the ability—and the clout—to raise hell on the students' behalf. Which is often enough.

IF A FRIEND'S IN TROUBLE: HOW TO HANDLE IT

You can't make somebody else happy. You can give someone everything—flowers, gifts, money, candy, the moon, your time and your love—but happiness. That has to come from within.

However, you may be able to point somebody on that right road, the one that will lead to happiness. If she's angry, you can hear her out; if he's upset, you can offer a hug or a shoulder to cry on; if she's scared, you can be there, giving moral support; and if he's in trouble, you can try to help him.

Note: "Try" is the key word here. Give it your best shot. But also know that if it doesn't work out it's not going to be your fault.

One of the toughest lessons we've ever learned is that sometimes you have to let people bottom out. You can't stop an alcoholic from drinking; only he can stop himself. You can't stop a bulimic from binge-eating and purging; only she can do it. But you can urge your friend to get help. Or, if the problem's bad enough, you can go over your friend's head and bring in the big guns—the resident adviser or your friend's parents, for instance, or even, as a last resort, the police (if your friend is doing something illegal, such as using or selling drugs, or something unsafe, such as getting beaten up by her boyfriend). You can be there to pick up the pieces, when your friend is finally ready to seek help.

Another word of advice: Know what you can handle, and what you can't. If your friend lays a major emotional or ethical burden on you, there's no shame in talking to someone else (a counselor, resident adviser, or professor) about it. This doesn't mean you should violate your friend's confidentiality and blab to the whole school that he's tested positive for AIDS, or that since her parents' divorce, she's been talking a lot lately about suicide. That would be cruel, exploitative and definitely not the way to treat someone who trusted you to be a friend. But what this does mean is that you shouldn't get

SUICIDE: ONE FRIEND'S STORY

"Last year, when I was a senior in high school," says Erica, an Indiana University freshman, "I was dating this guy named Paul, who was kind of needy—clingy, you know what I mean? We weren't serious or anything, and he felt a lot more for me than I did for him. I started to get kind of irritated with him, and I was pretty much ready to end our relationship. Well, one night he called me, and I wasn't too nice to him. Then, about an hour later, he called me back, and I felt guilty about the way I'd treated him before, so I was very caring.

"The next day, he wasn't at school. That afternoon, he called me—from the hospital!" It turned out that Paul, who was upset by his divorced father's new relationship with a younger woman and his mother's extreme, toxic bitterness toward his father, had tried to kill himself by taking all of his mother's Valiums. (Actually, a doctor tells us, this probably wouldn't have killed him, but still, the thought was there, and it was acted upon.)

"Paul said that I had stopped him! That because I had been so nice to him, he told his mother what he'd done, she rushed him to the hospital, and they pumped his stomach. He said he was alive because of me!"

Erica, as she tells it, became intensely angry at what Paul had done. "I was 17 years old; I couldn't handle the responsibility. It overwhelmed me. I wanted to say, 'Look, what you did, you did all by yourself, not because of me. It was your choice; you are responsible for your own actions.' But I didn't. I didn't know what to say. I told him I loved him. I lied. I didn't ever want to see him again. Actually, my mother ended up talking to him a lot more than I did; she wanted to help him, but I know she also wanted to help me."

Erica continued to date Paul for several more months, until she felt he was over the suicide attempt. "Then I broke up with him. I said I would be his friend, but not his girlfriend. Maybe I shouldn't have done it, but I didn't want to be in charge of his mental health. I felt like he was trying to bring me down, too."

Erica's decision may not be the right one for you. Only you know what that would be. Also, she didn't make it spontaneously; she agonized over what to do and spent hours talking to her clergyman as well as her parents.

overwhelmed by the magnitude of someone else's problem; just shifting the load over to you is not going to make the problem go away.

Here are a few problems your friends (or you) might encounter:

Suicidal talk

He keeps talking about ending the pain, about what it would feel like to be dead. It gives you the creeps, but you keep listening because you think you're helping him. What should you do? You're totally stressed out over this. Lately, you've dreamed that you walk in the door of your dorm room and find him hanging from the light fixture.

Well, this talk may be an attempt to gain attention, and it's almost certainly a cry for help that should be taken seriously. It's also too much responsibility for you to attempt to handle on your own. Professional counseling is urgently needed—perhaps for both of you—and it is available. Virtually every campus has access to highly trained psychologists and/or psychiatrists who can help students begin to get at the reason for their depression. (Note: Your friend's depression might be a medical problem; see "Help for Emotional Problems," page 219.)

If your roommate or friend won't seek help voluntarily, then you should alert the counseling center and/or the health clinic in your roommate's behalf. It would be better for your relationship if you got permission first—but obviously, this is a secondary consideration. "Look, buddy, you need to see a professional about your problem. Now, If you don't make the call, I will. I don't want you to think I'm ratting on you, but this is just too important to ignore." It's also too important for either of you to try to solve on your own.

Important note: Just because your friend or roommate has involved you doesn't mean his living or dying is your responsibility. It isn't, and don't let him make you part of the decision.

Suicide can be an end to pain; it can also be an incredibly hurtful and two-faced action, if someone does it in a pathetic attempt to "get back" at someone else or to "show them." Ultimately, it's his decision. Not yours. And if, God forbid, the worst happens, it's not your fault—no matter how much you may be tempted to blame yourself or to punish yourself for what he did.

Signs of anorexia or bulimia

Whether the problem is anorexia nervosa (a disorder that happens mainly in women, in which someone who is unreasonably terrified of being or becoming too fat refuses to eat much of anything at all, and begins literally wasting away) or bulimia (the binge-purge disease, which also mainly strikes females, in which someone gorges huge amounts of food, then either vomits or takes laxatives to avoid gaining weight), your roommate or friend needs professional help. It's a medical problem. Are you a doctor? No? Then you're neither medically qualified nor emotionally equipped to deal with a depressive condition of this magnitude and complexity.

Once rare, anorexia and bulimia are now being diagnosed on campuses across the country. Medical experts estimate that as many as 7 million women will suffer symptoms of bulimia at some point in their lives; college counselors believe that as many as 10 percent of the coeds on some campuses are bulimic. (Men do suffer from this, but the incidence is much lower.) Your friend might look healthy now, but she's probably already suffering (or will suffer, if she doesn't get help) from internal disorders and may be prone to other psychological disturbances, which frequently manifest themselves in suicide and alcohol and drug abuse. Both diseases, in other words, can be deadly.

First, urge your roommate or friend to seek professional care. Beg. Bribe. If your entreaty doesn't work, then notify your resident adviser and, if it becomes serious, the counseling center or health clinic. And then, if your roommate will not get help, you may want to move to a different room. It sounds callous, but it might be that the alternative—trying to live with someone who urgently requires treatment—is bad for both of you.

Why should you sacrifice yourself on the altar of your friend's mental illness? If she's determined to self-destruct, are you somehow less of a friend if you don't sit right there and watch it happen? No. *(Remember the first rule—somebody else's happiness is not up to you.)* Those for whom staying thin is an illness usually don't make good roommates. (If you think about it, your friend is pretty self-involved; she's got to know what she's doing is hurting you and others, but she keeps right on. That's not great mutual friendship.) Their frequent, uncontrollable urge for food often leads them to steal

BULIMIA: ONE FRIEND'S STORY

"The total, absolute denial of her problem really got to me after a few weeks," says Melanie. During the first semester of her freshman year, she lived with Eileen, who was bulimic. (Eileen transferred to another college at the end of the semester.)

"It was so creepy. I knew what Eileen was doing in the bathroom; I could see her feet under the stall—so she was facing the toilet. And she knew I knew. One night I stood there for an hour, banging on the door, screaming at her to come out. I stood up on the toilet in the next stall and shouted down at her. She was completely silent, and wouldn't look up. She pretended like I wasn't there. I was shaking and crying, I was so upset. When I finally went away, she came out and acted like nothing had happened."

Melanie became increasingly distressed as she watched her roommate waste away. "One afternoon, I saw her walking on campus from a distance, and I noticed how skinny her legs were for the first time. They were like twigs—like the people you saw on the news in Somalia. And I thought, 'She's killing herself.' " Melanie talked to an official in the housing office about Eileen, "but I don't think anything ever came of it. He suggested that I should get counseling to deal with my anger toward her!"

Melanie lost touch with Eileen almost immediately; they hadn't been that close, and Eileen left no forwarding address. "To tell you the truth, I'm glad she left. I know something bad was going to happen to her, and I'm glad it didn't happen in front of me. I tried to help her, and she wouldn't let me. I worried a lot about her, and I felt guilty that I couldn't reach her. I still do."

KNOW WHAT YOU CAN HANDLE AND WHAT YOU CAN'T

If your friend lays a major emotional or ethical burden on you, there's no shame in talking to someone else (a counselor, resident adviser, or professor) about it.

This doesn't mean you should violate your friend's confidentiality and blab to the whole school that he's tested positive for AIDS, or that since her parents' divorce, she's been talking a lot lately about suicide. That would be cruel, exploitative, and definitely not the way to treat someone who trusted you to be a friend.

But what this does mean is that you shouldn't get overwhelmed by the magnitude of someone else's problem; just shifting the load over to you is not going to make the problem go away.

from others, roommates included. Worst of all is the emotional damage they intentionally or unintentionally inflict on those around them.

In extreme cases, the treatment may require hospitalization and antidepressant medication; under tightly controlled conditions, the patient gradually learns to eat normally. In addition to medical treatment, psychological help—getting to the emotional causes of the problem, and rebuilding the patient's self-esteem—is crucial. In any event, what your friend needs is a lot more than what you can offer; she needs professional attention. And you might, too, if you try to cope alone with a situation that could lead to a devastating outcome.

A friend with a positive AIDS test

First, fight the pariah syndrome: You probably know this already, but we'll say it anyway: You can't get AIDS by being friends with someone who has it.

You can't get it from a squeeze of the hand or a hug. You can't pick it up from eating food prepared by someone with AIDS, or through drinking glasses or dishes. Actually, the virus is a real weenie compared with macho bugs such as the common cold virus—it can't survive more than a few seconds outside the human body. Also, it's easily killed by heat, alcohol, and contact with other solutions, such as bleach.

And yet, with all we've learned about the disease in the last decade, there remains this terrible dread of AIDS that can cause us to shrink away from someone who has it. Most of the fears are ignorant and unfounded, but they persist. Because they do, many people with AIDS have been treated shamefully—like pariahs. (Several years ago, a worried professor we know once tried to propose a policy change that would protect professors from having to teach in the same classroom as a student with AIDS. Fortunately, the professor was soon persuaded that the virus is not known ever to have been passed along during an academic discussion.)

Having HIV, the virus that causes AIDS, doesn't mean someone's life is over—far from it. In fact, people with HIV can live for years without having any symptoms of AIDS at all. With better medicines and treatments to bolster the body's immune system, the prognosis and life expectancy should get even brighter in the years to come. Urge your friend to get in touch with a medical center where new drugs and treatments are being studied. (Some resources are listed in Chapter Eleven.)

Another important thing you can do is urge your friend to share this diagnosis with any sexual partners he or she may have had—not to accuse them of passing on the AIDS virus (it's a little late for that), but so they can get tested, too. This is the responsible thing, and your friend owes it to them to do it.

Finally, the best thing you can do for your friend is to continue to be a friend. Don't turn away. Your friend is going to be struggling with some major personal and medical issues. Now more than ever, your support is going to matter—a lot.

FRIENDLY CONTACT DOESN'T SPREAD AIDS

Careful studies of people sharing the same household as a family member with AIDS turn up absolutely no evidence that the virus could be spread by hugging, kissing, sharing of bathroom and kitchen facilities, and other close, but non-sexual, contact. Mosquitoes can't spread the disease, either.

You can get AIDS from an exchange of body fluids during unprotected sex (when a condom wasn't used, or used improperly) or from injecting yourself with a dirty needle. (For a discussion of AIDS, see Chapter Eleven.)

CHAPTER 13

Making Plans for the Long Haul

As important as college is right now, in the long run it's just a stepping-stone in your life. A big stepping-stone, but a stepping-stone all the same. So was high school. So was kindergarten.

When one of us played high school football, he spent a lot of time in a training room lined with hand-lettered slogans designed to inspire fever-pitch bloodlust and macho bravery and to quell any rational thoughts about the possibility of, say, being maimed by the drooling, 200-pound, no-neck linebacker breathing down his throat and threatening to kill him:

"No pain, no gain."

"When the going gets tough, the tough get going!"

"A team that won't be beat can't be beat."

"Winners never quit, and quitters never win."

One of those slogans, however, actually hit home: "What you are going to be," it said, "you are now becoming."

Your personality, your level of ambition and drive, your priorities and choices—they're all beginning to form a pattern. Nothing's set in stone yet, which is good. This means that no bad habits are irreversible and that it's not too late to work on something you'd like to change about yourself. But a trend is definitely being established. You are moving toward who you're going to be.

So now is a good time to begin thinking about some decisions that you'll be facing soon—what you want to be when you grow up, and who you want to be.

COLLEGE AND ETHICS AND MORALITY

So much lip service has been paid in recent years to the catchy-sounding concept of "traditional values," that the phrase has been watered down almost to the point of having no meaning (but it still sounds good, which makes it ideal for political use). So let's not use it. Let's talk, instead, about ethics and morality—without which, civilization as we know it is pretty much of a crap shoot. By ethics and morality, we mean: Standing for something. Believing in something, and living your life to reflect that belief. Having a personal code.

More than a generation ago, a professor we know said, "We call ourselves higher education. We do a pretty fair job of teaching people how to make a living. We don't do a very good job of teaching people how to get along together and behave in a decent and honorable way." This was years before Watergate, before the insider trading scandals on Wall Street, before Whitewater or Intern-gate, before talk shows and TV movies gave some legitimacy to notoriety, and before the word "sleaze" became such a familiar part of our national vocabulary.

But it hasn't been ever thus—the academic world hasn't always taken such a "hands-off" approach. Universities used to take decidedly strong stands on moral and ethical issues. In fact, America's earliest colleges were thought of by settlers mainly as training grounds for ministers and devout laymen in the faith. Eventually, political leaders realized that more people than ministers needed advanced education. State-supported colleges and universities represented one response to the problem. But even in the state schools, many professors saw themselves as keepers of the flame—sentinels of social traditions and values. Lectures reflected a stern moral tone. Outside the classroom, student behavior was closely monitored (colleges acted *in loco parentis*—in place of parents) and disciplinary codes were tough.

Aren't you glad you didn't go to college back then?

The sixties, of course, changed all that. Ever since then, students have demanded, and gotten, far more freedom outside the classroom. And professors have redefined their role. Most professors now feel their job is to inform students—not preach to them or attempt to tell them how to live. The pendulum has definitely swung back the other way. Has it swung too far? Consider:

- The conflict of interest charges that plague every Presidential administration

Nothing's set in stone yet, which is good. This means that no bad habits are irreversible and that it's not too late to work on something you'd like to change about yourself.

By being so committed to the idea of tolerance, that—unwilling to offend anyone—they've created mini-moral vacuums. By being ethical weenies.

- The bribery, corruption, and illegal trading activities that recently rocked the financial world (specifically, the insider trading and savings & loan scandals)
- Medicare kickbacks, unnecessary surgical procedures, and other embarrassments to the medical community
- Shady arms deals that led to shakeups within the military and intelligence establishment

And so on. Such acts aren't committed by underprivileged high school dropouts; these and similar offenses almost always represent the work of some highly educated individuals—men and women educated at some of our country's most prestigious institutions—who achieved technical brilliance but, somewhere along the way, lost their moral compass.

It could be said, by those who look for accountability (also a popular buzzword), that colleges have failed such people—if not by actual commission (and let's face it, no college actually teaches a course called "Corruption 101"), then by omission. By hedging. By being reluctant to take stands. By being so committed to the idea of tolerance, that—unwilling to offend anyone—they've created mini-moral vacuums. By being ethical weenies.

What colleges have done, instead of bringing ethics into every course, is to create and emphasize separate courses in ethical behavior, which are usually offered in specific disciplines (in schools of business, law, medicine, education, and mass communication). These classes explore means of setting standards of behavior in the workplace; they also provide students with methods for developing moral judgments about professional dilemmas. Business and political science students, for example, learn ways to combine material success with social consciousness. Mass communications students analyze a whole boatload of gritty ethical dilemmas, including freebies, junkets, shielding the confidentiality of news sources, unwarranted invasions of personal privacy, and avoiding bias in reporting the news.

Most of these courses are designed to confront students with a barrage of ethical quandaries, but no easy answers. It's usually up to the students to come up with solutions on their own, helped by much outside reading and research. A well-taught ethics class is tough.

But the reward can last a lifetime, if it helps you determine your personal values and standards—because ambiguity, complexity and uncertainty are part of adult life (not that being a child and teenager was simple). And success is measured—or at least it should be—not only by what you accomplish, but how you do it. Thus the ethics course.

We should note that the idea of ethics courses—what one ethicist calls the "ghettoizing" of ethics—itself may be changing. For example: The Johns Hopkins School of Medicine recently completed a major curriculum overhaul that adds an ethical dimension to the study of nearly every subject. So instead of simply studying embryology, students will also address the bigger picture—causes of congenital malformation, how to prevent them, the family impact of a disabled child, and challenging issues related to genetic screening. Also, Vanderbilt University recently announced endowment of a multidisciplinary program, involving the schools of management, divinity, law and medicine, aimed at developing leaders with a greater sense of morality and vision. Such programs and innovations are springing up at colleges throughout the country as, in torrents and trickles, ethics is going "mainstream."

WHAT DO YOU WANT TO BE WHEN YOU GROW UP?

Decided yet? Huh? Come on, declared a major yet? Huh? What do you mean, you don't know?

Well, if you don't know now, as a freshman, you might as well hang it up. You're finished. Life as you know it is over.

WAIT! We were just kidding! It's okay if you don't know. In fact, it's perfectly fine. It's very common. So if you're not sure now, don't worry about it. You've got plenty of time to decide. Don't think you're the only one out there who ever spent freshman year as an "undecided" major—you're not. Don't worry about those people out there who seem to know, almost from birth, exactly what they want to do with their lives: "I'm going to finish my degree, work for two years, then take some time off to start a family; I will conceive in the summer, so I can have the baby in the spring, before it gets too hot outside." (Honest, we really do know people who plan things down to this level of detail!)

Don't think you're the only one out there who ever spent freshman year as an "undecided" major—you're not. Don't worry about those people out there who seem to know, almost from birth, exactly what they want to do with their lives.

So what if these people spend their college years in efficient, untroubled preparation for their careers? So what if their lives are meticulously organized? Don't let that intimidate or depress you. Don't consider yourself a failure if you don't have your life all planned out by the end of your freshman year.

Choosing your major: points to consider

Think about this: A major, or field of concentration, is simply a series of courses designed to provide you with a strong background in the academic area you're most attracted to. That's it—a bunch of courses in a specific area. A chunk of your overall curriculum. (Generally, declaring a major is an easy process: All you have to do is indicate your choice on your registration form, and the administration takes it from there.)

A major is just one part of your college education. You'll probably devote only a quarter to a third of your total course work to your major field; most of your hours will be consumed by general requirements and elective subjects.

In some career fields, your undergraduate major may not even matter much in the long run.

In some career fields, your undergraduate major may not even matter much in the long run. Law is one of these. Most law school admission policies recognize that a background in almost any field of study can be valuable. Advertising is another case in point. Highly successful advertising people are known to have majored in business, where they learned marketing; in journalism, where they got some understanding of the mass media; in English, where they studied great writing; in fine arts, where they were exposed to creative concepts; or in psychology, where they learned behavior patterns.

For other lines of work, however, the undergraduate major is the direct—and possibly the only—route that leads you into your chosen field. If you want to be a grade-school teacher, the sooner you declare a major in elementary education, the better. Fulfilling rigid teacher certification requirements will take up most of your course schedule, and a late decision could delay your degree. Engineering students also face a tough, complex set of requirements; so do students in music and a number of other areas.

By and large, though, your schedule probably does have some breathing room. So before you declare a major, you may want to consider the following:

- **Don't be anxious if you're not sure.** The worst move you could make right now would be to declare a "panic major." So what if the academic bureaucrats are hovering over you for a decision? (Don't blame them; they're just trying to shuttle your records over to the right department and assign you an appropriate faculty adviser.) You can usually fend them off for a while by declaring yourself "undecided."
- **Don't hesitate to take advantage of the academic counselors and aptitude testing resources available on your campus.** This is why they exist—to help you figure out what you want to do with your life. Once you've narrowed it down to a career, or even a general field, like Public Health, the problem of choosing a major (in this case, your choices could include epidemiology, biostatistics, health promotion, or environmental public health) usually takes care of itself.
- **Think of the long-range marketability of the major.** There are a lot of interesting, nontraditional, or esoteric majors out there— American studies, women's studies, ethnic studies, environmental studies. But before you declare such a major, think about the bigger picture. What are you going to do with your degree? What kind of job are you looking for? You may be planning to continue your education—for example, to take your bachelor's degree in women's studies and go to law school. In and of itself, however, the degree in women's studies—while certainly a worthy subject—may not open up as many employment opportunities for you as more traditional majors.

  Don't get us wrong: We're taking no stand here; we just want to make sure you have a plan, and that you don't graduate with a degree you can't use.
- **Consider minoring in the less marketable subject and majoring in something more directly related to your planned career.**
- **Think beyond the entry-level job and be careful not to limit your options.** If your dream is to be a television sportscaster, don't just limit yourself to

DESIGN YOUR OWN MAJOR

Choose a theme and then develop it with courses from a number of departments. (Individualized majors usually involve additional course work and endorsements from a faculty adviser and a dean.) Say, for example, that you're interested in becoming an expert on Latin America, and you get approval to develop an interdisciplinary major in this area. The courses for your major, in this case, would be drawn from such departments as political science, history, economics, foreign languages, sociology, and geography.

Choosing an individualized major can be a sign of intellectual creativity and curiosity, determination, assertiveness, industriousness, and other characteristics that potential employers (and admissions committees at graduate and professional schools) look for.

required journalism and communications courses. You'd do better to develop a course of study that also includes TV programming, management, accounting, communications law, and broadcast production. Who knows? Twenty years from now, you could be running the station.

Changing your major

It happens all the time. Changing your major may alarm your parents ("I wish Nicholas would just make up his mind about his future—why can't he be more like his big brother, Johnny, who knew from the day he started college that he wanted to be an orthodontist . . ."), but it really shouldn't. After all, college is your golden opportunity for growth and exposure to new subjects and different ideas. It's perfectly natural that, as you learn more, you may become fascinated with a field you never even knew existed a year ago. If this is the case, college is doing its job; it's broadening your horizons. Let it.

Academically, changing your major is no big deal—at least in your freshman and sophomore years—because no matter what your major, the general requirements (which you've probably been taking all along) are probably the same.

Academically, changing your major is no big deal—at least in your freshman and sophomore years—because no matter what your major, the general requirements (which you've probably been taking all along) are probably the same. It's no big deal from the college administration's point of view, either; to them, a change of majors is simple—a routine bookkeeping transaction.

All you'll probably need to do is the following:

- Notify the department in which your records are currently kept that you're making the change and request that your records be forwarded to the new department
- Request (and make sure you get) a faculty adviser in the new department
- Indicate your major on the enrollment form the next time you register.

Note: Before you do anything, make sure you won't have a problem getting admitted into the new department. At many universities, there are high-demand departments that have tightened their admissions standards, so do some checking before you make your final decision.

Suppose, for example, you want to switch your major from English in the College of Arts and Sciences to marketing in the College of Business Administration. But Business, faced with too many majors, has adopted a stringent policy that all entering transfers must have at least a 2.5 GPA, while yours is only a 2.3. You might ask for a waiver and try to get in anyway, but unless your petition is approved, you may be shut out of that major. (In which case, it's possible that you could still minor in it. Or, work on your GPA—if you have the luxury of time to do this—and apply again.)

If you're otherwise qualified, however, you'll find that changing your major is a relatively quick and painless procedure. This doesn't mean it should be done capriciously. While trying to decide whether to change your major, you might discover that the new department has an entirely different set of requirements—additional courses that could keep you in college for another year or more. For this reason alone, it's a good idea to hold off declaring a new major until you're reasonably sure of your commitment to it. While you're making up your mind, you can list yourself as "undecided." This way, you'll still get a faculty adviser—probably one who has a broad understanding of just this kind of problem—and you can profitably spend your time working away at those general distribution requirements.

Studying a foreign language

A well-known southern college football coach, reluctantly sitting through an all-faculty curriculum meeting, once silenced the room by grumbling: "I don't know why my players have to take a foreign language in the first place. After all, if English was good enough for Jesus, it's good enough for me!"

Sadly, the coach's comment—though appalling and, historically inaccurate—pretty much sums up what many Americans believe. It's true that English has indeed become hugely popular around the globe. (The Cable News Network is beamed around the globe, right?) English *is* spoken by an estimated half-billion people worldwide, which seems a whopping figure until you realize that the other 90 percent of the world speaks something else.

Americans, like our misguided friend the football coach, tend to be a little arrogant about our culture and to embrace an almost contemptuous attitude toward language—we expect everybody else to learn ours and spare us from having to learn theirs.

Even colleges, supposedly islands of understanding and wisdom in a sea of chaos, are often ambivalent

GOOD REASONS FOR ANOTHER LANGUAGE

Languages offer great potential. In the wake of the fall of Communism and in the increasingly global economy, international marketing departments of many corporations are expanding fast, scrambling to establish themselves in previously untapped consumer markets.

Languages are becoming necessary. In some parts of this country, speaking Spanish is almost a prerequisite for being hired and succeeding in some fields, including teaching, social work, journalism, and even law enforcement.

Other good reasons. Studying somebody else's language helps you understand that person's culture and way of thinking. Perhaps most importantly, it helps smooth a major stumbling block between you and that person and makes true communication possible.

"I don't want to be an interpreter or a translator or a foreign language teacher. So why should I have to study a foreign language? Why should I have to memorize sentences about Jacques and Gilles riding their bicycles and eating bouillabaisse?"

---

about foreign languages. Many students in arts and sciences view required foreign language courses as unnecessary time-wasters—something to be endured, like a flossing session in the dentist's chair. As one student we know commented during an advising session: "I don't want to be an interpreter or a translator or a foreign language teacher. So why should I have to study a foreign language? Why should I have to memorize sentences about Jacques and Gilles riding their bicycles and eating bouillabaisse?"

Well, actually, Jacques and Gilles aside, there are plenty of reasons, especially for students who can combine their language skills with something else.

Languages are practical. In a competitive job market, any little edge—anything that makes you stand out from the dozens of other candidates competing for the same entry-level position—can be the deciding factor in who gets hired and who keeps on living at home, unemployed, with Mom and Dad after graduation. You name the career field—business, industry, marketing, advertising, science, education, international law, health services, social work, missionary and religious fields, and travel and tourism, for starters—and opportunities abound for people who are fluent in a second or third language.

So why aren't more students signing up for these courses, thereby making themselves more marketable? It's that pesky old national myopia again. Many students simply can't see the need. Less than 4 percent of public high school graduates have had more than two years of a foreign language. Compared with other countries, our national track record in mastering languages other than our own is pretty bad. As a result, we're losing out in all kinds of ways, particularly in political, social, and commercial opportunities.

Why liberal arts courses matter

Being able to recite the poetry of Tennyson, having a working knowledge of the novels of Faulkner or the plays of Shakespeare, understanding what makes painters such as Van Eyck and Botticelli "masters," or appreciating the mathematical precision of Bach and Mozart probably won't help you too much when you show up for work at your first entry-level job after graduation. Nobody's going to give you a quiz—"Here are two architectural columns: Which is Doric, and which one's Ionic?"—or, probably, even care that you've got this knowledge floating around in your head.

What's the point? So why take liberal arts courses? Because you're at college, not a trade school. Not that there's anything wrong with trade schools, but the focus is different. You're here to broaden your horizons—to learn many things, to look at the bigger picture and try to understand your place in it—not simply to master a skill in the single-minded pursuit of a job. Humanities courses can enrich you. They can give you the scope and depth and mindset that will help you move beyond that first entry-level job and achieve great things.

Humanities courses and postgraduate education. So you want to go to medical school (or law or business or graduate or divinity school)? You don't see the point of wasting your time on anything other than classes related to that goal? Go ahead, take what you want, do as you see fit. But realize that you might not get into the professional school of your choice because you might be perceived as "pigeon-holed" and not broadly educated.

Many professional schools are working to abolish the "trade school" image of their students by changing the criteria they look for in potential students. Increasingly, they're looking for well-rounded students, not trolls. For example, in 1985, the Johns Hopkins School of Medicine stopped requiring the Medical College Admission Test as an entry requirement. The school felt, quite simply, that students who were broadly educated in the humanities made better doctors than mere Stanley Kaplan-programmed premeds who could ace the MCAT.

This statement, which appeared in the Bulletin of Yale University a decade ago, sums it up pretty well:

> "In our complex society and rapidly changing world, a sound education must prepare students for an unpredictable future, not merely by preparing them for particular careers, but by teaching them how to learn. . . . At its most fundamental level . . . Yale's purpose is to nourish in its students the motivation and affection for learning which will lead them to continue to develop their intellectual, creative, and moral capacities throughout the whole of their lives."

IN DEFENSE OF LIBERAL ARTS

An Indiana University president named Herman B. Wells once testified before a committee of the state legislature on behalf of his school's proposed budget. One of the lawmakers objected to funds earmarked to support "all those liberal arts courses."

"I don't want to be associated with any university," Wells is said to have replied, "that trains people to live and work throughout their lives without once asking why."

He got the money.

IF YOU STOP OUT

This is a serious step, far more serious than this relatively brief discussion may indicate, so make some plans beforehand. Set goals, such as: "During my stop-out, I intend to decide on a new career objective and a new major; I want to see if I would enjoy a job in sales." Make the time count for something; ideally, you should do more with this hiatus than just drift along aimlessly. Above all, keep in touch with your parents in a positive, constructive way during this period.

Tip: Don't burn your bridges. Make sure you leave school on good terms. Don't blow off your grades at the end of the semester or year ("The hell with this, I'm leaving school next month anyway"), or do something stupid (like give the college dean a one-digit salute on your way out) that you'll regret later. Your transcript and college record will be there waiting for you when you get back.

Let the appropriate officials—the registrar, dean, your faculty adviser—know you'll be away for a time, but that you do expect to complete your studies. Under these circumstances, it's entirely possible that you'll be able to reclaim your financial aid package, among other benefits, when you return.

IF YOU WANT TO TAKE A YEAR OFF

Square peg, square hole. Round peg, round hole. Square peg, round hole—oops! This peg doesn't fit the mold!

Our educational system is programmed to move people directly out of high school and into jobs or college. Those who do go on to college generally have about four years in which to decide on the careers they want to follow and to prepare themselves for the road ahead. Then, at some reasonable point after the commencement ceremony (so the theory goes), they should glide smoothly into their chosen businesses or professions.

Stopping out. But maybe you don't fit this mold. Maybe you want to take some time out, withdraw from the system and interrupt this rhythm so you can travel, rethink your goals and priorities, gain a new sense of perspective. Maybe you don't want to drop out, you want to "stop out." Stopping out, as opposed to quitting school, can be a positive, even life-changing, experience.

But there are risks, many of them financial. For one thing, your parents may object and order you to move out of the house and make your own way. ("When you get back in school and know what you want to do, I'll help. But I won't support you while you're doing nothing.") Also, you may not be able to land much of a job; employers might see you as a transient, somebody who won't be around too long and who therefore won't be a good use of their money—as soon as they get you trained, you'll be out the door. Or, you'll be in competition for the better positions with people who already have their degree.

If you do get interesting work, you may then find it tough to return to school once you've tasted independence and begun to earn your own money, thus defeating the purpose of your stop-out.

However, stop-outs who do come back to school are often happier and more successful students. Their work experience helps them in the classroom. (Some even get college credit for it through an experiential education program.) They've got some perspective. They're usually better organized, more mature, and more sure of themselves.

SUMMER SCHOOL

The most obvious advantage of summer school is that it gives you the chance to pick up additional courses or to repeat courses you didn't do well in the first time. Summer school can help you get back on schedule or even ahead of schedule, if you want to graduate early.

Some students use summer school to concentrate on a really tough subject (organic chemistry is a popular summer school choice) they don't want to tackle in addition to all the distractions of the regular academic year. If you hit the books hard during the summer term—and really, there isn't much else to do on campus in the summer but study because it's usually quite dead—you might fatten up your GPA. Many hard-pressed students who have been slapped on academic probation use the summer session to scramble back into good standing.

If you're the adventurous type, the summer session can be ideal for exploring new territory. Admission is kept relatively open and simple. Consider enrolling for the summer at an Ivy League school, for example, or at a campus in a different and exotic part of the country.

Of course, there is a downside. (Isn't there always?) For one thing, summer school costs money, and you could use the summer to work and save for next year. For another, the campus is quieter (okay, it's duller) and hotter, and some dorms and classroom buildings aren't air conditioned. They're ovens. Also, many top professors jealously reserve their summers for their own research, so the teachers you get in summer school may not always be the top of the line. Finally, there's the burnout factor—not to be underestimated. Going to college year-round can get old fast. A hot, boring, fatiguing summer school may leave you in a foul mood as you begin the fall term—particularly as you see everybody else breeze back to school rejuvenated and excited about the new year, when all you want to do right now is take it easy.

The upside. Despite its drawbacks, many students actually find summer school refreshing. The learning environment is different. Classes are small, they meet every day, and good relations between student and teacher are possible—as opposed to some of those huge classes where you just feel like a face in the crowd. Your professors are relaxed, accessible, and almost always in

THE BEST OF BOTH WORLDS?

Summer session options vary at colleges throughout the country. At the University of Mississippi, for example, students may attend one or two six-week summer terms, while the University of Kentucky offers one four-week and one eight-week session. Summer students at Cornell University can choose from courses offered during three-week, six-week, and eight-week sessions, along with dozens of special programs of varied lengths. Given all these possibilities, you may be able to attend summer school and get in some vacation or job time as well.

Note: It's often necessary to prearrange for a transfer of summer school credit from one college to another, especially when it involves a course in your major; so clear your plans ahead of time with your faculty adviser.

YOUR SCHOOL RECORDS: WHO GETS TO LOOK?

Relax. Thanks to a series of privacy laws enacted during the last two decades, only a very few individuals have access to your student files. Basically, the list begins and ends with you and a handful of college personnel with legitimate educational interests in you—most notably, your faculty adviser and your dean. The materials in your files should be open to you, and you have the right to challenge any record you believe is inaccurate or misleading, such as a mistake on your grade transcript or an erroneous announcement that you were once placed on academic probation. These things happen.

Your files (which may be kept in various offices throughout the campus or on one centralized computer system) contain a lot of information, including your grades, fee payment records, faculty adviser's notations, entrance test scores, any financial aid requests and supporting data you've provided, letters of recommendation, and other related documents. The college must maintain this information, but there's no need to worry that a prospective employer (or even some nosy relative) will go snooping into your files. They can't. The laws are very clear on this.

At the University of South Carolina, for example, according to the Family Education Rights and Privacy Act of

a good mood because—take it from a professor—during summer school, there is no committee work for faculty members, and those who teach get extra pay. So while summer school may or may not be for you, your teacher probably likes it fine!

CORRESPONDENCE COURSES

If you need an extra course or two, and summer school isn't convenient or affordable, then correspondence study might be a good way to go. You can take correspondence courses at almost any time, even while you're taking classes during the regular school year (although you'll need to get your dean's approval for such a workload). For most correspondence courses, you receive a study guide and a reading list. You work through the written assignments at your own pace (there are usually about twenty-four assignments for a three-credit course) and then you mail them in—one or two at a time—to an instructor who grades and returns them. When you've finished all your assignments, your teacher will arrange for your final examination to be administered near your home by a local school official.

Distance education. Your school may have its own correspondence study office. Some universities now offer "distance education"—interactive, televised instruction, with live classes transmitted over state and local educational television channels. If your school doesn't, someone on your campus (begin with your academic dean) will have access to *The Independent Study Catalog*, which lists the thousands of courses offered by member schools of the National University Continuing Education Association. With the help of this guide, you should be able to find the specific correspondence course you need.

Costs. Correspondence courses administered by colleges and universities are fairly cheap—about $75 per semester hour and more for classes involving videocassette work and telecommunication—with nominal fees for transferring credit to or from another institution. Home-study courses sold by commercial correspondence schools may be far more expensive.

The downside. Again, as with summer school, there are drawbacks. There's no classroom environment, no direct contact with a teacher, no discussion, no fixed schedule, no fellow students going through it with you for support. Each lesson may require three hours or more to finish, and the entire responsibility rests on your shoulders. *You should know before you take this step that a lot of students drop out of correspondence courses; it takes a disciplined, self-motivated person to see them through to completion.*

However, despite the obvious difficulties, correspondence instruction continues to gain in popularity among college students. The low cost, flexibility, and convenience make them well worth considering.

TRANSFERRING TO ANOTHER SCHOOL

You won't be the first, and you certainly won't be the last. Thousands of students transfer from one school to another every year. (In fact, one student we know was on his fourth college by his sophomore year!) Some transfers work out brilliantly; others leave students disappointed. All transfers, however, improve with adjustment and planning. Here are a few tips that may help:

- **Start by checking out other colleges on the Internet.** Browse their home pages. Some of them even allow you to apply on-line. Look for student activities, pictures and layouts of dorms, and names of people (faculty and students) you can contact if you want to learn more. Then send off for more information, including their catalog.
- **Familiarize yourself with the degree requirements at the new college,** through careful study of the catalog and visits to admissions people. Know that your present academic requirements become irrelevant when you transfer, and only your new institution's requirements apply. If the college you're planning to transfer to requires you to complete four semesters of a foreign language, for instance, then you might want to work on that requirement now—even if your present school doesn't require a foreign language.
- **Don't be surprised if you lose some credits when you transfer.** Not all courses are automatically accepted for credit by every college. You'll go

1974, students have the right to "review, inspect and challenge the accuracy of information kept in a cumulative file by the institution unless the student waives this right." This law also ensures that records can't be released in other than emergency situations without the student's written consent, except:

- To other school officials, including faculty within the educational institution or local educational agency who have legitimate educational interests;
- To officials of other schools or school systems in which the student intends to enroll, upon condition that the student be notified of the transfer, receive a copy of the record if desired, and have an opportunity for a hearing to challenge the content of the record;
- To authorized representatives of the Comptroller General of the United States, the Secretary of Education, an administrative head of an education agency, or state educational authorities;
- In connection with a student's application for, and receipt of, financial aid;
- Subpoena;
- Parents of dependent children.

At the University of South Carolina and many other institutions, students also have an opportunity to block the release of "directory information," which includes: "A student's name, mailing address and telephone number, semesters of attendance, enrollment status (full- or part-time), date of admission, date of graduation, school, major and minor fields of study, whether or not currently enrolled, classification (freshman, etc.), type of degree being pursued, honors, awards, degrees received, weight and height of members of athletic teams, and whether the student has participated in officially recognized activities and sports sponsored by the University."

through a transcript evaluation when you arrive at your new campus (or it will be done by mail beforehand), and an admissions officer will tell you which courses are transferable and which aren't. Most degree programs are flexible enough to allow a considerable number of credits to be counted as electives.

If you're lucky, you won't lose much by transferring, although you may find that the transferred credits will sharply reduce the number of elective credits you'll have for the future. As a general rule, basic courses such as Freshman English and Biology 1 are acknowledged much more readily than electives like Basket Weaving or Student Publications Practicum. And remedial courses probably won't transfer at all.

- **Expect some scheduling problems when you arrive on your new campus.** By the time you enroll for classes at the beginning of the semester, most students will have preregistered months before—which means they're far more likely to have been given their choices of professors, courses, and class times. Many class sections will have been closed before the transfers arrive, and the pickings can be pretty slim.

- **If you have a choice, transfer in for the fall semester, if only for social reasons.** It's easier to adjust and make new friends in the fall when many other people—freshmen and transfers—are new to the campus, too.

- **Don't panic if your grades slip a bit during your first semester at your new school.** This is normal. Chalk it up to adjusting to a new grading system and a new environment. Most transfer students recover nicely after one semester. One experienced admissions officer, a man who has examined thousands of student records over the years, tells us that the final grade point averages of transfer students—on his campus, at least—are virtually indistinguishable at graduation from those of students who had been at the same school for four years.

HOW DOES YOUR SCHOOL RANK NATIONALLY?

This question seems almost an obsession with some students and with some parents. Obviously, you want to go to a good school: An undergraduate education, for those lucky enough to have a chance at one, comes along only once in a lifetime. You want to make it count; you want it to be the best it can be.

But it's hard to rank schools comparatively. To begin with, few colleges are uniformly good or uniformly bad throughout their various academic and professional departments. Indiana University, for instance, has an excellent reputation in music, just as the University of Missouri is noted for its School of Journalism. Photography is considered an important strength at such schools as East Texas State and Western Kentucky, and Johns Hopkins University is considered a biomedical engineering powerhouse. This doesn't mean that the other departments at those universities are weak—far from it. But very few institutions are wealthy enough, or lucky enough, to develop a top-notch faculty in every single field of study.

Which are the best schools?

If that's the question, our answer is "best at what?" Even then we're on shaky ground. Some studies have been conducted in which college presidents or faculty members across the country were asked to list the best colleges or most distinguished departments. One of the more famous of these peer-ranked surveys is done each year by *U.S. News & World Report* magazine. But what does "distinguished" actually mean?

Frankly, to a large extent, it means distinguished in terms of published research—or, worse, general reputation. As you've probably learned on your own already, just because someone has a glittering reputation as a research scholar doesn't mean he or she is a good teacher. Some of the country's outstanding researchers prove to be total disasters in the classroom—particularly when the classroom is filled with undergraduates. A professor can have a well-deserved international reputation for research and yet at the same time be embarrassingly incoherent when trying to explain theories to freshmen in classes.

Also, there's no assurance that the distinguished faculty members—the university's token Nobel laureate,

Bottom line: The "top" college for you is the one where you feel most comfortable, and where you are challenged to do your best work. It's as simple—and as complicated—as that.

There are fine teachers on every campus—even on those campuses that don't boast strong reputations for scholarly research.

A trip overseas, whether it's a quickie tour or a semester or year of study at a foreign university, can be a wonderful experience and usually proves to be a highlight of your education. The great majority of students return from a trip overseas with their spirits lifted, their eyes opened, and their sights raised.

for example—will even be accessible to you. You might enroll at a famous university in order to study with Professor X only to learn that Professor X has (1) disappeared from the country on an extended sabbatical leave, (2) become a full-time consultant or dean, or (3) reduced his or her teaching load to one or two advanced seminars—open only to graduate students.

None of this is to detract from the world-class faculties at the best-known colleges. But the point is that there are fine teachers on every campus—even on those campuses that don't boast strong reputations for scholarly research. Many students have become academic misfits in their attempts to satisfy somebody else's notions about the value of getting a degree from one of the "top schools in the country."

JUNIOR YEAR ABROAD

Just about all overseas travel-study programs look good and most of them are. The difficulty (this is a problem most of us would love to have) comes in fitting your needs and your budget into just the right foreign-study package.

For help and some guidelines about what to look for in a program, find the study-abroad center or coordinating office on your campus.

At such centers, students can examine an extensive collection of reference materials and get plenty of advice and help in making this dream come true.

While the federal government isn't in the business of officially recognizing and evaluating foreign travel/study programs, it does suggest some guidelines that make sense in "Study and Teaching Opportunities Abroad" (see box on next page), including:

- **Know the sponsor.** Check with students who have participated in this program before you. Make sure you identify the agency that bears legal responsibility. Look into the program's history. Don't hesitate to ask questions. A reputable organization will welcome your inquiries. (As opposed to some guy barking with an irritated, loud sigh, "Look, college boy, I ain't got all day, you gonna go or what?")
- **Check the sponsor's finances.** Be sure you understand whether basic fees will cover all

expenses for travel, or whether there will be some add-on charges later (for taxis, buses, side trips, etc.). Will medical and accident insurance be covered by the basic fee? What provisions are made in case of cancellations?

- **Consider the contingency plans.** Find out whether arrangements exist for students who are in difficulty. Would they be sent home? At whose expense? Would there be extra charges or penalty fees for returning early?
- **Investigate housing and study facilities.** Knowing where you'll be living is important. In foreign countries, as here at home, there are wildly different opinions as to what constitutes adequate housing.
- **Compare the sponsor's objectives with your own.** Some programs emphasize travel and sightseeing, others concentrate on foreign language study, while still others focus on a specific subject area, such as music, art, architecture, the mass media, or literature. Be sure your interests are compatible with the priorities of the program.
- **Critically review the program of study.** If your objective is to study at a foreign university, find out whether you will actually work with the top people there. Will you be taught by temporary replacements or part-time staff members? To a great extent, the success or failure of an overseas study program depends on the teachers, so you need to know who you're going to get. Also, make sure you know the language of instruction and have a good idea of the academic demands that will be placed on you.

And perhaps most important of all, find out who the other students will be and how they were selected.

FOR MORE INFO ON STUDYING ABROAD

You can get more good help from the U.S. government, which publishes a booklet called "Study and Teaching Opportunities Abroad." It's available for a small fee from the Government Printing Office, Washington, D.C. 20402.

In addition to the evaluation criteria you'll find in nearby text, "Study and Teaching Opportunities Abroad" contains a helpful listing of information sources regarding travel tips, financial assistance and work opportunities.

CHAPTER 14

Working Toward the Next Degree

You know what you want to do with your life, and you're looking ahead to a few more years of education before you can get to do it. In some fields, even if a graduate degree isn't actually required, having that extra piece of sheepskin hanging on your wall can certainly improve your chances in the job market and bring you a higher starting salary.

What's there to know, you may be thinking—graduate school is just like staying a few extra years in college, right?

Wrong. There are big differences—in environment, intensity, even the admissions process—between college and graduate or professional schools. Here's a brief overview to get you started:

Graduate School

First, there's the time commitment—the better part of two years for a master's degree, four years or more for a Ph.D. For some people, this could amount to educational overkill. Depending on your career objectives, you may be better off moving immediately into the job market for some work experience instead. (Sometimes it's better, in other words, to quit warming up in the bull pen and get into the game!)

So one big decision to make is when to go to graduate school. Is it better to move straight through? Or should you get a few years of career experience under your belt first? There are good arguments on both sides, and you should take them into account—along with all the other considerations about personal and professional matters that go into a career decision of this magnitude.

Where to go? Presumably, every professor you have is an expert on the subject of graduate school, and most will probably be happy to talk with you about it as you attempt to make up your mind. Get as much information and advice as you can. The academic world is fairly small, and you're likely to find professors on your own campus who are familiar with practically any graduate program you're considering.

No matter where you attend graduate school, you'll discover an environment entirely different from the one you're in now. Instead of large lecture classes, you'll be placed in small, competitive seminars. You'll be expected to work harder, and far more attention will be paid to you by the senior members of the faculty (a decidedly mixed blessing!). And, because you may receive a teaching or research assistantship (as many graduate students do), you become much more involved with the staff and the workings of your department.

Graduate school will also change your intellectual and professional outlook. During your undergraduate years, you are essentially passive. No offense—it's the nature of this stage of education. Even though, compared to high school, college requires much more initiative, knowledge is still primarily dispensed to you, and your job is still, by and large, merely to understand and store it (at least until the next test!). As a graduate student, though, you'll assume a more active role. A big difference—you'll begin to learn how to generate new knowledge. There is a strong research emphasis in most graduate degree programs.

Graduate instruction is highly personalized and, therefore, costly for the institution. This is one of the main reasons most graduate programs are small and selective. Graduate admissions committees will want a great deal of information about you, which means you'll have to put a lot of time and effort into preparing your application.

Acceptance or rejection by a graduate school will hinge on some combination of factors, including your undergraduate grades, especially those you earn in your major field in your junior and senior years; your performance on the Graduate Record Examinations (GRE); recommendations from your professors and others who know your work; and the statement of purpose you submit as part of your application.

You should also be doing some careful selecting as well. Check into the quality of the program—not as it might have been when your favorite professor did graduate work there, but as it is today. Examine specific degree requirements, which will vary greatly from one place to another. (There can be literally years of

Acceptance or rejection by a graduate school will hinge on some combination of factors, including your undergraduate grades, especially those you earn in your major field in your junior and senior years; your performance on the Graduate Record Examinations (GRE); recommendations from your professors and others who know your work; and the statement of purpose you submit as part of your application.

Depending on your career objectives, you may be better off moving immediately into the job market for some work experience instead. (Sometimes it's better, in other words, to quit warming up in the bull pen and get into the game!)

difference among various universities in the length of time realistically needed to complete a graduate degree program.) Cost is always a consideration for graduate students, and so is the extent of financial support offered. In many cases, the dollar value of the graduate assistantship/fellowship will become the deciding factor.

If you're serious about graduate study, apply to a number of schools. (If you aren't serious, get a job instead. Graduate school is tough enough even if you love it!) Applying is a time-consuming and expensive business; the forms are lengthy and there's a processing fee for each application, but you'll need to open as many options as you can. Also, it's best to start as early as the fall semester of your senior year, if you can. (This means you'll need to do your preliminary screening and send for catalogs and application forms well before then.) Many graduate schools begin awarding fellowships and assistantships by mid-February for the next academic year. You might still get accepted into the program if you apply late, but your chances for financial support are much slimmer.

Note: Strongly consider moving to another school for your graduate work. Even though you may have to give up convenience and familiarity with your surroundings, there's a lot to be said for getting a new point of view through exposure to a new environment and a different faculty.

Law School

The absolute, guaranteed, surest way to prepare for law school is ... well, there isn't one prescribed way. Almost all law schools require that their applicants be college graduates, but the bachelor's degree can be in virtually any field of study. Essentially, law schools are looking for students who can reason and analyze with great skill, who can think critically, who have an understanding of human institutions and values, and who are able to express themselves well. The most common prelaw majors include political science, English, history, accounting, business administration, and journalism. No matter what the major, writing and speaking skills are critical.

Grades are important in determining who gets accepted; so is your performance on the Law School Admission Test (LSAT). But schools consider other factors, as well. For example, the trend of the grades is often taken into account. If, for example, you start off poorly as a freshman but improve markedly in later years, you're likely to be judged more favorably than another student with the same GPA but a record of level or declining performance. Letters of recommendation can help—or hurt. The reputation of your undergraduate school may be taken into account; some colleges are known to demand more of their students than others (therefore, a "B" average at one school may mean just as much as an "A" average at another). A heavy load of outside work can be a plus; admissions officers are impressed with students who have helped support themselves through college. Involvement in extracurricular activities can also be a good sign. "After all," as one law school dean explained, "lawyers don't work in a vacuum. They must understand people and appreciate their problems."

What are your chances of getting into law school? That depends on where you apply. If you're only interested in one specific institution, you may have a problem. If you're flexible and willing to apply to a number of schools, however, your chances are better. (Note: At state-supported institutions, priority must be given to applicants from that state—so in-state people have the edge. Residency quotas don't normally apply at private law schools.) For much more information, look for a copy of the *Prelaw Handbook,* prepared by the Law School Admission Council and the Association of American Law Schools. It's available at college bookstores or through the Law School Admission Service, P.O. Box 2000, Newtown, Pennsylvania 18940.

Medical School

Nearly every campus has a premed adviser who can help you chart your course toward medical school. There's no specific premed major. Although about two thirds of the country's medical school applicants major in one of the sciences, many medical schools are becoming interested in people with backgrounds in the humanities. So your major may not be that important—if, and this is important, you've had some core science classes, including a full year each of general chemistry, organic chemistry, biology, and physics (each with labs). Some medical schools may tack on additional requirements such as calculus, but as a general rule, you're free to major in anything from agriculture to English, as long

Essentially, law schools are looking for students who can reason and analyze with great skill, who can think critically, who have an understanding of human institutions and values, and who are able to express themselves well.

GOT ANY COLLEGE LOANS?

Speaking of financial aid, here's an important monetary note to consider: Some student loans may require that, after a certain "grace period" (usually six months to a year), you start paying them off when you've left school. If you take a six-month hiatus from college, you may use up this grace period, which means that, when you graduate—or even before, if you stay away from school long enough—you may end up having to make payments on your loans right away, job or no job.

as you cover those basic science courses. Some medical schools will admit you after you've finished 90 semester hours (the idea here being that, once you're admitted, you can relax and take some fun courses); others require a bachelor's degree.

With a few key exceptions, virtually all U.S. medical schools require or strongly recommend that you take the Medical College Admission Test (MCAT), a daylong, standardized exam. It's administered twice a year, and should be taken about eighteen months before you plan to enter medical school. Scores are evaluated and used differently by each school.

Undergraduate grades are very important; in fact, many schools regard them as key predictors of your medical school performance. However, other factors also weigh heavily, such as personal and professional traits, or a steady improvement in academic performance toward the end of your undergraduate years. The personal interview could also make or break a medical school applicant—although if academic and/or MCAT performance isn't convincing, applicants usually don't make it to the interview stage. During the interview, the committee will look for evidence of such things as social and intellectual maturity, leadership, drive, initiative, common sense, and—perhaps most of all—whether you have any idea of what you're letting yourself in for by seeking a career in medicine.

A good premed adviser will urge you, from your freshman year on, to challenge the desire you think you have to practice medicine. Spend time at a clinic or hospital, and while you're there, get as involved as you can in the treatment of patients. Know what you're getting into.

For more information, including detailed descriptions of programs at every accredited medical school in the U.S., get a copy of *Medical School Admission Requirements* from the library. (Or, you can order one from the Association of American Medical Colleges, One Dupont Circle, NW, Washington, D.C. 20036.)

Business School

A typical M.B.A. curriculum calls for at least one full year of tough, competitive graduate work in such subjects as organizational behavior, managerial economics, financial/managerial accounting, marketing management, legal and regulatory environment, business conditions analysis, production management, and quantitative business analysis.

If you're thinking of going on for an M.B.A., you should prepare by taking a full year of accounting and at least one semester of calculus. Some M.B.A. programs require additional undergraduate course work, but most schools may permit you to be conditionally admitted for M.B.A. study while you work on any undergraduate prerequisites you may have missed. It's not necessary to major in business—many liberal arts graduates are excellent M.B.A. candidates—but if you do have your bachelor's degree in business, you'll probably be able to complete the M.B.A. work more rapidly.

In many schools, it's possible to earn the M.B.A. degree as either a full- or part-time student. A number of M.B.A. programs, in fact, are geared for men and women who are already working in the business world. Many schools offer other degrees in business as well, such as the Doctor of Business Administration (D.B.A.), for those interested in research, teaching business at the college level, or business accounting.

Your admission to an accredited M.B.A. program will be based on such criteria as your undergraduate record, your performance on the Graduate Management Admission Test (GMAT), your accomplishments or experience at work, recommendations, and such intangibles as motivation and talent for leadership.

The Graduate Management Admission Council publishes *The Official Guide to the M.B.A.,* which contains descriptions of most M.B.A. programs in the country. Your library or business school should have copies. Or, you can order one from the GMAT Program Direction Office, Educational Testing Service, Princeton, NJ 08541.

Theological/Divinity School

There are about 160 accredited seminaries in the U.S., all members of the Association of Theological Schools. These schools all require that you have a bachelor's degree before beginning their programs. Ideally, your transcript should reflect a strong showing in English, history, philosophy, psychology, and sociology, as well as some aptitude for language study. Many seminaries will require you to take Greek and Hebrew; a few of them assume that you're already familiar with one or both of these languages.

In many schools, it's possible to earn the M.B.A. degree as either a full- or part-time student. A number of M.B.A. programs, in fact, are geared for men and women who are already working in the business world.

Among theological semi-naries, there can be huge differences in doctrine—even among seminaries representing the same religious denomination. A few of these differences are over some volatile issues, including God's gender (or lack thereof) and the church's stand on such heated topics as homosexuality, abortion, and the right to die.

Most professional and graduate schools differ in relatively small ways—in resources, in quality of the professors, in the level of accomplishment expected from students, in class size. But among theological seminaries, there can be huge differences in doctrine—even among seminaries representing the same religious denomination. A few of these differences are over some volatile issues, including God's gender (or lack thereof) and the church's stand on such heated topics as homosexuality, abortion, and the right to die. Even on quieter issues—the specifics of rituals like baptism, for example, or the revamping of hymnals and prayer books to include nontraditional or gender-free creeds, ceremonies and hymns—there can be great disparity.

So make sure you know—and are comfortable with—a school's point of view before you apply. In many cases, faculty members have developed a comprehensive statement that explains how religious issues will be interpreted and presented. If the theological stance at one seminary disturbs you, you should probably consider applying elsewhere.

The primary purpose of most seminaries, of course, is to prepare men and women for the clergy. The professional degree normally granted is called the Master of Divinity, and it requires three full years of study. However, not everyone who enrolls in a seminary necessarily wants or expects to become a member of the ordained clergy. Many students, including those who are simply interested in the study of religion, enroll in a two-year program leading to a Master of Arts. There are still other degrees and options offered around the country.

An interesting historical note: Traditionally, enrollment for religious study rises and falls with the times. During relatively quiet, prosperous years, many seminaries operate at less than capacity. Wars and depressions, however, bring on big increases in numbers of applicants.

THE JOB HUNT

By now, you know that we hope you'll savor college. That you'll enjoy every bit of it—even the hard parts—and that college will open up the world for you. But that doesn't mean you shouldn't think concretely about the next step—your career—until college is over.

What are the jobs? If you need some help finding a job—or just figuring out what jobs to look for—start with your professors. Many professors are nurturing types; they got into this business because they like to teach, they want to help students and, like academic gardeners, they love to see their little seedlings (you) grow and thrive. And most professors spend many hours counseling students on career possibilities and writing reference letters to prospective employers. So take advantage of their willingness to help, and their interest in your future; ask for their suggestions, and appreciate their time and help—even if you end up not using their advice.

Then get to work. Figure out what you have to offer an employer. Everybody's got something to sell—knowledge, experience, talent, skill, or time. The tricky part comes in packaging your assets effectively and directing them to the employers who are most likely to be interested in buying your product—you.

Where are the jobs? One school of thought suggests that the employment search, like charity, should begin at home. "Use your family, your friends, your contacts," one university placement director urged some students we know. "Use any kind of personal or business or family or political influence you can. I know there are students who don't want to do that. They say, 'I'm not going to take advantage of my family situation. I want to prove I can make it on my own.' Sorry, but I think that's baloney. You'll have the rest of your life to prove yourself. Your family can't keep a job for you once you've got it. That part is up to you and your abilities. But if your family or friends can help you get your foot in the door, then let them!"

Ask your teachers and faculty adviser for help, too, especially those who do consulting work or maintain close contact with the "real world." Engineering professors, for instance, routinely guide students in to permanent or summer jobs in industry, as do professors in the business school, journalism department, etc. Ask them to keep an ear to the ground—to pass on any job openings that come to their attention. Even if they can't help you personally, they may be able to direct you to a colleague who can.

Introduce yourself to visiting lecturers, if what they're talking about—book publishing, photography, etc.—interests you as a career possibility. If they give you a

Figure out what you have to offer an employer. Everybody's got something to sell—knowledge, experience, talent, skill, or time.

business card, keep it. You never know; it might come in handy later. (It's infinitely preferable to call someone and say, "You may not remember me, but we met at Dr. Blair's lecture . . ." than to say, in effect: "Uh, you don't know me from Adam, but, uh, I'm looking for a job . . .")

Pore over departmental billboards. Many employers ask colleges for help finding new employees. But they do it in a diffuse way—they send out a notice or brochure, which usually gets photocopied and stuck up on some department's billboard. For example: Thousands of jobs are available each year in local, state, and national government. But getting information on these departments means doing some legwork. Some notices may be sent to the political science department; others may go to the College of Agriculture, the sociology department, or some other academic units. To find out about such jobs, your best bet may be simply to trudge around the campus, making periodic inspections of departmental bulletin boards.

Investigate online "help-wanted" billboards. The number of these is expanding all the time. On the Internet alone, for example, there are dozens. And what a time-saver! You can check these anytime, and it's one-stop shopping. In one sitting, you could get a lead on several possible jobs.

Get to know the placement office. At many schools, this is a great clearinghouse for news about job openings and internship programs. Lists of vacancies and interview schedules are posted or updated on the university's computer network, often—weekly or even daily at some campuses—so you'll need to check in at regular intervals.

Don't overlook newspaper classified ads. Your school's library subscribes to many newspapers—probably including one published in the city where you'd like to work. Tip: Don't waste your time with weekday or Saturday editions; many employers only spend their money on ads in the Sunday paper. Also, check out the classifieds in trade and association journals related to your prospective career field.

Take the initiative, and write directly to the company you're interested in. You don't have to wait for notice of a vacancy to appear. Sometimes, a well-crafted letter and good resume will strike a responsive chord with a key executive. Even if they don't have an opening available at the moment, they may hang onto it for future reference, or they may even invite you in for an interview—which could lay the groundwork for a job later.

Be patient. Understand that job hunting requires time, effort, imagination, and a range of strategies. Don't give up—believe that the right job is out there, waiting for you. And do your best to find it.

Advice From the Placement Office: Don't Wait Until You're a Senior

There is a fact of life of which your college or university is acutely aware: Its reputation is directly linked to the career successes of its graduates. The bottom line, as always (we hate to sound cynical, but, hey, if the shoe fits . . .) is money. If an inordinate number of alumni from your college wind up flipping burgers at the Big Moo Barn Grill (get it? bar 'n' grill?), the university gladhanders aren't going to be able to drum up many donations from nostalgic graduates at class reunions.

With this in mind, your college or university most likely operates a placement office, which is open to everyone connected with the institution—from freshmen to alumni. Check into it. You can find a wealth of information here on job-hunting techniques, individual companies, graduate study, summer and short-term employment, and career opportunities in general. In addition to supplying reading material, placement office counselors often hold seminars and clinics on interviewing techniques, career planning, and related vocational topics. Note: Your placement office or Career Center will probably require you to buy a software disk (which costs about $35) to help you write your resume and to get you into the institutional database.

A major bonus, at many schools, is an informal job placement network. (Similar to the "old boy" club, it's the "old school" club.) This consists of alumni who either use their own professional connections or colleagues in other fields to help launch your career. They may not be able to hire you, but they can often get your foot in the door—by helping you get an interview or even an internship in the field (or, with luck, at the particular company) of your choice. And sometimes a little helping hand is all you need: a chance to be seen by the people actually doing the hiring instead of having

Many professors are nurturing types; they got into this business because they like to teach, they want to help students and, like academic gardeners, they love to see their little seedlings (you) grow and thrive.

The simple fact that you're a student is often all it takes for someone to look more kindly upon you. Leap on this fact. Make it work for you.

your resume screened by some company's personnel office (which may or may not pass it on to those people in charge).

What's amazing, considering the scope and potential of these resources, is the fact that most undergraduates don't take full advantage of them. "My biggest problem," says a placement director we know, "is that students wait until they're seniors to come see us."

That is a shame. There is a point you need to absorb now, so you can use it to the utmost: *People like college students. They want to help them.* The simple fact that you're a student is often all it takes for someone to look more kindly upon you. Leap on this fact. Make it work for you. Translate it into summer jobs. Internships. "Informational" interviews. (In this kind of interview, it's understood by both parties—you and the interviewer—that you're not looking to be hired for a specific job; instead, you're getting a valuable consultation (on your career, your potential, how your resume reads) from a professional in a career field you hope to enter.

The other side to this truth is that the day you graduate, you're no longer a student. You're entering the job market. You're fresh, young, energetic—and, to some people, a potential threat or, at least, just another applicant. You may never get as much help or goodwill in your life as you could be getting right now.

Another point: Don't get us wrong; we're not saying you should spend your college years in an obsessive, single-minded quest for a job. As we've said all along, your educational career should be far broader than this, and college should do far more for you than just land you a nice job somewhere. But we do believe that it's a mistake to ignore your career plans entirely. One of the authors of this book, in fact, in decades as a faculty adviser, has seen too many tearful graduating seniors who put off thinking about life after college until the last weeks of the last semester. ("It's pretty depressing," says a friend of ours, "particularly for a journalism professor, to see an unemployed college graduate, who frittered away four years of her life, come back and ask to get an article published in the school newspaper, just so she can have a clipping—one clipping!—for her portfolio. One wonders what she did for four years, and what kind of job she expected to get—or if even she thought about it at all!")

So plan ahead. Make the most of any and all resources available to you. Check in with your placement office early; find out about what kinds of specific advice and resources you can count on later. Also, you may want to do some preliminary reading about various types of careers, so you can start to narrow your range of choices.

If you're completely at sea about the types of work you may be best suited to do, check in at the counseling office. Your first interview here should provide a trained psychologist with a good idea of your background and interests. Afterward, you may be encouraged to take a battery of aptitude tests that can be used in follow-up sessions as your career goals begin to take shape. There may be a charge for processing the tests; the counseling itself is normally free. The tests will suggest several occupational areas for which you appear to be suited—and, just as important, point out other career fields that you probably wouldn't like or might even hate. Testing won't reveal any magic, sure-fire career formula for you to follow, but it can provide helpful information. Most important of all, you'll actually be doing something about planning your career, instead of just waiting around passively in hopes that lightning will strike and a booming voice from on high will tell you what to do with your life.

A major bonus, at many schools, is an informal job placement network—similar to the "old boy" club, it's the "old school" club. This consists of alumni who either use their own professional connections or colleagues in other fields to help launch your career.

THE RESUME

The resume is your life in two pages or less. It's a summary of your qualifications, carefully selected and usually presented in outline form. The general rule is to make it as brief as possible (two pages at most, so it can be read easily and quickly by someone who must skim through a whole stack of these and who has neither the time nor the inclination to know your entire life story) yet comprehensive enough to supply the specific information your prospective boss will need to make a judgment about your background. (Note: Take the time to proofread. In fact, have somebody else give it the once-over. A resume with major typos or other glaring errors isn't going to inspire an employer with confidence or a burning desire to hire you.)

It's a nice touch to have your resume printed on good paper; you can do it yourself with a laser printer. If you

Note: It's not legal for an interviewer to ask your age, marital status, religion, or sexual preference. So if for any reason you don't want to provide this information—you don't have to.

don't have one, a quick-print shop like Kinko's can fix you right up. (Hint: It's not a good idea to give out an obvious photocopy; this may suggest that you've given the original to somebody else—and that whoever gets the obvious photocopy isn't worth the trouble of an original.)

There's no one best way to prepare a resume. Some employers are demons for conciseness and believe a resume should be limited to a single page. Others prefer more information, a fuller account of your background and credentials. (For more ideas and samples of different types of resumes, consult your campus placement office.)

But no matter what model of resume you choose, here are some of the basics you'll probably want it to include:

- Identifying information. Your name, address and phone number (both on campus and at your permanent home). Some people include additional personal data, such as their date of birth, marital status (optional), hobbies, etc. Note: It's not legal for an interviewer to ask your age, marital status, religion, or sexual preference. So if for any reason you don't want to provide this information—you don't have to. (On the other hand, you don't have to make a federal case out of it, either. Be polite, and give or don't give the information; it's up to you.)
- Your job objective. This doesn't have to be terribly specific (like "Women's Sportswear Buyer at the White Marsh Mall branch of Macy's department store"); just mention the type of work you hope to find, such as "sales," or "public relations." And feel free to tailor your resume to fit each specific job application. If you're applying for summer work as a lifeguard at the beach, you wouldn't want to list your ultimate job objective, which may be in nuclear physics. If your immediate objective is to land a temporary job as a lifeguard, let your resume say so.
- Your educational background. List the high school from which you were graduated and the college or university you're currently attending. Point out courses or subjects you've completed that pertain to your job objective. Also, mention extracurricular activities (these can indicate

well-roundedness and leadership potential), honors, and scholarships you've won. (Note: We know we don't even have to mention this, but: Don't pad your resume. Not even a little. Somebody will probably find out eventually, and your credibility will be seriously—perhaps even irreparably—injured.)

- Your work history. Make a separate entry for each job you've had, beginning with the most recent, then the next most recent, etc. Briefly mention the tasks you performed and highlight all the positive features you can. For example, you might want to include the fact that you supervised other workers or that you received a letter of commendation. Any type of work is important, by the way. Don't omit a job just because you think the work was too menial to mention. (One magazine editor we know always includes the fact that he helped support himself in college by working as a maintenance man. When asked about it, as he often is, he comments wryly that cleaning up "refuse," or something to that effect, taught him how to recognize it whenever he sees it.) There's no shame in honest work, as your grandfather might tell you. And as a rule, employers tend to look favorably on people who have shown the initiative to find jobs of any kind.

- On the other hand, don't feel obligated to include everything. It's extremely likely that, when you get to a certain stage in your career, your resume will no longer include that six-month job as a salad girl at York Steak House or your sojourn as a seller of Twizzlers and popcorn at the Fayette Mall Cinemas. For one thing, you'll probably have forgotten the managers' names by then; for another, the employers you'll be applying to probably won't be interested in ancient history. Such data will be unnecessary. But even now, there's nothing that says you absolutely have to put down every single bit of employment you've ever had, particularly if it didn't turn out well. We're not saying that you should lie or do anything dishonest, and we unconditionally advise against erring the other way and embellishing your resume. But if there's an employer you'd rather not mention or a reference you'd rather not

Don't pad your resume. Not even a little. Somebody will probably find out eventually, and your credibility will be seriously—perhaps even irreparably—injured.

Take the time to proofread. In fact, have somebody else give it the once-over. A resume with major typos or other glaring errors isn't going to inspire an employer with confidence or a burning desire to hire you.

SCANNED RESUMES

At many companies, resumes are scanned by computers to identify key words and target specific kinds of applicants; there are also many Web sites on the Internet where you can post your resume. This is a terrible practice, in our opinion, but it's happening, so you should be aware of it. If a computer is going to get the first crack at you, try to make it happy. Use nouns that can be picked up and checked off, such as "marketing," "accounting," "management" and "analysis." Avoid words such as "clerical" and "secretary" like the plague. (For example, if you handled the mailing list and some minor typesetting duties for your school's alumni magazine, it would not be out of line to call yourself an "editorial assistant.") The computer is looking for skills and keywords. Are you fluent in another language? Good at public speaking? An excellent organizer? Put it in there. It may ring some computer's bell. So grit your teeth and make yours a "scannable" resume. The whole goal is to survive the first cut—and actually have the chance to talk to a human being.

have checked (unless you're applying for a government job), it's okay if you leave it out.

- Miscellaneous qualifications and experience. Here is your opportunity to list any special skills you may have, such as knowledge of a foreign language or the ability to operate various office machines. This is also a good section to mention any volunteer work you may have done.

- References. Give the names, addresses, and job titles of three people who know you and the work you've done. Teachers and former employers are good choices. (Note: Before you do anything, check with the people you're listing! For one thing, it's only common courtesy; for another, you don't want to get sandbagged with a surprise scathing appraisal instead of the warm recommendation you thought you could count on.) Some people prefer a simple line that says, "References available on request." An advantage of this is that you can tailor your references to the particular job. For example, for a writing job, a prospective employer may be more interested in what your English or Journalism professors have to say than in the glowing character reference your football coach could provide.

Once you do make it to the interview, beware of another new trend: The "Behavior-Based" question. Have some stories ready to go. Have you survived a really big personal challenge that tested your mettle and found you to be worthy? Trot it out. Be prepared to give an example of how some crisis arose in your life and how you met it. Needless to say, the story should be quick and upbeat, and, if at all possible, the ending should be happy—but not sappy.

SAMPLE RESUME

Bradley Truman

118 Columbia Terrace
Lexington, KY 40502
606-361-4137

Home Address:
504 Sisk Ave.
Louisville, KY 45353
502-276-1643

Job Objective: Advertising Sales

Educational Background

University of Kentucky, Lexington. Expected graduation: May 2001.

- Advertising staff, *Kentucky Kernel*, independent student daily newspaper. Serve approximately 25 clients. Design layouts. Develop sales presentation. Some market research.
- Member, Kappa Sigma social fraternity. Vice president of pledge class in freshman year. Currently Assistant Rush Chairman.
- Have completed Principles of Advertising (grade of A) and one introductory course in marketing.

Tates Creek High School, Louisville, KY. Was graduated in May 1997.

- Ranked 23rd in class of 634.
- Varsity basketball, three years. Won "110 percent" award in senior year.
- Member, Beta Club.
- Member, National Honor Society.
- Vice President, Spanish Club.
- Advertising staff, *The Masthead*, student newspaper. Sold ads for three years. Designed layouts.

Work History

August 1997-present. Advertising salesman (part-time), *Kentucky Kernel*.

June 1997-August 1997. Sir Pizza, Crossroads Mall, Lexington, KY. Served three weeks as night counter supervisor.

May 1995-June 1997. Turfland Mall Cinemas, Lexington, KY. Worked nights and weekends while in high school as ticket taker, assistant cashier, and salesclerk in concessions.

Miscellaneous Qualifications

Familiar with WordPerfect and Word, ad layout, newspaper production. Fluent in spoken and written Spanish.

References

Prof. Mary Lou Dennis
Department of Marketing
University of Kentucky
Lexington, KY 40506

Mrs. Sally Ann Wentz
Director of Publications
University of Kentucky
Lexington, KY 40506

Ms. Winton Robertson
Manager, Sir Pizza
Crossroads Mall
Lexington, KY 40502

Mr. Logan Brockman
Manager, Turfland Mall Cinemas
Turfland Mall
Lexington, KY 40503

SAMPLE LETTER OF APPLICATION

Ms. Carole A. Ayre
Director of Advertising
Milwaukee Times
Times Plaza
Milwaukee, WI 58989

Dear Ms. Ayre:

I am writing to apply for a position in your Summer Intern Program. I believe that working for the *Milwaukee Times* would be a valuable learning experience. I hope one day to work as an advertising sales representative for a metropolitan newspaper.

The enclosed resume lists my qualifications. Please note that I am currently a part-time advertising salesman for our student daily newspaper here at the University of Kentucky. In this capacity, I have developed sales presentations and serviced about twenty-five active accounts.

I believe that this experience, combined with my own enthusiasm for the field, would make me a useful member of your Summer Intern team, and I can assure you that I would make the most of this exciting opportunity.

Please let me know if I can provide any additional information. Thank you in advance for your consideration.

Sincerely,

Bradley Truman

Prepare for the interview, just like you would for a test, because this is a test—of you.

THE JOB INTERVIEW

Congratulations! Your resume and letter of application clicked with a prospective employer, and you've got an interview all set up. How do you make the most of this important meeting? (That is, in addition to being ready to spew stories of your competence at a moment's notice, as previously discussed in "The Resume.")

First, do your homework. Don't just show up and expect them to hire you. Show your interest in the company by finding out about its products or services, the kinds of jobs it offers, what's happening in the industry as a whole, and what's happening with this particular organization. (Tip: If the company has a public affairs office, call and ask them to send you any available literature, including an annual report. Then read it.) Employers are pleased when someone has taken the trouble to become familiar with their business—and, conversely, are not too thrilled when they discover that someone hasn't bothered.

Prepare for the interview, just like you would for a test, because this is a test—of you. Get your thoughts together, and try to anticipate some of the questions that are most likely to come up. Some of the more typical questions include: Where do you hope to be in five years? Ten years? Why should we hire you? What can you do for us? Why do you want to work for us? What has been your most enjoyable experience in college? What are your biggest strengths? Weaknesses? (We have to smile here, because we remember a friend of ours who racked her brains to answer a similar question when being interviewed for acceptance to medical school. She wound up by saying, "If I have a fault, it's that I just care too much." She got in, but GEEZ! Give us a break!)

Hoping to put you at ease, some interviewers will begin by asking you simply to talk about yourself. In any event, you need to think about your qualifications and about the type of job you're looking for and why.

There might be a segment of the interview when it's your turn to ask questions. So have some intelligent ones ready. (A question like, "How long do you get for lunch?" is probably not the greatest question if you want to stun them with your personal acumen.) Find out what the position involves, what opportunities for advancement may be open to you now or in the future, and anything else you'd like to know about the job.

What to wear? If you can, visit the office beforehand (better yet, drop off your resume and cover letter in person). And while you're there (you probably won't get to speak to anyone; you'll probably just hand your resume to the receptionist and leave), sneak a peek at what other employees are wearing. Then use your own best judgment. (The rule is to dress neatly and conservatively, but there are some exceptions. If you're applying for a job in which creativity is a premium—a graphic designer, for example—then you might not want to show up looking like you just escaped from IBM.) Try to avoid being either too formal or too casual. And when it comes to the interview itself:

Positions are lost when common courtesy and tact are missing from the interview.

- Be pleasant and friendly but businesslike. Don't be too friendly; it's not appropriate at this first meeting. You're not pals, you're not there to bond, you're interviewing for a job. Be respectful. And please: Attempt a good, firm handshake. Even if you get a flaccid, clammy-fish handshake in return, at least you'll have made the effort.
- Let the employer control the conversation. Your answers should be complete but brief. Don't ramble, and avoid dogmatic statements. ("I'd never work for a company that doesn't have an on-site daycare program. Oh, you don't? I mean—I have a friend who'd never work for a company that doesn't . . . Not a good friend . . . And anyway, I tell her she's crazy making such rash statements! I reprimand her, yes, I really do . . . The interview's over, isn't it?") And don't interrupt. Even if you're itching to, control yourself. Positions are lost when common courtesy and tact are missing from the interview. If the interviewer can't keep the upper hand in a half-hour interview, why should she want to subject herself to you every day?
- Stress your qualifications without exaggerating. The employer's questions will indicate the type of person wanted. Pick up on these cues and present your credentials accordingly. For example, if you're being interviewed for a management trainee position and the employer mentions that the job might require some contact with

customers, respond by mentioning any experiences or courses that have prepared you to deal with people.

- Don't bad-mouth. Ever. In discussing your previous jobs, courses or other experiences, avoid criticizing former employers, professors, or fellow students. "In a few years, what bad things will he be saying about me?" the interviewer may—justifiably—wonder. Show some class. If you can't think up anything nice, then stick to the facts. ("I worked for Mr. Johnson for two and a half years. The job involved meeting some interesting people." No need to mention that one of those interesting people was Mr. Johnson's alcoholic wife, who used to call you up and rant in an angry, slurred voice.)
- Don't discuss your personal, domestic, or financial problems. For one thing, it's inappropriate. For another, it could be a real turn-off, and it could distract the interviewer from noticing the worthy qualities that would make you an ideal candidate for this job. ("Oh, yeah, that's the kid with the crazy girlfriend," instead of, "Did you notice that guy? He seemed really on-the-ball. Asked some sharp questions.")
- End on a positive note. Shake hands again, and thank the employer for taking the time to talk with you. If the employer does not definitely offer you a job or indicate when you will hear about it, ask when you may call to learn the decision.

Other tips: If you're really nervous about the interview, you may want to rehearse beforehand. Have a friend pose questions to you and criticize your responses. Some college placement offices offer free TV camera and studio facilities so you can videotape yourself in a practice job interview. You can play back the tape in private and plan ways to improve. ("What was that thing I was doing with my hair? How distracting! Now I'll remember to keep my hands folded on my lap," etc.)

And finally, read up on other interviewing techniques. Look for helpful guides for successful job interviewing; they're available in all college libraries and most bookstores.

And Finally . . .

What else is there to say? You've read the book on the freshman year, now get out there and live it!

No matter what the orientation speakers (or even this book) may tell you, the freshman year—like the entire college experience—isn't necessarily a crossroad for the rest of your life. But usually, the freshman year does present the biggest hurdles and greatest set of challenges you'll have to face. If you can make it through this year, the rest should be smooth—or, we should say, smoother—sailing.

If you need help, seek it. Know that your college is making an investment in you, and that, as you've probably suspected all along, colleges in general are greedy places. They want to get their money's worth: They want you to stay in school and do well. They want to retain you as a student; they don't want you to drop out or transfer elsewhere. And then they want you to graduate, to become an alum who will do them proud. So if you run into trouble—academically or otherwise— talk to somebody. If you don't get answers right away, keep asking.

One final note, if we may, at the risk of sounding like a bad fortune cookie message: Temper your journey with humility. Oswald Chambers said nearly a century ago, "If your cup is sweet, drink with good grace." As you're figuring out all the answers, avoid becoming smug. Instead, make an effort every now and then to cut some slack to those lower on the totem pole than you—next year's crop of freshmen. Because hey, you've been there, and done that, and you can help.

In the movie *Animal House* there is a statue of the founder of Faber College, with this insightful motto: "Knowledge is good." Well, it *is* good. But in a way, knowledge itself is irrelevant—it's what you do with it that counts. The writer Marya Mannes once declared, "What I have will do; what I make of it is up to me."

Believe in your own worth. What you have is, or can be, plenty. Here's hoping college helps you make the most of it and that you have a great time along the way.

Index

Help, 210–37
Hepatitis B, 192, 214–15
Heroin, 205–6
Herpes, genital, 192
Highlighters, 13
Hitchhiking, 43
HIV (human immunodeficiency virus), 190–91, 236–37
   test for, 193–94
Home, living at, 50–51
Homesickness, 82–83
Homosexual roommate, 30
Hopelessness, 221
Hot pots/plates, 14–15
Housekeeping, 19–22
Humanities courses, 246–47
Human papilloma virus, 192

I

Ibuprofen, 8–9
Identity theft, 57–58
Immunizations, 94, 214–15
Incompletes, 104–5
Indiana University, 253
Insects, 22–23
Insurance, on personal belongings, 23
Interest, on credit cards, 62, 64
International students
   advice for, 168–69
   meeting, 167–68
International study, 254–55
Internet, 134–36, 264
Interviews, job, 274–76
Intramural sports, 163–64
Invitational parties, 169–71
Involvement, 161–69
Irons, 10

J

Jackson, Shirley, 79
Job hunting, 262–67
   application letter sample, 273
   interviews, 274–76
   resume for, 267–72
Jobs, school and, 144–45
Jogging, rape and, 196
Johns Hopkins University, 14, 44, 241, 247, 253
Junk food, 86–87

K

Keyboards for computers, 133–34

L

Lamps, 14
Language study, 245–46
Laptop computers in class, 127
Laughter, 221–22
Laundry, 8, 10–12
Laws. *See also* Legal *entries*.
   on disabilities, 226
Law school, 258–59
Law School Admission Test, 258
Learning disabilities, 226
Leases on apartments, 45–48
Lecture notes, 124–27
Legacies, 169
Legal advice, on apartments and leasing, 46–48
Legal assistance, in sexual harassment and discrimination, 231–33
Liberal arts courses, 246–47
Libraries, 137–38
Life experience, credit for, 145
Lighting, 14
Lincoln, Abraham, viii
Linens, 8
Living arrangements. *See* Dormitory life; Off-campus living.
Loans
   consolidation, 68
   paying off, 260
Location, of apartment, 43
Long-term planning, 238–55

M

Majors
   changing, 244–45
   choosing, 241–44
   designing, 243
Management, self-, 124–48
Marijuana, 205–6
Marriage, 187–89
MasterCard, 58
Math anxiety, 223
M.B.A. degree, 260–61
Meal package, 69–70
Medical assistance, 211–18
Medical College Admission Test, 260
Medical school, 259–60

image/view of, 112
office hours of, 100–101, 118–19
phoned at home, 118–19
politics and, 116
publish-or-perish demand on, 116–17
sex with, 228. *See also* Sexual harassment
    and discrimination.
tenure for, 114–16
test objectives of, 156
Promiscuity, 192
Pronouns, 131
Publications, research, 137, 138
Public transportation, 43

R
Race, minority student groups, 164–65
Ranking of schools, 253–54
Rape, 194
    action after, 199–201
    avoiding, 195–97
    date, 195–99
Ray, Oakley, 81
Reader's Guide to Periodical Literature, 137
Readiness for college, quiz on, x–xi
Reading skills, 128–30
Recordkeeping, 58
Records, school, 250, 251
Refrigerators, 15
Registration for classes, 91, 96–98
Rehabilitation Act of 1973, Section 504 of, 226
Relationships. *See* Friendships; Sexual activity
Religious fellowship, 166–67
Reputations of schools, 253–54
Research, 136–38
    teaching and, by professors, 116–17
Resident adviser, 28–29
Respiratory problems, 213
Responsibility, of roommates, 32
Resumes, 267–69
    information in, 268–70
    sample, 271–72
    scanned, 270
Roaches, 22–23
Rohypnol, 198–99
Roman Catholic Newman Center, 166
Roommates, 24–36
    for apartments, 47–49
    best friend from high school, 33–35
    changing, 29–30
    choosing vs. random assignment, 24–28

concerns about, 24
contracts with, 26
drug use by, 204
fun and, 34–35
gay, 30
getting along with, 30–33
interviewing, 41–42
privacy and, 33
problems with, 28–30
Rush Week, 169–70, 172

S
Safety, rape avoidance, 195–97
Sales and Marketing Management, 138
Scholarships, for sophomores, 74–75
School rank, 253–54
School records, 250–51
Security, apartment, 44
Security deposits, 44–45
Self-management, 124–48
Sensitivity, of roommates, 32–33
Settling in, 2–23
Sewing kit, 10
Sexual activity
    abstinence, 199
    dating, 184–87
    disease transmission and safe sex, 190–94,
        214–15
    drinking and, 177
    obscene/prank phone calls, 201–4
    panty raids, 204
    pregnancy, 189–90
    with professors, 228
    rape, 194–201
Sexual harassment and discrimination, 228–33
Shelving, 17
Shoes
    athlete's foot and, 7
    paraphernalia, 10
    storing, 18
Shopping, on Internet, 135
Shyness, 35–36
Sickness, 211–18
Smith, Red, 130
Soap, liquid dishwashing, 20
Social life. *See also* Sexual activity.
    costs of, 73
    as learning experience, 79–80
    meeting international students, 167–68

Visa (credit card), 58
Visual impairment, 226
Vitamins, 214
Voice mail, 16
Volunteer work, 165–66

W
Waking up, 14, 16
Wall decorations, 16–19
Wardrobe, 2–4, 275
Water, 88
Weather, 3
Web sites, 134
Wells, Herman B., 247

Western Kentucky, 253
White-out, 13, 19
Withdrawal from class, 102–104
Word-processing programs, 133
Work. *See also* Job hunting.
    school and, 144–45
    volunteer, 165–66
Working, for room and board, 40–42
Workshops, 210
Work-Study, 142
Writing skills, 130–32

Y
Yale University, 38–39

Notes

Notes

Notes

Printed in the United States
55873LVS00005B/97-296